William J. Fay

Agape in the New Testament

VOLUME III

CESLAUS SPICQ, O.P.

AGAPE IN THE NEW TESTAMENT

Volume Three
Agape in the Gospel, Epistles
and Apocalypse of St. John

TRANSLATED BY
Sister Marie Aquinas McNamara, O.P.
AND
Sister Mary Honoria Richter, O.P.

B. HERDER BOOK CO.
St. Louis and London

IMPRIMATUR ✝ Joseph Cardinal Ritter
Archbishop of St. Louis, June 8, 1966

Introduction

The meaning of the inspired books can never be exhausted. The more the letter of Scripture is considered, the more clearly its spirit emerges, and what God intended to say to men comes to be better understood through exegesis. God revealed his love best in the last writings of the Canon, and there the semantic of *agape* reaches its definitive stage.

The earlier values of *agape* remain constant, from its first classical meaning of hospitality, through its fundamental meaning in the Septuagint of fidelity and observance of the commandments, to the properly Christian values of gift and self-sacrifice which St. Paul emphasizes. In the writings of St. John, however, there is one aspect of *agape* which is brought out in singular relief—the aspect of manifestation and proof. Most of St. John's uses of the word should be translated "manifest love," "love which proves itself," or "the economy, the development of the divine love."

The meanings of words always follow the evolution of ideas, and the meditations of the apostles gradually enriched the term "charity" with all the teachings of the life and doctrine of the Savior. The new depth of the notion of *agape* arose directly from the progress of Christology. The new faith recognized in Jesus the manifestation and gift of the Father's love. God's messenger is himself the epiphany of God's *agape*, so that *agape* becomes at once the model and the source, the archetype and the cause, of the love proper to the children of God. Consequently, the Christians' charity necessarily tends to declare itself, to act, to be productive, like the charity of the Father who is in heaven. Believers cannot speak the word *agape* without singing its seminal quality, its energy, its proofs. That is why the world can recognize the disciples of Jesus Christ by the manifest love which unites them with one another and which will be, till the end of time, the "mark" of God's Church most deeply intended by its founder.

C. S.

Contents

Chapter V: Conclusion, 157

CHAPTER I

Charity in the
Apocalypse

WE BELIEVE—though the matter is of little importance for the present exegesis—that the Apocalypse, the fourth Gospel, and the three Johannine Epistles were all written by the same author: the apostle St. John, brother of James the Great, son of Zebedee and Salome. It is more important, and more difficult, to determine the chronology of these works. The Apocalypse was probably written at Patmos (1:9) around 94–96; the Gospel, at Ephesus in the last years of the first century, after the death of Domitian; and the Epistles, shortly after that.

The Apocalypse uses the noun *agape* four times and the verb *agapan* twice; the adjective *agapētos* does not appear at all. The Apocalypse is an entirely different genre from the Epistles. An analysis of its texts concerning love will permit us to see whether the Johannine and the Pauline notions of *agape* are homogeneous. Thus we shall be able to discover the common conception of *agape* as it existed at the end of the apostolic age which closed revelation. Did Christian love —the revealed reality which comes from the Lord—receive a personal interpretation from each apostle, or is it a sacred revelation faithfully transmitted by all the witnesses of Christ and preserved as an unchangeable deposit by the whole Church?

1. Christ's permanent charity for believers

To him *who loves* us and has freed us from our sins through his own blood and has made us a kingdom, priests for God (Apoc. 1:5).

At the beginning of the greeting addressed to the seven churches of proconsular Asia (1:4), St. John exalts Jesus Christ, witness and redeemer, in a magnificent threefold title: he is the trustworthy witness of the Father's entire revelation, the first to rise from the dead, and the sovereign of the kings of the earth.

The acclamation—glory and power—of the seven Churches is addressed not so much to the only-begotten Son or to the Pantocrator as to "him who loves us." *Ho agapōn hēmas*, "he who loves us," is Christ's direct title to the gratitude of the redeemed, the new priests. The context is one of worship, and there is a whole world of difference here between *philein* and *agapan*. *Agapan* is a religious, divine love which manifests and proves itself. It is, besides, a love of predilection (*hēmas*, us) by which the Sovereign deliberately and gratuitously accords his favors to his subjects.

The use of the present participle is extremely forceful; it shows the permanence and constancy of Christ's charity. The Son of God who delivered himself to death out of love (Jn. 15:13) had promised his disciples that he would continue to love them after his death (*agapēsō*, 14:21; cf. 13:1: *eis telos*). Now that he has risen, his charity for his own endures (15:9-10). Henceforth, his *agape* shares the immutability of heavenly realities. It is part of the eternal present, and Christ can be truly described, therefore, as loving his own forever and unceasingly.

The context allows us to fill out this exegesis. As the "First-born from the dead," Christ is the Living One par excellence (*ho zōn*, Apoc. 1:18; 4:9, etc.); since he is at the right hand of the Father, his life is the life of one who has been glorified. As glorified, he envelops Christians in his love, the authentic love of the one witness faithful above all others (v. 5; cf. 3:14). We can put complete trust in him who came upon this earth to bear witness to the truth (Jn. 18:37). Finally, his love is full and overflowing, as befits the king of the kings of earth (cf. 17:14; 19:16), who bestows his favors with the munificence of the Sovereign of the entire universe.

St. John's acclamation is directed particularly to the generosity and manifestations of Christ's love. There is a close connection between "to him who loves us," *agapōnti*, "to him who has freed us," *lysanti*, and even "he has made [us a kingdom]," *epoiēsen*, of verse 6. Jesus' love is proved in his twofold gift. He has delivered us from the slavery of sin and, as it were, broken the chains which blocked our way to God. He has made us share in his sovereignty and raised us to a royal and priestly dignity.

Christ's extreme generosity is comprehensible only in terms of his love for us and, more immediately, of his death on the cross, *en tōi haimati autou.* St. Paul had already frequently made the association between *agape* and Calvary,[1] particularly in Rom. 8:37, where he says that Christ loved us, Christ who also died for us (vv. 34–35). St. Paul also often associates God's election and his charity, as the Septuagint did, and as St. John does too in the triple repetition of "us": "He loves us; he has freed us from our sins; he has made us a kingdom." The Christ of St. John has an extraordinary predilection for the believers: "He loved his own" (Jn. 13:1). Here his love is the love of the heavenly Lord for the members of his kingdom. His transcendence is no obstacle to the warmth and watchfulness of his charity. In any case, the faithful can know the *agape* of Christ from the twofold privilege they possess here and now: the royal priesthood and freedom from sin. Their gratitude is immense.

[1] Gal. 2:20; 5:2, 25; cf. 2 Cor. 5:14.

2. The lessening of fraternal charity

Nevertheless I hold this against you that you have given up the *love* you had at first (Apoc. 2:4).

Christ praises the Church of Ephesus warmly for its fidelity to true doctrine—it had not compromised with false teachers—and for its courage in persecution. "I know your conduct, your toil, and your patience" (2:2). Conduct, *erga;* toil, *kopos;* and patience, *hypomenē*, are reminiscent of 1 Thess. 1:3, and the similarity suggests that the essentials of the Christian life were flourishing in the first city of Asia Minor. In fact, this praise makes the great reproach which follows it almost unintelligible. St. John says that this Church has abandoned or neglected charity, the only virtue that matters (1 Cor. 13:1–3). What does he mean?

The interpretation of the verse depends on what *agape* and *aphiēmi* mean. *Aphiēmi* was a very common verb and it had several different meanings. Here it could mean "renounce, desert" or "neglect, disregard." Both senses were frequent during the Hellenistic period. *Aphiēmi* was used of a man who had been abandoned [2] or of a patrimony which had been definitely renounced.[3] Usually, however, it had the simpler meaning, "to release, to let go";[4] for example, to open a sluice gate and let the water flow through.[5] It was a technical term for exemption from a public charge or dispensation from a public service. In 254 two citizens of Antinoopolis explained to the *stratēgos* of Oxyrhynchus that they had well-established rights to be free (*aphiēmi*) from all public duties.[6] Philonidus wrote to his father, Cleon, that he

---

[2] Jn. 10:12; Mt. 26:56.
[3] *Cessio bonorum*, cf. Jer. 12:7; P. *Colomb*, 123:53.
[4] P. *Karanis*, 518, 14; P. *Zen. Colomb*, 1: 6, 14; P. *Lille*, 7:17; P. *Ent.* 84:17.
[5] P. *Pet.* 2:13, 15, 2; cf. 37, 1b, 11; P. *Ryl.* 4:561, 3.
[6] P. *Oxy.* 8:1119, 17.

should make every effort to be permanently relieved of his duties.[7] Finally, in conformity with classical usage, the verb meant "to neglect, to abandon out of neglect or contempt." In the third century A.D. a woman reproached her brother, Petechon, for not taking care of the funeral arrangements for another of their brothers.[8] More important, in 99 Gemellus rebuked Epagathus for not having worked the field at Apeas and for having neglected (*aphiēmi*) it.[9]

This reproach for negligence seems to be the best parallel to the reproach in our text, especially if we take the similar lukewarmness of the Church at Laodicea into account.[10] In addition, according to the juridical usages cited above, the "relaxation" of the Ephesians is more a progressive disobedience or a shirking (cf. *hypostolē*, Heb. 10:39) of their rigorous obligation than an absolute rejection of it, properly speaking.

It is equally difficult to determine exactly what the Ephesians have let go. St. John contrasts their present charity with the *agape* they had when they were converted or when their church was founded. They have suffered a decline in their charity that is like the decline in the fidelity of their young widows (1 Tim. 5:12). In the beginning their love was fervent, and as time passed—*dia ton chronon* (Heb. 5:12)—and they practiced charity (Heb. 5:14; cf. 1 Tim. 4:7–8) frequently (Heb. 5:14), their virtue should have developed and borne fruit.

The Church of Thyatira had grown in just this way: "I know your achievements, your faith, love, service, and patience" (Apoc. 2:19). The Lord is asking the Church of Ephesus to return to its former works, *ta prōta erga poiēson* (2:5). We may conclude—and semantics confirms—that there is no question about their interior fervor; their religious enthusiasm had not diminished. *Agape* never has a purely sentimental sense. Apoc. 2:5 and 2:19 expressly associate *agape* and *erga*, "works." It is the manifestations and con-

---

[7] *P. Pet.* 2:13, 19, 8.   [8] *P. Oxy.* 7:1067, 5.   [9] *P. Fay.* 112:13.
[10] *Chliaros*, Apoc. 3:16.

crete accomplishments of love which are diminishing. But love for whom?

If we refer, with E. Lohmeyer and D. W. Hadorn, to Jer. 2:2, "I recall your youthful devotion and your bridal love (*agape*)," [11] St. John would seem to have the reciprocal love of God and the faithful in mind; he would mean their delight in one another. "The youthful charity" of Israel and of the Ephesians was in the beginning a total, joyful gift, but it no longer showed the same signs of attachment and zeal. Nevertheless, it seems preferable to understand "works," *erga*, of Apoc. 2:5, to which we must return, in the same sense as "works," *erga*, of Apoc. 2:19, where works are associated with *agape* and *diakonia*, service, and refer unmistakably to "works of charity" for one's neighbor, particularly for the poor (Oecumenius). St. John's words are a reference, then, to the commandment of fraternal love prescribed and accepted from one's first adherence of faith (2 Jn. 5–6). "He who loves his brother abides in the light, and so he has no cause for stumbling" (1 Jn. 2:10). In this sense, the whole moral conduct of the Ephesians is affected by their decline in charity for neighbor. *Agape* is the basic constituent which gives consistency and vigor to all the virtues (Col. 3:14). If *agape* gives way (*aphēkes*)—or if its vital breath grows weaker—the best efforts, patience, and orthodoxy itself lose their value. The change becomes all too evident.

In other words, the Ephesians are excusing themselves more and more frequently from the eminent public service imposed on every disciple of Christ as his own law (Jn. 13:35)—the service of neighbor. It is not said that *agape* itself diminishes, but that it no longer gives the same signs of its presence. Its manifestations become more and more rare, less and less generous, and it falls the victim of a kind of lethargy or sclerosis. The Ephesians are in the same state as the Hebrews who were sluggish and slow to understand, *nōthroi* (Heb. 5:11). Their capacity for loving divinely re-

---

[11] This would not be the "engagement period," as this expression is usually translated, but rather the early period of the marriage.

mains, but they are lazy about using it. Their conduct falls far short of their potential. They sin by omission (cf. Heb. 2:8).

3. The works of Christian charity

I know your achievements, your *love*, fidelity, service, and patience. I know, too, your latest achievements which outnumber the early ones (Apoc. 2:19).

No other Church was initially praised more highly than the Church of Thyatira (cf. E. Lohmeyer), but it is difficult to determine whether each word in the list of achievements has its proper value or whether St. John is quoting a traditional list of virtues. There are ten such lists in the Pastorals,[12] and all ten contain the word *agape*. All except 2 Tim. 1:7 associate *agape* and *pistis*, faith, and three associate it also with *hypomonē*, patience.[13] Nevertheless, this comparison does not allow us to give charity the supreme place accorded it in most of the Pauline epistles. Just as *pistis* here is principally loyalty (Moffatt) and fidelity (Bossuet, Allo, Wikenhauser) rather than faith properly speaking, so charity is considered in its practical accomplishments. It is more moral virtue than theological virtue. However, the pair *agape-pistis* shows that the practical accomplishments of charity are in direct relationship to the union of the soul with God and Christ. The "charitable and faithful" Christian believes in Christ and loves him personally (cf. Heb. 6:10).

There can be no doubt that in this text St. John is praising the "works" of the Church (2:1; 14:13); he introduces their description with the word *kai*. Since the first word after "works" is *agape*, *agape* must be considered in its acts or manifestations, and it is more than likely that the other virtues are simply exercises of love, particularly of love for

---

[12] Cf. C. Spicq, *Agape in the New Testament*, vol. II, pp. 406–407.
[13] 1 Tim. 6:11; Tit. 2:2; 2 Tim. 3:10.

neighbor. In any case, *diakonia*, service, must refer to service
of the poor and the afflicted,[14] and *hypomonē*, patience, may
refer to the strength of endurance which the Sermon on the
Mount and Saint Paul (*panta hypomonei*, 1 Cor. 13:7) both
presented as characteristic of *agape*.

The Church of Thyatira has done more than persevere
and hold fast; it has also made progress. Its latest works sur-
pass its earlier ones in number and quality. The community
has already reached a certain maturity, and its past can be
compared with its present. At Ephesus there had been a diminishing of charity (2:4), but at Thyatira religious and
moral conduct, particularly the achievements of *agape*, are
better than they were at the beginning. According to this
text, Christian love can be recognized by its dynamism, just
as a good tree is known by its abundant good fruit.

4. Christ's love for Philadelphia

They will know that *I have loved* you (Apoc. 3:9).

In Apoc. 1:5 the Christian faith, which recognized in the
death of the Savior his great love for those he redeemed, acclaimed his signal charity. Here, Christ himself makes a
declaration of love to the humble Church of Philadelphia,
and the converted Jews could recognize the Lord's love for
the community which had received them.

Once again *agape* is discovered through its manifest signs,
but in contrast with Apoc. 1:5, here the pronoun *egō*, "I,"
makes the statement very forceful. The speaker is he "who is
holy and true" (v. 7); he can be trusted absolutely. Furthermore, his love is not presented in relation to the passion or
some gift of grace; it is absolute. Any qualification would
weaken the impact of the declaration. Finally, the Lord repeats for his Church exactly the same words which Yahweh

[14] Acts, 11:29; Rom. 15:25, 31; 1 Cor. 16, 15; 2 Cor. 8:4; 9:1; Heb.
6:10; 1 Pet. 4:10.

had addressed to his people (Is. 43:3) to account for his victorious providence for them: *kagō se ēgapēsa*.

5. The heroic choice of the Martyrs

"They despise (*ouk ēgapēsan*) life even to the point of being willing to die" (Apoc. 12:11).

The angels celebrate the victory of the faithful Christians who will conquer Satan through the blood of the Lamb and their own sacrifice, which is expressed in almost the same terms which Jesus used many times in talking with his disciples.[15] In his Gospel, St. John would write: "He who holds his life dear (*philōn*) destroys it; he who sets no store by his life (*misōn*) in this world will preserve it for eternal life" (12:25). To describe love of life, St. John used the verb *philein;* but the twenty-four elders, who were probably the singers of the hymn, knew Greek better than the Evangelist and very correctly used *agapan* instead. Here *agapan* has its classical sense of "to prefer" and "to appreciate, to esteem." [16] In the negative, then, it means "to despise, to condemn." It is a synonym of *kataphronein*,[17] which recalls Mt. 6:24: "A man cannot be the slave of two masters. He will either hate the one and love the other, or, at least, be attentive to the one and neglectful of the other." The martyrs love their souls, of course, but they set no store by their life in this world (Jn. 12:25) and do not shrink from the face of death. Their deliberate and fully conscious contempt for temporal life is simply another aspect of their preference for the eternal life of the soul,[18] and the angels praise their choice. The union of charity and renouncement, which is both evangelical and Pauline, should be noted.

[15] Mt. 16:25; Mk. 8:35; Lk. 9:24.
[16] Cf. C. Spicq, *Agape, Prolégomènes à une étude de théologie néotestamentaire,* Louvain, 1955, pp. 3, 43, 46, 52, 55.
[17] Cf. C. Spicq, *Agape in the New Testament,* vol. I, pp. 16 ff.
[18] Jn. 12:25; cf. Prov. 15:32.

6. Jerusalem, the preferred city

They went up over the broad plain of the earth and surrounded the camp of the saints and the *beloved* city (Apoc. 20:9).

Assembled by Satan, all the pagan nations surround Jerusalem, which is called the holy city (21:2) or the city of God (3:12) because its members belong to God, who dwells in the midst of them (14:1). St. John is applying to the new Sion, the image of the Church,[19] the name which the Old Testament had applied to the first Sion, the city chosen and preferred by God,[20] and to Jacob (Deut. 32:15). These Old Testament usages often contain a reference to the divine providence and solicitude. The "camp" of the saints will not be invaded by the hordes of the devil. Because the people of God are beloved, they are secure. *Égapemenē*, "beloved," is a title of confidence as well as of honor.

The Apocalypse stresses the opposition between Christ and Satan. The book seems to be dominated by the divine anger, yet the charity of God and our Savior is affirmed in it with unequalled force. God is presented as permanently loving and caring for the Church as the "camp of the saints." [21] The importance of the declaration of love which begins this book of prophecies cannot be overstressed. Christ is he who loves us, *ho agapōn* (1:5), with a constant love which no vicissitude can alter and which summarizes all his relations with the Church. He has proved his charity by giving his life on Calvary, and his love is as efficacious as it is generous, since he has purified his elect from all sin and made of them a royal, priestly people. Christians cherish his favors and the love from which they proceed; therefore they praise

[19] *Ita* Oecumenius, Bossuet, Swete, Allo, Moffatt, Bonsirven, Brütsch . . .
[20] Sir. 24:11; cf. Ps. 78:68; 87:2; Zach. 1:14.
[21] Apoc. 20:9; the perfect *ēgapemenē* suggests a stable condition.

the Christ who has loved them, *tōi agapōnti hēmas.* This verse expresses the faith of the primitive community and its conception of the glorious Lord. If St. Paul had written it, he would probably have added some theological elaboration of the idea. St. John simply states two facts—that the risen Christ is filled with love for his own and that the disciples' adherence of faith is an attachment and gift of themselves to their loving Lord. For Christians, Jesus is, without any doubt, "he who loves us." Their sure trust gives rise in them to an absolute confidence in Christ's fidelity and help. In even the worst trials, each Christian's courage is sustained by his sure knowledge of the all-powerful love which surrounds him. The Christian's conviction is the fruit not only of his contemplation of the cross (5:9–10), but also of the belief suggested to him in his everyday life by the Holy Spirit (22:17) as he hears Christ, the truest of witnesses, say and repeat categorically, "I love you." [22]

Knowing themselves to be chosen, loved, protected, and lavished with gifts by God and Christ, the first Christians knew that they were the beneficiaries of a signal mercy and an honorable, fruitful new Covenant. Above all, they understood Christ's *agape* in its strongest and most precise sense: it is love, a reciprocal, total, definitive union. They dared compare their relation with Jesus to the relation of a bride to her beloved.[23] The metaphor had been used in the Old Testament,[24] of course, and even in the Gospel,[25] but the Apocalypse is concerned with the last days, and it is remarkable that *agape* should be presented with such tenderness in a book which is in many respects so tragic. This union cannot be understood except in the light of Christ's having loved men first (1:5; 3:9). All these considerations show that at the end of the first century *agape* underwent a decisive semantic evolution, or, rather, that the ardent passion it formerly conveyed in exceptional cases, as on the lips of the

---

[22] Apoc. 3:19.   [23] Apoc. 19:7; 21:2, 9.
[24] Cf. *Prolégomènes,* pp. 113 ff.
[25] Mt. 22:1 ff.; 25:1 ff.; Mk. 2:19; Jn. 3:29.

spouse in the Canticle of Canticles or in Philo,[26] became
purified and raised to the religious level, where it retained its
extreme fervor. All the many modes of man's loving can be
permeated and animated by the divine love. The good Samaritan whose heart was moved by the misery of his neighbor was one example of this fervent love, but the greatest
example is the crucified Christ uniting himself to his Church
as a husband loves his wife (Eph. 5:25 ff.). The Apocalypse
does more than repeat this teaching; it shows its reality as
it is lived by the people of God and shows it in so spontaneous and normal a fashion that there is no need for any explanation.

In modern terminology, we would say that Christians
"adore" their Savior, thus adding enthusiasm to the ideas of
religion and total love. The disciples cry out their passionate
wish "to the Christ who loves us"—"to him be glory and
power for ever and ever" (1:6). They are profoundly aware
that they are consecrated to him body and soul; indeed, the
martyrs prefer to despise life itself and all its goods rather
than to be unfaithful to him (12:11).

Christ's charity is singularly demanding. St. Paul had already made it plain that the Lord wants a Church that is
pure, without spot or wrinkle or anything of the sort (Eph.
5:27), but the Apocalypse makes Christ intervene in local
communities to judge them on their charity (2:4, 19), the
essential virtue which contains the whole Christian life. In
fact, from the moment of his conversion the believer is defined in the eyes of God by his spontaneous charity, especially toward his neighbor. As the years pass, his love should
grow and be more and more frequently exercised and displayed. There is always a danger that it will not be productive enough. It must produce works. Just as Christ's charity
for his own is provident and efficacious, so his disciples'
charity must perform more and more works, more and
more good actions of better and better quality—something
only the infallible Judge can truly evaluate.

[26] Cf. *Prolégomènes*, pp. 74 ff.; 175 ff.

There was real generosity in the Church at Ephesus, especially in its endurance in trials, which was praiseworthy in itself but also insufficient, because it was not inspired by true charity. The Ephesians' case is similar to 1 Cor. 13:1–4, which states that only *agape* can make even heroic action valuable. Moreover, love which does not express itself in devotion and effective service for neighbor was found wanting, and this is similar to 1 Cor. 13:5–7, where *agape* is said to direct all virtuous activity. For St. John, as for St. Paul, charity is essentially active and dynamic even in very difficult circumstances. Its work, *ergon,* is a labor, *kopos,* an effort, a strain.[27] After all, its model is the blood shed by the Savior (1:5) which the martyrs followed so faithfully, even in the face of death, *archi thanatou* (12:11).

[27] Apoc. 14:13; cf. 2:2–3; 1 Thess. 1:3.

CHAPTER II

Charity in the
Fourth Gospel[1]

U<small>NLIKE</small> the synoptic Gospels, the Gospel of St. John does not contain the adjective *agapētos*. However, it has the verb *agapan* thirty-seven times and the noun *agape* seven times, six of them in the Discourse after the Last Supper.

One of the many difficulties which must be resolved by a commentator of this Gospel before he can proceed to the text itself is the problem of its composition, and particularly the problem of determining the original order of the pericopes. During the last fifty years a great variety of often overly-daring hypotheses have been proposed to restore their logical and supposedly primitive sequence. These fanciful conjectures have tended to discredit the thesis of dislocated pages in St. John's Gospel. Nevertheless, there are at least two examples of out-of-order pagination: 1) Chapter 5, which interrupts the story of the Galilean ministry and breaks the unity of chapters 4 and 6, should be placed after chapter 6, as Ludolph the Carthusian pointed out. 2) In the Discourse after the Last Supper, the Lord says, "Rise; we must be going on our way" (14:31), yet the Discourse continues in the same setting (15:1). Later the Lord reproaches the Apostles. "None of you asks me: 'Where are you going?'" (16:5) even though Peter had already expressly asked him that very ques-

---

[1] This chapter will be confined to the religious uses of *agapan* and *agape*.

tion (13:36), etc. Therefore, choosing from among the many valid solutions we shall adopt the transposition of Spitta,[2] followed by J. Moffatt and J. H. Bernard: [3] 13:31a; 15–16; 13:31b–38; 14; 17.

1. The primacy and the fullness of God's love for men

So marked, indeed, has been God's *love* for the world that he gave his only-begotten Son: everyone who believes in him is not to perish, but to have eternal life (Jn. 3:16).

It is agreed almost universally that the words of this pericope, vv. 16–21, are not Jesus' but John's. The Evangelist is commenting on Jesus' talk with Nicodemus, and he wants to state explicitly the nature of the Son's mission. He writes as a theologian explaining the mysterious declaration, "The Son of Man must needs be lifted up" (3:15). What does "must needs," *dei*, mean? Is it some kind of tragic necessity or is it some constraint forced upon Jesus? [4] By whom and why and with what intention? [5]

So marked indeed has been God's love

Christ's mission and redemptive work proceed from God's love for men, from his *agape*, which is the most generous, constant and universal love there is. In the Greek text of Jn. 3:16, the verb *ēgapēsen*, "[God] loved," precedes the

[2] *Zur Geschichte und Literatur des Urchristenthums*, I, 1893, pp. 156–204.
[3] *The Gospel according to St. John*. Edinburgh, I–II, 1928, pp. xvi–xxxiii.
[4] According to Heb. 12:2, Jesus chose the cross freely; according to Jn. 10:18; 14:31, he chose it because of his adherence to the Father's will.
[5] St. John Chrysostom saw this connection clearly: "Do not be surprised that I must be raised up so that you may be saved; it is in fact the will of the father who loves you." (Col. 159)

subject. Its emphatic position shows that the point of the sentence is in God's charity, in the nature, extension, and accomplishments of so exceptional a love. *Agape* is God's own love, proper to God alone. The word *theos, God,* is preceded by the article *ho,* so that it must be given its transcendent sense. It refers to the Holy One, to the Creator as distinct from his creation, *kosmos,* to the person of the Father in his relation to the Son. The Old Testament had shown that God's mercy was in proportion to his majesty,[6] but St. John shows the eternal charity of God, which is the reason for all his undertakings, manifesting itself in a twofold intervention in history. Both the Incarnation and Christ's death on Calvary must be considered epiphanies of the divine *agape* (1 Jn. 4:9). The first words of the sentence, *houtōs gar ēgapēsen ho theos* . . . , could be translated, "The divine charity proved itself in this way, namely. . . ."

For the world

The first thing revealed about this love is its object; it reaches the whole world, *ton kosmon.* The use of *kosmos* (three times in v. 17; cf. 1:10) excludes every idea of limitation. God's *agape* is no longer simply Yahweh's predilection for Israel (Deut. 14:1–2 etc.), or even the heavenly Father's love for his children (1 Jn. 3:1); here St. John means God's love for all humanity, for each and every human being (1 Tim. 2:4). His use of *agape* in a phrase which expresses ideas as far removed from each other as "God" and "the world," *ho theos ton kosmon,* brings out the paradox in his love. Concretely, this is a world of sinners, of God's enemies, and the divine decision to manifest his charity is made toward men who are, above all else, guilty. "God proves his love for us, because, when we were still sinners, Christ died for us" (Rom. 5:8). The Lamb of God will come to take away the sins of the world (Jn. 1:29).

[6] Sir. 2:18.

That he gave his only-begotten Son

If it is surprising that God should love the whole world, it is stupefying to realize that he delivered up his own Son to sinners. The point of St. John's affirmation is in the correspondence between God's love and his signal gift: "so marked has been his love that he gave . . ." His love is the cause of his gift. Used alone, the word "that," *hōste*, means dependence or result, but with "so marked," *houtōs, hōste* shows an effective realization exactly corresponding to the intention of the person acting. It shows both manner and degree, so it would be an error to consider it simply the introduction to a result clause. It expresses the writer's feelings: God has loved men in *this* way and to *such* a degree—under this staggering form—that he has really and in fact given us his Son. The human mind would never have conceived such a thing.

God gives to men the Person who is most dear to him. The verb *edōken*, "he gave," refers to a free decision taken in the other world and enduring forever. The use of the aorist tense, which corresponds to the aorist *ēgapēsen*, shows that the decision was carried out in this world. The verb should be taken in its usual sense of "to give a present," which is appropriate for the respect which a sovereign's *agape* for his subjects includes. There is no constraint in the initiative undertaken by the All-powerful. He loves everyone, and he offers his Son to believers (cf. 1:12). The divine love which manifests itself in a precise moment of time is the Son himself, made flesh (v. 14) among us (1 Jn. 3:16), come down from heaven because he has been sent.[7] The verse refers primarily to the incarnation, the epiphany of charity (Tit. 3:4), but God's gift is so total and complete that it includes Jesus' death as well as his birth. St. John is stressing the "abandon" of the gift. He uses the verb *didōmi*, which is the root of the verb *paradidōmi*, used by the Apostles to describe

---

[7] *didonai = apostellein;* cf. 3:13, 17, 19; 14:16; 1 Jn. 4:9–10.

the sacrifice of Calvary.[8] In addition, he explains the typology of the bronze serpent. "Just as Moses lifted up the serpent in the desert, so the Son of Man must needs, *hypsōthēnai dei*, be lifted up, that everyone who believes in him may have eternal life" (Jn. 3:14). To the "exaltation of the serpent" correspond the coming and immolation of Jesus. If love can be judged by its gifts, then the immensity of the Father's charity is evident in the sending of a victim (Lk. 20:13).

Naming Jesus "his only-begotten Son," *ton huion ton monogenē*, shows not only his dignity and divinity but also his intimacy with the Father (1:18) and the Father's great love for him. The only-begotten Son is the Son loved before all others, *ho agapētos* (Mt. 3:17). God loves men so much that he gives them his only Son, his Beloved par excellence (Col. 1:13). The giving is total, and the gift shows the infinite extent of God's love. The Father sacrifices his own Son.

Everyone who believes in him is not to perish,
but to have eternal life

The Father's intention and purpose in sending his Son are explained in the second part of the verse: in order that no one may perish, that everyone may live. The double statement of the idea, once positively, once negatively, amounts to a superlative; salvation is to be universal, immediate, and definitive. There is no clearer way of saying that the divine *agape* is a "willing of good" for others. God's desire is so real and strong that he consents to a truly absolute sacrifice in order to achieve the "good" which is eternal life, participation in the life of God himself, the giving of love for love. The final words, "that everyone who believes in him may have eternal life," are the accomplishment of the intention implied in the words, "so marked has been God's love." The Father's love, his gift of the Son in his incarnation and death, and eternal life are rigorously intertwined (cf. Rom. 8:30) in the divine plan and the economy of salvation. Nevertheless,

[8] Rom. 8:32; Gal. 1:4; 2:20.

it remains for men to take advantage of the salvation which has been offered them. Faith, *pas ho pisteuōn*, is the only response the divine initiative asks of them—faith in the person of the incarnate Christ. According to the context, the believer confesses that Jesus is the only-begotten Son only after he has received the Lord (cf. 1:12) and seen him as the epiphany of the Father's charity. God reconciles the world to himself in Christ (2 Cor. 5:19). St. John says that each person's salvation is determined by whether he welcomes or rejects God's love offered in Christ, its revelation and victim. Living faith believes in love. St. John expresses this idea clearly in 1 John 4:16; cf. 3:16, etc.

This verse has been correctly considered a summary of St. John's Gospel, and the verb *agapan* has been considered the key to all revelation—to the mystery of God, of Christology and Soteriology. Love is the union between God and man, between eternity and history, between heavenly things and earthly things (Jn. 3:12). In Christ the believer knows God and lives with his life.

No text of Scripture tells more about charity than Jn. 3:16, which reveals love as an attribute of the Father. Love is eternal because it exists before the sending of the Son; it inspires the plan of salvation. It is universal because it is for the whole world. It is completely gratuitous, with no motive other than itself. It is gentle and merciful, active and powerful. In its desire to prove itself, it seizes the initiative. The facet of God's love most clearly revealed in the text is its immensity. There is no doubt that St. John wishes to suggest to his readers that God's love is infinite, as St. Thomas, following St. John Chrysostom, understood: "This verse gives four reasons for the immensity of God's love: 1) The person loving; 2) the condition of the one loved; 3) the greatness of the gifts; 4) the greatness of the fruit."

Yet despite God's remarkable and abundant love, some men are lost. St. John tries to account for the scandal of incredulity in commenting, "Everyone *who believes* in him is not to perish." He contrasts those who believe with those "who refuse to believe" (v. 18). What distinguishes those who welcome God's gift from those who reject it?

2. The hateful choice of unbelievers

And this is how the sentence of condemnation is passed; the light has come into the world, but men *loved* the darkness rather than the light, because their actions were wicked (Jn. 3:19).

This condemnation is not an arbitrary sentence which will be pronounced by the Sovereign Judge at the end of time, but a decision which each person makes for himself here and now. In making it, the unbeliever condemns himself (v. 18). The choice is quickly made. The light comes into the world which God wishes to save (v. 16). The light is the Word incarnate who remains among men forever (as the perfect *elēluthē*, "has come," shows) as a witness to God and permanent source of salvation. It is impossible not to have an opinion about him. Believers welcome him, recognizing what he is—the only-begotten Son (v. 16; 1:12). Another group of men, however, apparently the greater number, reject his person, his message, and his work because they prefer the darkness. . . .

In the phrase "men loved the darkness more than the light" the Greek text places the predicate before the subject. The emphatic position of the unbelievers' *agapan* is in contrast to God's *agapan* in v. 16—"So marked has been God's love for the world"—suggesting the monstrousness of the wicked choice. Men respond to the saving divine initiative with a preference for darkness and perdition. They are not victims of a blind and unconscious tendency which they cannot resist—*amor meus, pondus meum*—but are making a lucid judgment and deliberate choice. *Agapan* has its double classic sense of "to esteem, to appreciate" and "to prefer" (Apoc. 12:11). Most commentators correctly construct *mallon*, "more," with the object, *to skotos*, "darkness," rather

than with the verb *agapan*. The comparison does not con-
cern degrees of love. Men are not "more" attached to darkness; they choose darkness "rather" (cf. 12:43) than light.
The verb is in the aorist because it refers to a concrete
choice made at a particular moment. No one can evade an
eventual meeting with the Christ who is coming. Everyone
must either welcome him or reject him. Faith, *pistis*, and
love, *agape*, define an attitude of soul and decisive orientation of life. To love darkness is to shut oneself up in darkness forever, just as to believe in the light means to be
attached to light until death.

How is it possible for anyone not to love the light? St. John
gives a psychological explanation in terms of the principle
that like attracts like. If a man lives badly, he fears the
light which will penetrate his secret life, reveal and condemn his evil deeds (v. 20), and demand his repentance.
"Wicked actions," *ta erga ponēra*, does not necessarily mean
flagrant immorality or a life of debauchery, much less an
isolated act or two. The expression refers to an orientation
of life which is perversion of religion: a malignity which
can come only from the devil (7:7; 1 Jn. 3:12; 5:19). A
person who chooses evil necessarily resists the divine light.
Wickedness, *adikia*, blinds him and prevents him from receiving the truth (Rom. 1:18). The idea is the same as St.
Paul's earlier teaching about unbelievers: Those who perish
have not wished to receive the love of truth which would
save them (2 Thess. 2:10).

In the final analysis, a man's salvation or perdition is accomplished as a function of a twofold love. The divine
charity gives Christ, the revelation and the redeemer, to all
men. Some accept him by faith—and their welcoming him
has no need of explanation. Others refuse (*ho apeithōn*, v.
36) because their love for evil is the stronger love. Their
love makes them impervious or even hostile to the object
of faith. Everything is determined by the fundamental love
of the heart. "Where your treasure is . . ."

3. The Father's love, source of Jesus' sovereignty

The Father *loves* the Son and has put all things in his hand (Jn. 3:35).

This third use of the verb *agapan* in St. John's Gospel is again the evangelist's own commentary.[9] There is an echo in it of the heavenly voice heard at the Lord's baptism and transfiguration.[10] At the Jordan and on Tabor the Father's charity was primarily delight, *eudokein*, but here it is limitless generosity. God gives all things to his well-beloved Son. The Son is considered in his humanity, undoubtedly, but loved as the only-begotten Son in an evocation of the relationship of the Trinity. Moreover, the verb "loves," *agapai*, in the present, contains no determination of time. The love which God eternally bears his Son moves him to confide everything here on earth to him. The gift is in proportion to the Father's love. It is final, as the perfect *dedōken*, "has put," shows. Jesus himself tells us the content of the "all things," *panta*, put into his hand.[11] In a word, they are the sovereign power, the *exousia*, which Jesus exercises over every creature.[12]

Because his charity manifests itself by great favors and the granting of the highest prerogatives, *agapan* can be translated "to honor," as it is in classical usage when applied to a superior granting his favor to a subject and treating him generously. When the Father exalts and glorifies his Son, he is showing him *agape*.

Consequently, Jesus' declaration in John 5:20, "The Father dearly loves (*philei*) [D: *agapai*] the Son, and lets him see everything he is doing," is not an exact parallel to our

[9] The section 3:31–36 must have been accidentally transposed; it is directly connected to vv. 16–21; St. John continues his personal reflections.

[10] Mt. 3:17; cf. *Agape in the New Testament*, vol. I, pp. 37 ff.

[11] The judgment (5:22, 27), life (v. 26), the disciples (6:37, 39), the commandment (12:49); the divine name (17:11), glory (v. 24).

[12] Mt. 28:18; cf. 11:27; Jn. 13:3; Jn. 17:2.

text. John 3:35 (cf. v. 16) speaks of the solemn manifestation and official gift of God's love, but John 5:20 uses the
verb *philein* to emphasize its confidence and intimacy. The
Son who is in the Father's bosom (1:18) sees the Father
act (5:19); the Father shows the Son everything. The communication of secrets is expressed more exactly by *philein*
than by *agapan*.

4. Exegetes without love

I know you through and through; you do not have the *love*
of God in your hearts (Jn. 5:42).

The Scribes and Pharisees were extremely religious and
zealous for the honor of God. They pored over the Scriptures, yet they were unwilling to accept the testimony of
the Father's messenger, of him whom the Old Covenant
announced. Jesus explained why they did not believe: You
do not possess authentic charity.[13] "Charity" here is not so
much love properly so-called as the religion and worship
required by the first commandment. "Thou shalt love the
Lord thy God with all thy heart, with all thy mind . . ."
(Deut. 6:5). In Greek the articles before "love" and "God"
make the Lord's statement in John 5:42 the equivalent of a
quotation which refers to the true love of the one true God.
The Jews were zealous in their exegesis of Scripture, but
they were not sincerely jealous for the honor of God (cf.
Jn. 12:43). True *agape* implies, then, integrity and purity
of intention. Certainly it is full of fervor for the beloved.
The text indicates especially that a loyal love predisposes
to the true knowledge of faith (2 Thess. 2:10). If the lack
of charity leaves one blind,[14] vital possession of *agape* sharp-
ens one's spiritual perception and gives a sense of divine

[13] Along with the great majority of commentators we consider *tou
theou* as an objective genitive, "love for God"; cf. Lk. 11:42.
[14] Cf. Jn. 3:19; Mt. 23:6; *Agape in the New Testament* vol. I, pp.
119 ff.

realities.[15] If they had had charity, these exegetes could have studied God's plan intelligently (3:16), identified (*dokima-zein*, Philip. 1:10) his only-begotten Son, and recognized the Savior sent by God (Jn. 5:43; 8:42). Exegesis without love leaves one unbelieving before the fact of the Incarnate Son, but the Holy Spirit—who infuses charity (Rom. 5:5) and "fathoms all things, even the depths of God" (1 Cor. 2:10) —searches God. With this love, the reader of Scripture "recognizes" Jesus.

According to Hoskyns, this sentence of the Lord is the most devastating of all the condemnations of the Jews. "You are doomed, Pharisees, . . . because you disregard . . . the love of God" (Lk. 11:42). In addition, it points out that the abyss which separates Christ from his adversaries is insuperable, for Jesus was totally devoted and loving to his Father.[16]

5. Divine sonship and love of Christ

If God were your Father, you would *love* me, for it is from God that I came and am now here (Jn. 8:42).

This sentence is often studied together with the preceding one, John 5:42, which it is thought to complete. Jesus had said that a man who loves God knows the Son (5:42). Here he would be adding that a man who knows God loves the Son. In general, this interpretation is correct, but it must not be forgotten that the two contexts are different. From 8:33 on, the Master's entire polemic rests on the notion of authentic sonship. The Jews claimed to be sons of Abraham (vv. 33, 37) and even sons of God (v. 41); really, they were sons of the devil (v. 44). The criterion is this: The true son *does the works* of his Father (vv. 38, 41a)—he acts like his Father, thinks like his Father, speaks like his Father. If the Father loves and honors the Son (3:35), the Jews ought to

---

[15] Cf. Eph. 3:17–18; Philip. 1:9; Col. 2:2.   [16] Jn. 4:34; 17:25–26.

love him in the same way and "receive with honor" the one
sent to them by God.

This is the usual—and classical—meaning of *agapan* in
this context. It does not refer to love properly speaking, but
rather to a receiving with respect and joy. The welcoming of
Him who comes (1:11) presupposes a discernment which
can recognize Jesus as Son and messenger (1:10). *Agapan*
implies an evaluation, a deliberate judgment which makes
one determined to honor and be attentive to the person who
comes. Authentic divine sonship proves itself by its knowledge of Jesus Christ. That is why the Lord immediately
explains that the sons of the devil do not know or understand his language (v. 43). Love alone, which the Jews do
not have, controls spiritual perception and intuitive knowledge.

The hardest task of the exegete is to determine the link
between *agape* and God's paternity. If we understand that
having God for Father implies loving God, we can gloss,
"If they were sincerely attached to God as to their only
Father, they would love everything which concerns God,
and before all else they would love him who comes to them
from God." [17] This interpretation presupposes that Jesus is
more than a messenger or even a plenipotentiary. He must
be the manifestation and very person of God. We reach
the Father through the Son. It must be added that on the
moral and religious level, to be begotten by God implies
participation in his very spirit, which bastards do not have
(v. 41). The *pneuma* which God makes live in his children
(James 4:5) enables them both to hear—to understand the
words of Jesus (Jn. 8:47)—and to discern—to love the
person of the Son (v. 42). Once again *agape* ascends from
men toward God, their response to his initiative and presence.[18]

[17] F. M. Braun.
[18] A. Nygren commented neither upon this text nor upon the preceding one.

6. The Father's approval and gratitude

The Father *loves* me because I lay down my life to take it back again (Jn. 10:17).

The announcement of Jesus' death concludes the allegory of the good shepherd (*ho poimēn ho kalos*) and the hireling (*misthōtos*), which the Lord has just applied to himself (vv. 14–16). It corrects a too narrow application of the allegory. Jesus is not *like* the good shepherd; he alone is the true and perfect Shepherd.[19] The model is always superior to the copy and the type to the antitype. Unlike the hireling, Jesus has the entire ownership of his flock and entire responsibility for it (v. 12). More important, he willingly sacrifices himself for his flock. The emphasis is on his initiative, which was taken in complete liberty. An ordinary shepherd may have to risk his life, it is true. He does not run away from a wolf or a thief, but while he fights, he tries to save himself. The good shepherd, on the contrary, wishes to die. Not content with exposing his life (v. 11), he gives it voluntarily and lays it down of his own free will. What is far greater, he immolates himself amidst the worst of tortures.

According to the context, his death is an heroic act of love for the flock. Since it is God who sends his Son as a victim for the salvation of the world (3:16), Calvary expresses Jesus' obedience to his Father [20] and the complete conformity of wills [21] which only Christ's love for God could have accomplished. The Lord claimed full mastery and initiative in his sacrifice when he dealt with his judges and executioners, and he submitted himself out of love to the will of his Father. His adherence to God's plan is so profound that his act of giving remains perfectly free and totally his own.

"This is why the Father loves me." The Greek has *dia*

---

[19] Cf. Heb. 13:20; 1 Pet. 5:4.   [20] Philip. 2:8; Heb. 10:5–10.
[21] Jn. 4:34; 5:30; 6:38; 8:29.

touto followed by *hoti;* these words express the motive or reason for an emotion or act.[22] The divine love is affected by Christ's obedience and oblation. The relations within the Trinity are not modified or enriched in any way, of course, but here Jesus is speaking of the love which God manifests to him in history since his Incarnation, when Jesus told the Father that he had come to do his will (Heb. 10:5). Obviously, *agapan* is a motivated love which is the result of a new and clearly understood fact (cf. v. 15, "the Father knows me"). We might understand that the Father feels "infinite satisfaction" (Godet) at his Son's love but it is better semantics to see the Father's *agape* as perfect gratitude, like that of John 14:23: "Anyone who loves me will treasure my message, and my Father will love him, and we shall visit him and make our home with him." God is grateful to Jesus for loving sinners and adhering to the plan of salvation and thus proving his love.[23] It is "a sacrifice that has an agreeable fragrance." [24] Because all *agape* manifests itself openly, the loving gratitude of the Father expresses itself in the exaltation of Jesus.[25] Finally, the divine gratitude is aroused by Jesus' perfect accomplishment of the Father's command (*entolē*, v. 18), a command which is not in any sense an isolated precept or order, but is, rather, a word (Jn. 12:49) and communication of a plan and proposition, *thelēma* (Heb. 10:9–10) of a mission and program. *Entolē*, "command," is a synonym for *paraggelia*, "charge" (1 Tim. 1:5).

In order (hina) to take it back again

It is impossible to give a certain interpretation of the last part of the verse. Perhaps *hina* should be understood in the weak sense of *hōste*, as it often is in the *koine*. If this sense is correct, the resurrection—the taking up again of life—would be a simple consequence or a particular mode of Jesus'

---

[22] Cf. 5:16, 18; 6:65; 8:47; 12:18, 39. [23] Cf. Ex. 20:6; Deut. 5:10.
[24] Eph. 5:2. Cf. Ps. 116:15. [25] Philip. 2:9; Heb. 2:9.

death: "I lay down my life but in such a way that I will take it up again; I am and I will remain the absolute Master of my life." This interpretation fits the general tone of the text perfectly well. However, most of the modern commentators follow St. Augustine in giving *hina* its full value as a conjunction showing purpose or goal. They join it to *agapai*, "[The Father] loves [me]," rather than to *tithēmi*, "I lay down my life." They observe not only that the resurrection is a part of the divine plan and an act of the Father [26] but also that it is as much the cause of our salvation as Christ's death is.[27]

It would seem that these two aspects should not be contrasted. The perfect Shepherd gives his life only in order to be forever the leader of the flock in this world and the next. His immolation is only one step of his mission. The Father's love of gratitude expresses itself in not leaving his Son in Sheol and in "glorifying" him in his victorious passion. Jesus declares that he is sure of the Father's interventions (cf. 5:26), for, loved unfailingly, he can intercede efficaciously for his own (cf. Heb. 7:25).

7. Jesus' attachment to Martha, Mary, and Lazarus

Now Jesus *loved* Martha and her sister and Lazarus (Jn. 11:5). See below, Ch. III, "*Philein* in St. John," pp. 86 ff.

8. Preferring men's approval to God's

They *cared more* for the approval of men than for the approval of God (Jn. 12:43).

This is the fifth of the seven uses of *agapan* by St. John himself. He is explaining why so many prominent men who have been converted to Christ do not have the courage to

[26] Acts 2:24; Rom. 1:4; 6:4; Gal. 1:1.
[27] Rom. 4:25; cf. 1 Cor. 15:17; Heb. 10:12; 12:2.

announce their conversions. Psychologically, they feared the ostracism of the Pharisees, which had already been laid on the parents of the man born blind (9:22). Religiously, they preferred the approval of men to God's approval. The wording is the same as in John 3:19, and the thought, the same as in John 5:44; 1 John 2:15; James 4:4; Galatians 1:10; 6:14. In this context, *agapan* does not mean "to take pleasure in" (C. K. Barrett) but "to attach a price to." When it is used with *mallon*, "more," as it is here, it means to choose in preference to something else." The nuance of "to desire," which is frequent in the Septuagint, should not be excluded.

9. The supreme manifestation of Christ's unchanging charity

The feast of the Passover was now approaching, and Jesus knew that his time for passing from this world to his Father had arrived. He had always *loved* his own who were in the world and now he *loved* them to the end (Jn. 13:1).

This long verse of thirty-four words is not only a theological introduction to the last part of the Gospel but also its solemn preface. St. John loves to bring out the hidden significance of Jesus' actions. For example, the multiplication of the loaves and the healing of the man born blind show that Jesus is life and light.[28] Here, the washing of the feet, the Lord's confidences to his closest disciples, his last supper with them, and his passion (15:13) are presented as revelations of his charity. Both his actions and his words give instruction, and they must be interpreted one by one, as St. John intended; they are expressions of the Savior's love. Objectively, Jesus' death and resurrection are a manifestation of his glory and divinity,[29] but, subjectively, everything that the Master said and did during his last hours on earth was inspired by

[28] Cf. O. Cullmann, *Les Sacraments dans l'Evangile johannique*, Paris, 1951.

[29] Jn. 12:28; 13:31–32.

his charity. *Agape* must furnish the key, then, to the exegesis of chapters 13 to 19 of the fourth Gospel. The words "to the end," *eis telos,* of 13:1 are completed by Jesus' words in 19:30, "It is finished," *tetelestai.* During the last hours of his life, Jesus manifested to the supreme degree the love that he had always had for his disciples. Only the beloved disciple could authentically interpret the Master's feelings and be authorized to reveal them to the primitive Church.

Chapter 13, verse 1 begins with a double statement of the chronology of events. The first is Jewish, "before the feast of the Passover," *pro tēs heortēs;* it is distinct from Chapter 19, verse 14, "the eve of the Passover." The second, "and Jesus knew" (*eidōs*), is Christian. It emphasizes first Christ's perfect knowledge of the time and circumstances of his death and then the sequence of events. The moment, in fact, is completely precise; it was fixed by Providence for the return (v. 3) of the incarnate Word to his Father. The movement of the phrase demands both a causal and an affective nuance in the word *eidōs: because* Jesus knew that his hour was at last about to come. . . . He had always known his hour, but when it drew near (12:23, 27; 17:1) he hastened (Lk. 22:15) to accomplish the acts which lay ahead: to place in the hands of his own both the Eucharist and the ministry, his own body and the souls of others.

All these details and suggestions of time and circumstance are related to the principal action, Christ's charity. The object of this verse and of all the chapters that follow is to point out Christ's love. Precisely because the chronology of this Passover is so important, St. John defines the *agape* of Jesus in terms of the Savior's entire mission on earth and in heaven. Christ has loved his own from eternity. During his life his love never for a moment left him, and he spent his life showing it to his own. The aorist participle *agapēsas,* "he had loved," reflects all of his ministry, his preaching, and the miracles he had already worked, for *agapan* is concerned with manifest acts and signs.[30] His love here is a

[30] The verb *agapan* conveys this expression of love, and St. John

predilection for a limited group, for "his own," *tous idious*. His relations with the multitude and his public teaching are over (12:36). During his last hours, the Master gives himself exclusively to his own who have been privileged to receive his love and devotion (cf. 17:6, 9, 11, 20). The expression, "his own," *hoi idioi*, is much more limited than the "compatriots" mentioned in John 1:11. It can be taken to mean his disciples, *mathētai*,[31] since it emphasizes the idea of belonging,[32] but it has a theological meaning also: these men whom the Father has given and confided to me.[33] Finally, it has an affective nuance. Jesus loves in a very special way these disciples whom he has received as a precious gift from his Father and who have given themselves to him by the total consecration of their lives (cf. v. 13). There is an interior religious relationship between "to love," *agapan*, and "his own," *idious*.

The addition, "who were in the world," *tous en tōi kosmōi*, seems to emphasize the disciples' need for the love and support of their lord. They will go on living in a wicked world, which is opposed to the glory which will be the Lord's; they must live in solitude and trials (cf. 14:18). The charity of Christ had chosen some from among all men. He had withdrawn his own from the world and brought them together to draw them to himself. The words, "his own," the first elite of all believers to come, suggest the Church itself (11:52).

St. John's affirmation rests on the immense and decisive proof of love which Jesus was going to give his own in sacrificing his life for them: "he loved them to the end," *eis telos ēgapēsen autous*. The aorist indicative [34] refers to a particular act, a detailed gift whose preparations and fulfillment were about to be described: On the eve of the Pass-

---

must have had in mind the Lord's "service" of men throughout his life (Mt. 20:28).

[31] Mk. 4:34; Jn. 8:31; 13:23, 35; 15:8, etc.

[32] Jn. 15:19; cf. Acts 4:23; 24:23; 1 Cor. 3:8; 6:18. Jesus loves his own for the same reason the world hates them (15:19): They are "his."

[33] Jn. 6:37, 39; 17:11.   [34] Cf. 3:16; Gal. 2:20; Eph. 5:2.

over, as he was about to leave the disciples whom he cherished, Christ showed them all his charity and "in a sense surpassed himself in his expressions of his love." [35]

In these circumstances, the expression *eis telos*, which occurs only this once in St. John, obviously retains its temporal meaning, "unto the end, finally." A love that continues to such an "end," the voluntary death of a martyr, is heroic, and *eis telos* also has the sense of "completely, totally" (Deut. 31:24). This sense can be understood in two ways: "definitively, indefectibly" [36] or "to the highest degree, to the fullest possible extent." [37] In a phrase that is so precise from a chronological point of view (the tenses of the verbs, the Passover, the end of life) and at the same time so theologically profound,[38] good exegesis requires that *eis telos* keep its fullest meaning. However, following Augustine and Chrysostom, common exegesis correctly stresses the perfection of Christ's love, or, rather, its most complete manifestation. Jesus gave his disciples a proof of love that was both decisive and definitive. During these tragic hours, he forgot himself in thinking of his own, in consoling them and reassuring them (16:33). From the moment he had called them he had given them unmistakable signs of his affection, but at the last supper and above all through his death, he manifested his love for them perfectly and in an extraordinary way, crowning all his earlier signs of love. He was going to the limit of love, so to speak, beyond the bounds of every measure.

This Johannine teaching on charity in 13:1 is parallel to that of 3:16, and together the two verses constitute the theological framework of the Gospel. In John 3:16 God loves the world so much that he sacrifices his Son; in John 13:1 the Son himself loves his disciples so much that he

---

[35] Godet, who quotes Homer, *Odyssey* 23:214.

[36] *Eis telos* in the sense of perpetual, definitive, eternal, Ps. 9:19; 16:11; 49; 10; 77:9; 103:9; Dan. 3:34.

[37] Polybius 1:20, 7; 12:27, 3.

[38] St. Thomas analyzes with precision, "Tria tanguntur: Festum praesens . . . Mors Christi imminens . . . Christi dilectio fervens."

sacrifices his life for them. There is no need in a context like this for stressing the technical and religious meaning of *agapan* which is so markedly different from *philein* [39] and which agrees so closely with the meaning in the Septuagint. *Agapan* here is choice and predilection first of all, and then official manifestation and proof. The Evangelist's thought might be glossed: Since all love of *agape* is active and gives itself, perfect *agape* inspires total sacrifice. It includes magnanimity,[40] and this final note is all the more essential in that *agape* is perfectly conscious, *eidōs*, with complete freedom in the bestowing of its gifts [41] and in choosing the occasions of its manifestations. Finally, this love is unchanging and definitive. He who loves with *agape* is never unfaithful to his commitments. Once he has given his heart, he loves forever.[42] St. John expressly emphasizes that Jesus, who had always loved, *agapēsas*, his own, gave them the greatest proof of his love, *ēgapēsan*, at the last Passover, and that he will continue to love them eternally, *eis telos*. His death "immobilizes" his signal charity. Although its modes of expression vary, *agape* is permanent and unchangeable. In the Apocalypse, St. John calls Christ "him who loves," *ho agapōn* (1:5). *Agape*'s stability explains the belief of the apostles in Christ's charity, which is the whole of their faith.[43]

[39] Jesus' tender affection for "his own" is doubtless a sort of friendship, but it remains that of a superior for his subjects (13:13); the persons involved are too unequal for the relationship to be called a true *philia*; furthermore, the Greek notion of friendship is characterized by harmony, reason, and measure, and Christ's *agape* in death is the height of excess.

[40] Cf. *Agape in the New Testament*, vol. II, pp. 151–152.

[41] The revelation of the Father's secrets, i.e. the life of the Trinity (15:15); the bloody sacrifice (15:13), the eucharistic communication of life (15:1), constituting a people of priests and kings (Apoc. 1:4; 5:9–10) etc.

[42] Cf. *Prolégomènes* (*Index* under "Perseverance"); Fl. Josephus, p. 186; Eph. 6:24.

[43] 1 Jn. 3:16; 4:9–10, 16.

10. The disciple whom Jesus loved

Whom Jesus *loved* (Jn. 13:23). Cf. below, pp. 91–94.

11–15. Union with Christ and with one's brothers in charity

9. Just as the Father *has loved* me, so I *have loved* you. Remain in my *love*. 10. If you observe my commandments, you will remain in my *love*, just as I have perfectly observed my Father's commandments and remain in his *love* . . . 12. This is my commandment: *love* one another as I *love* you. 13. No one can give a greater proof of his *love* than by laying down his life for his friends. 14. You are my friends, provided that you do what I command you. 15. No longer do I call you servants for a servant is not in his master's confidence. But I have called you friends, because I have made known to you all that I have heard from my Father . . . 17. These things I command you: *love* one another (Jn. 15:9–17).

This entire section devoted to *agape*, union with Christ and Christ's disciples, is closely related to the allegory of the vine and forms a commentary on it. Jesus had just instituted the eucharist as the prolongation of his presence among his own. He compares his union with his disciples by the blood of the "eucharisted" grape to the union of a vine with its branches. The point of the allegory is the union. The only vital problem for the branches is remaining united to the trunk so that they can bear fruit.[44] Jesus explains more clearly that the union is effected by charity. The disciples must remain in his love (vv. 9–10) and they must love one another because of their common union in the love of him (vv. 12–17).

[44] Verses 2 through 8 each contain the idea of union; and verses 2, 4, 5 and 8 speak of fecundity.

V. 9 "Just as the Father has loved me, so I have loved you. Remain in my love."

The Master consecrated the last hours he spent with his disciples to his farewell to them. He assured them that his love for them would live forever. St. John had already recorded that the love which formed the extremely strong, close bond between Jesus and his own from the moment that he chose them (v. 16) had inspired and defined all their relations during his public life.[45] The Synoptics [46] and the Lord himself had made it clear that the Father manifested a signal charity of delight and gift toward his incarnate Son. It is love which summarizes the relationship between Father and Son,[47] and Jesus loves his disciples in exactly the same way as his Father loves him. The Greek word *kathōs*, translated "as," is stronger than *hōsper*; it is used of things which are similar in nature and consequently equal or analogous in action. The great revelation of this verse is that the charity of the Father, the Son, and the disciples is on one and the same level and flows from one to the other without any interruption. As the Father has loved me, so have I loved you. You, yourselves, remain in this *agape*. The verse implies that charity is a bond; charity creates the union between those who love one another. It tells us that "to be in Christ" (v. 2) means to be in his love. Above all, it presents the relationship of the Father to the Son as the type and source of Christ's relationship to his own disciples. There is so great a disproportion between the Son and the disciples that the statement is truly stupefying, but it is no arbitrary parallel or comparison. It is precisely the love most proper to God which reaches men through the intervention of Christ. God loves men in Christ, and they participate in his love and live from it in the most real sense. The allegory of the vine had already showed that the vine and its branches share one nature and are permanently

---

[45] *Hymas ēgapēsa* (15:9) recalls *agapēsas tous idios* (13:1).
[46] Mt. 3:17; 17:5.
[47] Cf. the verb in the present Jn. 3:35; 5:20; 10:17.

united in a vital relationship. Now it is stated that Christ's *agape*, like the Father's and derived from it, unites the disciples and vivifies them by maintaining them under its sway.

The Christian life, pure submission to the grasp of Christ's charity, is defined by union with the Savior. The only problem for the Christian is to be united and inserted "in me" (15:2). Rather, since Jesus has already taken the initiative by forming the union, the Christian has only to persevere in his belonging to Christ to maintain forever the union and communion in love. Christ makes an imperative call for the cooperation of his disciples: "Remain in my love." *Agape* is in any case a stable love,[48] but for Christians its permanence is the permanence of the eternal charity of the Father and the Son. St. Paul, in one of his usual active images, spoke of "pursuing" charity (*diōkete*, 1 Cor. 14:1), and St. Jude asked Christians to keep themselves in God's love (*heatous . . . tērēsate*, Jude 21). According to St. John, we must establish ourselves permanently in charity, preserve the union which has already been formed, and immobilize ourselves in *agape* (cf. v. 10; Eph. 1:4). The idea recalls Wisdom 3:9: "Those who are faithful will cling to him in love," and even more John 6:56: "He who eats my flesh and drinks my blood remains in me and I in him, *en emoi menei kagō en autōi*." It is important to make use of all available information that can throw light on the exact meaning of the verb *menein*, whose theological importance is so considerable in St. John.

Meno is used in the Septuagint almost eighty times, usually to translate the verbs *'âmad* and *qûm*.[49] Its first sense is "to live," "to remain in a place or near someone,"[50] and "to be on guard, immobile."[51] It also conveys the idea of duration and stability[52] in the sense of "to subsist, to con-

[48] Cf. *Prolégomènes*, pp. 44, n. 7; 93 n. 5; 114–118; 136; 186.
[49] Then *Yâschab* "to live" (Gen. 24:55; Ps. 9:8; 102:13; Zach. 14:10); *hayah* "to be" (1 Kings 8:16; Ps. 89:37; Ez. 48:8).
[50] Ex. 9:28; Judges 19:9; Jud. 7:20; 11:17.
[51] Judges 16:2; 2 Sam. 18:14; Jud. 7:5; 15:2; Tob. 8:20.
[52] Lev. 13:5, 23, 28, 37; Numb. 30:5, 9, 10, 13; Dan. 6:13; Wisd. 16:5; 18:20; Sir. 37:2.

tinue to be," [53] especially in the formula *menein en*, "to remain in," [54] or the superlative *menein eis ton aiōna*, "to remain forever." The superlative is often applied to divine creation and to the Fathers (Sir. 42:23; 44:13), but it is especially fitting for God himself, for his attributes of justice and fidelity, for his plan and his word which last forever.[55] In this sense, which may well be called theological, *menein* unites the notions of existence and continuity, so that we speak of the living God subsisting forever or of the new heaven and the new earth which will subsist before Yahweh.[56]

The author of the fourth Gospel was perfectly familiar with the profane meaning of *menein*, "to live, to dwell," which predominates in the Synoptics. The first question he asks Jesus is, "Where are you staying?" (Jn. 1:38). John also knows the sense, "to endure, subsist, persevere," [57] which is used of something which remains identical with itself,[58] and preeminently of Christ and his gifts which remain forever.[59] *Menō* appears forty times in John's Gospel, eleven of them in chapter 15, and twenty-four times in his first epistle. The great contribution of the Johannine language is the use of the formula *menein en*, "to remain in," in a new religious sense. *Menein en* describes the relationship between God and Christ: "the Father remaining in me" (14:10), and between God and Christians,[60] and Christ and his disciples. "One who remains in him," *ho menōn en autōi*, is a precise definition of the faithful man.

This definition had already been suggested by the welcoming of the word of God or of the truth which lives in the believer,[61] as John 8:31 says, "If you continue in (*meinēte*

---

[53] Wisd. 11:25.   [54] Eccl. 7:15; Wisd. 7:27; 19:18; 2 Mach. 8:1.
[55] Ps. 9:8; 33:11; 102:13; 111:3, 10; 112:3, 9; 117:2; Is. 14:24; 40:8; Prov. 19:21.
[56] Dan. 6:27; Is. 66:22.
[57] Sin remains (Jn. 9:41); fruit lasts (15:16); the Apostle survives (21:22; cf. Apoc. 17:10). Through faith one does not remain in darkness.
[58] The grain of wheat remains as it was, *autos monos menei* (12:24).
[59] Jn. 12:34; cf. 6:27; 1 Jn. 2:17.   [60] 1 Jn. 3:24; 4:12, 15.
[61] Jn. 5:38; 15:7; 1 Jn. 2:14, 24; 2 Jn. 2.

en) my word you are truly my disciples." The authentic
disciple clings to God and Christ by faith (1 Jn. 4:15), and
the whole purpose of the allegory of the vine is to define
the disciple by the permanence of his adherence and belonging: "You will become my disciples" (Jn. 15:8). The
disciple is so clearly "he who remains" that he is called "he
who says he abides in him" (1 Jn. 2:6) or "everyone who
abides in him" (1 Jn. 3:6). Perseverance in this union is
his salvation. "Abide in him." [62] That he may be able to
persevere, he possesses permanently the seed of God (3:9),
the anointing (2:27), the Holy Spirit (4:13), and *agape*
(3:17; 4:16). He eats the flesh and drinks the blood of the
Savior (Jn. 6:56; cf. Acts 2:42), and he observes the commandments (Jn. 15:10; 1 Jn. 3:24). By existing permanently
in God and Christ, the Christian keeps himself from sin (1 Jn.
3:6), receives whatever he asks for in prayer (Jn. 15:7),
and bears fruit. He "who does not abide" not only can do
nothing (Jn. 15:5), but also separates himself from the community of the faithful (1 Jn. 2:19); God himself cuts him
off (Jn. 15:2).

Menein en, then, means "to exist," but to exist by or in
another; it is what St. Paul called "to be in Christ Jesus."
The union is so intimate that it suggests reciprocal immanence. In fact, the same formula which expresses the dwelling and abode of the disciple in Christ or God designates the
consubstantiality of the Father and the Son (14:10–11). This
is not misleading, because the Lord asks his Father that his
own "may be as one . . . just as you, Father, are in me and
I am in you, so they, too, are to be one in us" (17:11, 21);
"that they may be one—I in them and you in me, that their
oneness may be perfect" (vv. 22–23). To abide in Christ is
to be in vital, mutual, indefectible union with him. *Menein
en* expresses both reciprocity and duration; it is an eternal
communion. The Father and the Son enter the believer to
establish their abode in him (14:23), and after his death the
believer will be received into the abode of the Father (14:2).

[62] 1 Jn. 2:28; cf. 1 Tim. 2:15.

In the allegory of the vine, Jesus stressed both the permanence of the union—one must never cease to *exist in* the community which has been established forever—and the *agape* which is itself the attachment and belonging. To abide in Christ—"Remain in me" (15:4)—is to abide in his love —"Remain in my love" (Jn. 15:9)—just as Jesus himself abides in the love of the Father—"I abide in his love" (v. 10). Verse 17 and the first Epistle of St. John attribute the same efficacy for life and salvation to fraternal charity.[63] Since the twelve were eager to bear fruit, it is understandable that it is more necessary for the Apostle than for anyone else to "abide in love." [64] Charity bears fruit more than all the charisms (1 Cor. 12–13). The primary teaching about *agape* is that it is the principle of subsistence. It forms and preserves the union between the Father and the Son, between Christ and his own, and between the Father and the disciple of Jesus. St. Paul cries out, "Nor can any other creature separate us from God's love for us which is in Christ Jesus, our Lord" (Rom. 8:39). This is the golden ring of charity.

Verse 10: "If you observe my commandments, you will remain in my *love,* just as I have perfectly observed my Father's commandments and remain in his *love* . . ."

Since God and Christ have taken the initiative in love, only one question faces the disciple: how to remain in unchanging charity? Jesus explains—by observing the commandments. The Septuagint had already taught that *agape* and fidelity are correlatives, if not synonyms. To love God is to belong to him exclusively, to serve him and obey him. In saying, "Observe my commandments," Jesus is calling on the personal charity of the disciples, you will live in my love by loving me in return with the true and effective love of fidelity and union of wills.

The words "precept" and "commandment" are ambiguous in that they stress constraint and obligation, but the example

---

[63] 1 Jn. 2:10; 3:14; 3:15, 17.
[64] Cf. *Prolégomènes,* pp. 91 ff., 124.

of the Lord—which proves that this fidelity is not impossible
or superhuman—makes their meaning clearer. According to
John 4:34 and 8:29, Jesus had only one desire, to do his
Father's will; he did exactly what would please God. His
whole life was directed by the agreement of their wills, in
the smallest details as well as in the supreme sacrifice (Lk.
22:42), and that is why the Father loved him (Jn. 10:17)
and why Jesus remains forever in his love (the verb *menō*
is in the present). Obedience is the expression and manifestation of love.

Far from imposing too heavy a burden on his disciples
(1 Jn. 5:3), the Lord is telling them the secret of his pure and
simple joy: "I have told you this, that my joy may be yours,
and your joy may be perfect" (v. 11). Jesus gives the example of perfect charity. Not only does his love abide in the
love of the Father, not only does it root itself there, prove
itself (13:1), and give itself forever to the disciples, but also
it reveals to them how they can love in their turn in response
to his kindness. Going further, it reveals its most intimate
secrets.

Jesus' soul is filled with joy—a great mystery. The last
hour the "man of sorrows" spent on earth was surely tragic
above all others. It was overshadowed by his approaching
agony and torture (Heb. 12:2) and made heavier by the
betrayal of his chosen disciple. His heart was already in anguish,[65] yet the Lord's joy remained, the result of his union
with his Father and the fruit of his *agape* of adherence and
fidelity (v. 10). His joy was fullness overflowing in the loving soul (v. 9) of him who had revealed the Father, of the
High Priest and Shepherd who gives his life for his sheep,
for "there is more happiness in giving than in receiving"
(Acts 20:35). This is the blessedness of charity.

[65] *etarachthē* (Jn. 13:21). Luthardt noted that "in the 17 verses of
this chapter, there is not one linking particle. This long *asyndeton* has
a special solemnity and betrays the Master's emotion during his farewell discourse. He speaks in detached phrases, as if to catch his breath
after each statement. A person who is oppressed by chargrin and tears
does not construct a 'discourse.' "

The Lord who was about to leave his own encouraged them wonderfully by revealing to them the secret of perfect joy: to abide in love and to observe the commandments. His legacy is perfectly real. Jesus intended his own unique and characteristic joy to pass into the hearts of his disciples and become their own. He wanted them to know and savor the joy he himself has in loving and remaining in unbreakable communion with his Father.

Precisely because Christ's joy is proper to himself—as previously the charity which the disciples were to share was his own—it could not conceivably be some ordinary kind of more or less deep feeling. What Jesus wanted was that the joy of his disciples reach its complete measure and be fully attained. His desire must not be thought of as a sudden impulse spoken in passing. It is one of the most deliberately expressed of the Lord's last wishes, and he stated it twice again: "Thus nothing will be wanting to your joy" (16:24); ". . . that they may taste my joy made perfect within their souls" (17:13). His desire is possible of fulfillment only because joy and *agápe* are intrinsically united. Like love, joy expresses communion with God and Christ; both are attributes of the disciple. If the soul becomes happy from the moment it adheres to the Lord by whom it knows it is loved, an entire life spent in loving fidelity must grow into joy without end. The ever greater ascendancy of Christ's charity over all the faculties of the soul develops the capacity for spiritual joy to enormous fullness. Joy is the delicious fruit of the union of branch with vine.

Verse 12: "This is my commandment: love one another as I love you."

After having stressed the relation of the branches to the Vine (vv. 1–11), Jesus could not neglect the relation of the branches among themselves (vv. 12–17) or, consequently, the "commandments" the disciples must observe to maintain themselves in reciprocal union. He was not in the least beginning a new theme, but rather developing the requirements and consequences implicit in union and insertion in Christ. To the first precept of living in Christ's love (vv. 9–10) he added the second of living in fraternal love. It would be unthinkable that the vine which belongs to God and is cultivated by him (vv. 1–2) could be nourished by anything except charity. Gift of the Father manifested and transmitted by Christ, charity forms the relation between the disciples as well as with the Lord himself.

The opening proposition is constructed like a definition, "This is . . . ," and its wording in Greek, *hē entolē hē emē*, "my commandment," strongly emphasizes the possessive "my." It might be glossed: "This is my own precept, distinctive for those who are my true disciples" (cf. 13:35). In verse 10 Jesus had used the plural "commandments," but here he uses the singular "commandment" to show that this precept is distinctive. The only condition for the continued existence of the branches is "to remain" attached to the vine, and the only law of life for the disciples is to love one another (*agapate allēlous*). The verb in the present subjunctive of duration suggests a permanent act or state, as it were, of unchanging love. The final "as I have loved you," *kathōs ēgapēsa hymas*, is even more important. It is commented on in vv. 13–16 and is directly related to the definition in v. 9: Christ's love for his own (13:1) is like his Father's love for him; it is of the same divine nature. Jesus had just mentioned his own love and asked his disciples to remain in it. Referring again to his love, he tells them to love one another because fraternal *agape* is the means of remaining united to him. Obedience to the commandments (v. 10) is reduced to fraternal love. In other words, it is not a matter of sensibility or purely interior affection but of religious love which gives and spends itself in imitation of the Savior's love (cf. Eph. 5:2). Its first characteristic is profundity and totality (Jn. 13:1). Just as the *true* vine has fruitful branches, so true and properly Christian love is active and generous. Its source is the Father's love for the Son, so those who love one another with *agape* love *sub specie aeterni* with a stability and fidel-

ity that nothing can alter. Finally, the immediately preceding
verse shows that fervor and lively joy in fraternal love are
also part of Christian love. "Behold how good and how pleasant it is for brothers to dwell together in unity!"

Verse 13: "No one can give a greater proof of his love
than by laying down his life for his friends. 14. You are my
friends provided that you do what I command you."

Jesus himself explicitly stated the two predominant qualities of his *agape*. They are gift and intimacy (vv. 13–16),
precisely the qualities stressed by St. Paul in Eph. 5:25–30.
The gift is made in the form of generous sacrifice of self. No
one can give a greater proof of his love than by laying down
his life for his friends. St. John in 10:11 had spoken of the
good shepherd who lays down his life for his sheep, and later
he commented, "From this we know what love is, that Jesus
laid down his life for us" (1 Jn. 3:16). In John 15:13, however, the proposition is general and does not refer directly
to Jesus. It is an aphorism. To go voluntarily to death for the
sake of someone else has been recognized from all time as the
most expressive possible sign of strong, sincere love and its
most unmistakable proof, *martyria*, for "nothing is more
precious than life." [66] *Agape* in verse 13 retains the traditional
sense it has in the Septuagint of "manifestation of love." The
verse as a whole means that there is no more telling sign or
manifest proof of love than the willingness to die. To give
one's life is not only the highest degree of love but also the
most expressive sign of love's sincerity and depth. It is a
gesture that the beloved cannot fail to understand. The
philoi in this context are not so much "friends" in the strict
sense as "those loved with a generous love."

The words "for his friends," *hyper tōn philōn*, in v. 13
should be taken passively and in the broadest possible sense:
"those whom one loves nobly and not for oneself." Verse 14
confirms this reading in presenting a condition for friendship: "provided that you do what I command you," and

[66] Euripides, *Alcestis*, 301.

verse 10 explains further, "You will remain in my love if you observe my commandments." There is a progression in the thought, however. For one thing, in verse 13 the disciples who respond to the charity of Christ by obedience and abide effectively in his love are called "friends," *philoi*, and between friends there is always reciprocity of love. More profoundly still, the opening categorical declaration, "You are my friends," not only refers to the beloved, privileged beneficiaries of Jesus' death (v. 13) but also identifies them as "friends" in a religious sense. By being faithful to Christ's commandments, especially to his commandment of fraternal charity, the disciples became the "friends" of their Master and Lord (13:13). His "you are my friends" is a real declaration of love—and it was so new to the apostles that they must have shown their surprise and so led Jesus to explain what their friendship was.

Verse 15: "No longer do I call you servants for a servant is not in his master's confidence. But I have called you friends, because I have made known to you all that I have heard from my Father."

Until then, the disciples' relations with Christ were those of servants, *douloi*, to their Lord, *Kyrios*—already an honorable position, given such a Master. The Messias was himself the Servant of Yahweh. In truth, the twelve will always be *servants*, receiving orders to carry out, never on a level with the Lord of glory. This kind of equality is proper to friendship in the strict sense, but a servant has to obey without knowing the intentions and plans of his master or the reasons for the orders he must follow. All he has to do is carry out his instructions without trying to understand. Jesus is calling his disciples "friends" in the sense of "confidants." "I have called you friends, because I have made known to you all that I have heard from my Father." The statement is as clear as one could wish. The Christ who made it was not so much the Christ-Teacher revealing the way of salvation (Jn. 14:6), as Christ the Son of God dwelling in the bosom of the

Father (1:18), initiating his own (13:1) into the secrets of
the divine life and into the realities which the Father has
communicated to him. The disciples are friends of the incarnate Word because as apostles and leaders of his Church,
they are entrusted with the secret of the mystery of the life
of the Trinity, of God's charity, and of his providential plan
for salvation in which they are called to collaborate. They
are "stewards of God's mystery." [67]

The accent is on the unlimited confidence implied in the
making of so exceptional, valuable, and total a revelation.
What Jesus taught to his disciples corresponded exactly to
what he had heard from the Father. The communication was
perfect and completely different from what he taught to the
multitude. Obviously, the meaning of "I have made known
. . . everything" should not be pushed too far; it is more
intensive than extensive. As St. Thomas observes, "If Jesus
had made everything known to them, it would follow that
the disciples would know as much as the Son." Actually, the
disciples still had a great many things to learn (Jn. 16:12).
When Jesus said, "I have told you everything; I have done
everything," he was speaking the language of the heart,
which uses absolutes to convey the essential.

The meaning of "friends" has evolved, then, in vv. 13–15.
From the simple, passive, profane, and completely general
meaning of "those who are loved" in verse 13, it has become
the disciples as such in verse 14 where it refers to reciprocal
attachment. The friend of Christ responds to Christ's *agape*
by obedience. However, this relationship is not friendship in
the technical and well-developed sense of the Greek *philia*,
at least not explicitly so, for Jesus himself explains: You are
my friends because you are my confidants, the recipients of
my entire confidence.[68] Christ's friendship, then, is that

---

[67] 1 Cor. 4:1; cf. v. 2; Lk. 12:42; Tit. 1:7.
[68] V. 15. "The true sign of friendship is that a friend reveals the
secrets of his heart to a friend. For when friends have one heart and
one soul, a friend does not seem to place outside his own heart what
he reveals to a friend . . . In making us sharers in his wisdom, God
reveals his secrets to us" (St. Thomas).

which is established between one who reveals a secret and one who receives it. It can exist between persons of disproportionate condition, like a master and his subjects. Many commentators correctly recall the royal title, "Friends of the King," a title which had nothing to do with friends in the proper sense, but was bestowed on officials, important persons, or persons more or less in the public eye whom the prince wished to honor. The analogy is valuable in so far as it stresses both the contrast between servants and friends in Jn. 15:15 and dignity of the twelve in the New Covenant. According to the immediate context and the conception of the ecclesiastical hierarchy in Jn. 13:3–17, these "friends of the *Kyrios*" should be understood less as "chief men," *dynastai*, or "nobles," *megistōnes*, than as intimate counsellors, *symbouloi*, and confidants.

In other words, this friendship, *philia*, is only one aspect and one special case of Christ's *agape*, just as the disciples' brotherly love, *philadelphia*, is a mode of the charity which the Holy Spirit infuses and which reaches to all persons, from God to enemies. It is not correct to identify *philia*—the word itself is not even used—and *agape* in St. John, as most exegetes have done. One might even assert, judging from this pericope alone, that the twelve and their successors are the only "friends," *philoi*, of Christ, for they are the only ones who have been personally chosen to receive and guard the deposit of the Father's revelations by the Son.

Verse 16: "You have not chosen me, but I have chosen you, and the task I imposed upon you is to go forward steadfastly in bearing fruit; and your fruit is to be lasting. Thus the Father will grant you any petition you may present to him in my name." Verse 17: "These things I command you: love one another."

Verse 16 underlines the disproportion which must always exist between the Lord and his own. He is the one who formed the friendship. He is the one who took and keeps the entire initiative in this intimate, generous relationship with the twelve, making them by his purely gratuitous gift part of the work of redemption, the greatest work there is, the work of God which Jesus came in person to accomplish.

In vv. 7–8 Jesus had reminded the apostles that prayer is their means of bearing fruit and fulfilling their vocations, for the Vine belongs to the Father who communicates his secrets to it (v. 15) and cultivates it so that it will bear fruit (vv. 1–2; cf. Is. 5:1–7). Only the Father can give the branches their proper fecundity. Jesus concludes the allegory of "the True Vine" by a formula that recapitulates its major teaching: "These things I command you: love one another . . ." (v. 17). *Tauta entellomai hymin, hina agapate allēlous.* If *hina* is taken as introducing a purpose clause, the sentence should be translated, "This is what I command you so that you may love one another." However, as Père Lagrange has observed, this meaning does not fit the context, since the Lord has not prescribed anything for the sake of obtaining fraternal charity. *Hina* should therefore be given the same meaning it had in vv. 12 and 16 where it is a synonym of *hoti* and introduces the content of the precept.

This verse is materially parallel to verse 12, "This is my commandment: love one another as I love you," but it emphasizes the imperative quality of the precept with the verb "I command," *entellomai*, which is stronger and more personal than "this is my commandment" in v. 12. "This is an order which *I* give you." However, the neuter plural demonstrative *tauta*, "these things," refers to more than just the earlier declaration of this precept of mutual love. It forms an *inclusio*, repeating the teaching of the allegory of the vine in a summary and conclusion and giving its practical implications. It refers essentially to the basic condition and spirit of the *disciples* (v. 8), who are to be and to remain in Christ. They have been chosen for this purpose, and they will bear fruit in joy, if they ask it of the Father. In a certain sense, the sap of this vine is *agape*. The disciples remain in Christ through love as Christ remains in the Father (vv. 9–10). Consequently, it is love which forms the union among the disciples just as it is love which forms the Father's union with the Son. After having told his own to remain in his unchanging charity, the last thing Jesus tells them is to love one another, for their love is the ultimate fruit of the Father's diligent cultivation of the vine. It is the reiterated and supreme will of Jesus (13:34–35) and the summary of all morality. Since the Vine was the national symbol of Israel, the allegory could not but close on the note of fraternal charity, the only law of the new people of God.

Thus the Father loves the Son; the Son loves his own; the disciples love one another. Love is the root, trunk, and fruit of the vine rooted in eternity which will someday cover the whole world (Mt. 13:31–32). The conversion and salvation of the world begin in the eternal love (Jn. 3:16) which is manifested in Christ. The apostles must communicate its attractiveness and power through their mutual charity. How could anything but *agape* be the single precept the Lord leaves to those who believe in him?

16–17. The new commandment of reciprocal fraternal love

A new commandment I give you: *love* one another; as I have *loved* you, so you, too, must *love* one another. By this all the world will know that you are my disciples—if you manifest *love* for one another (Jn. 13:34–35).

Critics like Loisy, Bauer, and Bultmann account for a certain lack of cohesion and some juxtaposed elements in John 13:33–38 by concluding that the pericope is a verbal patchwork, the result of a retouching of the original text. In reality, the entire section is dominated by the thought of the separation which is about to take place. Speaking both as Master and Father (Westcott) Jesus tenderly addressed his little children who, in their love, would seek him ardently after his death. He left them a task which would be their consolation until he returns (14:3)—the task of loving one another. The task is really a testament, a last will. It may be considered both a means and a pledge of future reunion with Christ (Loisy) or, more accurately, a substitute for the personal presence of the Lord among his disciples. Better still, the exercise of fraternal charity within the messianic community, which is organically linked with the Savior's departure, is "the normal occupation of Christians who await the Parousia and desire to prepare themselves for the judgment."

Jesus defines the duty of loving as a "precept," and the imperative force of the word "commandment," *entolē*, must surely be kept, but in context its meaning is much broader than that of a simple command. According to the Old Testament notion, Law is first of all the expression of the divine will; then an instruction and teaching received from the sovereign authority to serve as a rule of conduct for men; and finally a salvation-device, aiming in its fullness to procure the life of an individual or of an entire people. St. John uses *entolē* of the "commandment" which Jesus receives from his Father—in the sense of mission, revelation, eternal life [69]—and of the "precepts" which the Master imposes on his disciples and which are always connected in one way or another with *agape*.[70] Clearly, fraternal love is a function, a mission that the Master imposes upon his Church. More than a general rule, it is a new "economy" including doctrine and morality, an "institution" which defines both the constitution—or at least the spirit—of the Christian community and the whole life of each of its members. St. Paul called it "the law of Christ," *ho nomos tou Christou*, Gal. 6:2.

The substance of the precept—mutual love—is contained in the words: "love one another," *agapate allēlous*. The Old Testament had commanded love of neighbor (Lev. 19:18), and Jesus had extended that love to all men, whoever they might be (Lk. 10:29, 36), particularly to enemies (Mt. 5:43–48). Before leaving his own, he asked them to love one an-

[69] Jn. 10:18; 12:49–50; 14:31.
[70] Jn. 14:15, 21; 15:10, 12; cf. 1 Jn. 2:3–5; Rom. 13:9; Gal. 5:14; 6:2.

other. Their fraternity, *adelphotēs* (1 Pet. 2:17; 5:9), which constitutes them as a group apart because of their faith in Jesus, is characterized by their *philadelphia*.[71] The reason the word itself is not used is that it has no religious connotations. *Agape*, on the contrary, implies that the privileged reciprocal love among brothers (cf. Gal. 6:10) is possible and valuable only in so far as other Christians are loved "out of love for God" or for Christ, as the next verse states.

The essential words of the precept, "as I have loved you," *kathōs ēgapēsa hymas* (cf. 15:12), specify the way the disciples are to love. From the uses of *agape* in the Septuagint and especially from the Master's teachings recorded in the Synoptics, the apostles must surely have known that they were to love one another with charity, as they were to love their neighbor, *dia tēs agapēs* (Gal. 5:13) or *en agapēi* (1 Cor. 16:14). But Jesus was living his last hours in an intense expression of *agape* (13:1). He had just presented a model of love's humble service for his friends to imitate by washing their feet (vv. 14–15). Then he again added his example to his command, in order to show what he means by love, to make their imitating him easier, and especially to deepen the obligation of his own to love.

All the commentators agree that in "as (*kathōs*) I have loved you," *kathōs* does not have the sense of degree or intensity of affection. No one can love with the same intensity and holiness as Jesus; a copy is always inferior to the original. The love which the apostles are to show one another is to be of the same kind and nature as Christ's. They are to love and serve one another "in the same way" as the Master, a way that is specifically different from all other human love (cf. Jn. 14:27, *ou kathōs*). *Kathōs*, which is stronger than *hōsper*, does not show a simple comparison or an approximately correct analogy or a superficial resemblance, but rather a profound conformity. The example of Jesus is also the norm and foundation of love, as is suggested by "so you too," *hina kai hymeis*, which follows immediately. This is

[71] Rom. 12:10; Heb. 13:1; 1 Pet. 1:22; 2 Pet. 1:7.

another case in which current grammar had to be adapted to an original theological content. The language of revelation has its own structure. If the reciprocal love of the disciples is the same kind of love as the Master's love for them, then their love must be a participation in his. Their love for one another is decisive proof of the living relationship between them and Jesus (v. 35). Each person must love his brother with the same love with which Jesus loved (*ēgapēsa* is in the aorist) both of them during his life, with the love which St. John described in the beginning of chapter 13.

Consequently, the final "so you too must love one another," *hina kai hymeis agapate allēlous*, is not simply a restatement of the commandment but an addition to it which defines its spirit and mode. "Love one another, but with this love which is mine, which I have shown and proved to you." Henceforth the *agape* of believers is not only a divine, infused love (Rom. 5:5) but also a formally Christian love which the Master came to reveal by his teaching and his life. In all the world, only the members of the Church can live in his love.

This accounts for the emphasis in v. 35 on the distinctive quality of Christian charity. "By this all the world will know," *en toutōi gnōsontai pantes*. In the future, mutual charity will be the mark and the characteristic, perpetual, and universal sign of the disciples of Jesus Christ. Just as the Pharisees always wore phylacteries, John's disciples conferred baptism, and each Rabbinic school had its own shibboleth, so the distinctive mark of Christians is reciprocal love. The idea of "mark" presupposes an expression of *agape* that is constant, clearly visible, and unmistakable. The whole world, which may be living in hate or at least indifference, can detect and believe this sign. It will recognize the men who belong to another world. More precisely, the authentic, vital relationship of disciple to Master will be revealed in the disciples' manifest charity. The formula, "that you are my disciples," *hoti emoi mathētai este*, is very strong. "Disciple" should be taken as the highest Christian title (15:8). A Greek pupil received only instruction from the rhetor or the philosopher, but the disciple (*talmid*) of a Rabbi lived with his master and assimilated not only his teaching but also his "tradition," his style of life, and his religious faith. The disciple of Jesus Christ is even closer to his Master. He follows him (Mt. 8:21–22), shares what happens to him (Jn. 13:8), is united with him,[72] and, above all, believes in him—in his person and his doctrine.[73] Finally, the relations of his disciples to Jesus are not so much those of students to their Master as of believers who have given their whole faith to their Lord by consecrating their lives to him. They are called not only to be the first links in the chain of tradition transmitting the teachings of Jesus but also to be his witnesses by their way of life and by their preaching. Their truly correct name, "his own" (13:1), shows their absolute belonging to Jesus, and that is exactly what Jesus wanted to show by the emphatic wording, *emoi mathētai*, "disciples belonging to me," which must be glossed by the "in me," *en emoi*, of John 15:2. "All the world will know that you are my disciples" directs the thought to the disciples as well as to Jesus. When the disciples manifest fraternal charity, not only do they recall the love of Jesus for them (13:1), not only do they show themselves his authentic disciples and imitators closely instructed by his example and precept, but also they continue and prolong the very charity of the Savior himself. The last wish of Jesus was that the love of God which he showed to his own and bestowed on them during his entire life (15:9; 17:23) would continue after his departure. His disciples would continue the epiphany of *agape* forever.[74] That is why he founded his Church, a group of believers who always love one another in the way he has revealed, which is unique and so original that every unbeliever will recognize "his disciples" in them. Bultmann is correct in seeing here more than a simple historical characteristic; it is an essential predicate of the believer, a definition of his nature.

[72] Mt. 10:24–25; Mk. 8:34; Jn. 12:25.   [73] Jn. 2:11, 22; cf. 8:31.
[74] Tit. 3:4; 1 Jn. 4:9.

With this clarification made, it becomes possible to understand the newness of the precept. "A new commandment I give you" (13:34). 1) At first reading, the properly theological designation, "new commandment," places mutual love among the specific elements of the second economy of salvation, the "New Covenant" which replaces and surpasses in excellence the "old," which is finished (Heb. 8:13). 2) Love of neighbor was a secondary precept in the Old Covenant; it was not even included in the Ten Commandments. The "innovation" in the Christian institution is the giving it an unequalled place and making it the object of a fundamental and quasi-unique precept. 3) Leviticus 19:18 had prescribed love for one's neighbor—compatriots, Israelites, and proselytes. Henceforth, *agape* has a new object determined by the ties of faith, not blood. It is to be a religious love among believers and particularly among disciples. 4) In the Sermon on the Mount, the Lord had given the precept of love of enemies, but at the Last Supper he asked for reciprocal love (*allēlous, en allēlois*), fraternal love which will constitute the Church as a society of loving and beloved men. 5) However, the great innovation consists specifically in the nature and mode of the new love. The disciples will love one another *as* Christ loved them. "New" is the same as "as I have loved." The essential and original element in the disciples' *agape* is that it is rooted in Christ. 6) Consequently, there is no question of its being some added rule or additional reason for loving, for Christ himself loves us as his Father loves him (15:9). The mutual love of the disciples is divine in its origin and quality; it is an infused gift as well as a precept. One must love "in Christ," as a branch receives sap from the vine (15:5, 10, 12). Charity is the fruit of vital union with the vine, and it will be a "sign" of the disciple. 7) Therefore, the mode and the acts of love are changed. It is no longer a matter of "doing good" and praying (Mt. 5:44; Lk. 6:35), but of devoting and sacrificing oneself after the example of the Savior who loves "to the end" (13:1; cf. Gal. 2:20). The *agape* prescribed on the eve of Christ's death is intrinsically united to the Cross (1 Jn. 3:16; cf. 2 Cor. 5:14). Now the disciple must love his neighbor not "as himself," but "more than himself." 8) Finally, by the formulation of the new precept during the final hours of his life, Jesus defined perfect "justice," which he had announced in the Sermon on the Mount (Mt. 5:20). He explained how the Law and the Prophets are to be fulfilled—how to practice the morality proper to members of his Kingdom (Mt. 22:40). He gave the religion he was founding its specific and distinctive character. His commandment, *entolē*, of love constitutes the Church as truly as does the eucharist, his testament, *diathēkē*, in blood.[75] The eucharist, which he had just instituted, will always be the memorial of his going (1 Cor. 11:25), just as *agape* will always remain the sign of his presence. The eucharist is a meal of union among his disciples (1 Cor. 10:17), just as *agape* is the bond among believers (Jn. 17:21). The fraternal agapes (Jude 12) of the community are agapes of charity as well as of the eucharistic meal, "until he return" (1 Cor. 11:26) and drink with his own the new fruit of the vine in the kingdom of his Father (Mt. 26:29).

That is why charity, like the eucharist, is a substitute for the presence of the visible Christ (13:33). Charity was prescribed during the farewell dinner at which the eucharist was instituted. Both are perpetually re-given witnesses to the love of God for the world, in Christ, but acts of fraternal love will be an especial epiphany of the divine *agape*. Christ wanted the Christians' reciprocal, original love to reveal his presence and action forever.

From the semantic point of view, *agape* in these two verses receives its definitive, complete, and specifically Christian sense. It is a love so different from all other loves that everyone recognizes it as soon as it appears; it is forever new and unexpected in the world. It is impossible to define the disciples' *agape*, since it is a love like Christ's own love—it *is* his own love by which they also live. It is possible to say what *agape* is not, however. It is not concupiscence, *erōs*, or natural

[75] Mt. 26:28; Mk. 14:24; Lk. 22:20.

and spontaneous tenderness, *storgē,* or the measured, beautiful benevolence limited to close friends, *philia.* "*Agape* is from God" (1 Jn. 4:7). Only an authentic disciple receives it and lives from it in all that he does, as Christ, his model, did. Even though he cannot translate into words the nature of the fire he carries in his heart, its flame will never be extinguished (1 Cor. 13:8). Its force presses him to give himself in total self-forgetfulness. "The *agape* of Christ urges us" (2 Cor. 5:14). Fraternal charity is, without the slightest doubt, both the criterion of the new birth of the authentic child of God (Tit. 3:5) and the summary of Christian morality. "Walk in love as Christ has loved us" (Eph. 5:2).

18–22. Charity which is faithful toward Jesus and comes from the Father, the Son, and the Holy Spirit

15 If *you love* me, you will keep my commandments, 16 and I will ask the Father, and he will grant you another Advocate to be with you for all time to come . . . 21 He who accepts my commandments and keeps them—he is the one *who loves* me. And he that *loves* me *will,* in turn, *be loved* by my Father; and I *will love* him, and will manifest myself to him. . . . 23 Anyone who loves me will keep my word, and my Father *will love* him and we will come to him and make our home with him. 24 He who does not *love* me does not keep my word. And the word which you have heard is not mine but the Father's who sent me (Jn. 14:15, 16, 21, 23, 24).

The time for Christ's departure was very near (14:31), and the moment of separation had almost arrived. Chapter 14 describes the Master's final farewell to his disciples. He saw the anguish of his own—"Let not your hearts be troubled" (vv. 1, 27)—and he would not leave them orphans without help or consolation (v. 18). After having assured them that the necessary separation would not be permanent, (vv.

1–11), he promised them the presence and help of the three divine Persons (vv. 12–24). His last words became an exhortation to peace and confidence (vv. 25–31).

Verses 15–24, as Bultmann has noticed, form a unit. They bring together three promises so magnificent that they were able to strengthen the disciples in the tragic hours which were beginning and in their terrible trial of solitude. The Paraclete (vv. 15–17), Jesus himself (vv. 18–21), and Jesus with his Father (vv. 22–24) would come to the twelve and establish their home in the apostles' souls. Since their coming and dwelling are dependent on the disciples' *agape* for the Lord, *agape* is the essential definition of disciples, *mathētai:* they are simple believers, who cling to the person of the Revealer (8:31); they are vitally incorporated into Christ (15:8). Disciples are essentially those who love and remain faithful to their love, giving unmistakable proof of devotion by their obedience. The Holy Trinity responds to their total gift of themselves by a loving, consoling, strengthening presence. In a word, the Christian is one who loves Christ with charity and in whom God lives.

Verses 15–16 "If you love me, you will keep my commandments, and I will ask the Father, and he will grant you another Advocate to be with you for all time to come.

To receive the Holy Spirit, the fulfillment of two correlative conditions is required. One is subjective: the charity of the disciple; the other is objective: the prayer of Christ. The emphasis is on the first four words, "If you love me." Everything depends on the disciples' love for Jesus. If their *agape* is sincere, Christ will intercede for his own, and his own will be able to receive the Paraclete. In the Greek, *ean,* "if," is followed by the indicative *agapate,* "you love," so the clause expresses an already fulfilled condition and not a mere possibility or wish. It could be translated, "Since you love me." The verb *agapan* retains the religious and technical sense it had in the Septuagint. It is not a simple inclination of the heart—*philein* (cf. 15:14–15)—but rather an adherence of one's whole being in faith and worship, a definitive consecration. In fact, the context suggests that *agape* should be taken in the classical sense of persevering love: "If you continue to love me."

Agape, strictly speaking, is composed of clear-sighted predilection and active devotion, and that is why the word is so well-suited in both the Old and the New Covenants for defining the attitude of the faithful toward the Lord. However, Jesus stressed the second characteristic especially: If you truly love me, you will put my commandments into practice; or, as the future tense suggests, you will be faithful in your observance of my commandments. It is necessary to persevere in love, thus keeping the Master's precepts as the unchanging law of life. The word "commandments" should be taken in the broadest sense possible. "Commandments" means the revelation of the divine will as a whole, above all, of the "two great commandments"—love of God and love of neighbor (Mt. 22:38–40)—and of the spirit of the sermon on the mount. These are the commandments which we must believe, accomplish, await, and, finally, endure. The correspondence between "if you love *me*" and "you will keep *my* commandments" shows that Jesus was speaking as Revealer and Master (13:34), recalling all the teaching he had already given to the disciples who believed in his word. His "commandments" include two things, consequently: the explanation of the secrets and plans of the Father (1:18), and the pattern of interior attitudes and exterior behavior which characterizes life in the Kingdom. Nothing of these revelations and explanations must be lost, since they trace "the way" to reach God (8:51; 14:6). The disciples would have to prove themselves as disciples by observing the Lord's precepts with vigilance and fidelity.

The Jews would have acquiesced in the idea of "observance," [76] but Jesus, who had made his disciples' obedience to the commandments the condition of his own love (15:10), went on to explain that the test of the disciples' love for him

[76] *Prolégomènes*, p. 98.

is fidelity. "If you love me, you will keep my commandments." His statement defined the nature of the love he asked. It is not a sentimental love, but one as sincere and effective as his own (15:13). At that moment, when the twelve were so authentically displaying their affection by their open sorrow at the coming separation,[77] the Master educated their *agape* and explained that love is primarily union of wills and gift of self. A loving disciple obeys his Lord. True charity is necessarily faithful: If you wish to show me that you love me, continue to do what I have told you. It is clear that the precepts must always be observed out of love for Christ—that is the essence of his morality—and that loving fidelity is the means of remaining in personal, immediate communion with him. Far from being legalistic, obedience to the commandments is primarily the expression of ardent charity manifesting itself in works.

The loving fidelity of the disciples will be answered by the faithful love of Jesus, who will use his powers as mediator and intercessor with his Father on their behalf. Touched, so to speak, by the attachment and devotion of his own, he will not let himself be outdone in generosity. He will intervene with his Father to obtain the greatest possible gifts for them. The word *erōtaō*, "I ask," which Jesus always used when he addressed his Father, does not express a supplication made by an inferior to a superior, but an authorized request or demand made by a mediator rightfully exercising his official function. The future "I will ask" expresses both the new situation of the glorified Christ exposing his desire face-to-face with his Father and the conditional formation of the request: If you continue to love me and observe my commandments, I will intervene.

The fruit of Jesus' infallibly efficacious prayer (11:42) for his loving disciples is the Father's sending of the Paraclete, of an Assistant, a Protector, an Aid, an Auxiliary, a Defender. In naming him "another Advocate," *allon paraklēton*, Jesus makes him his successor to the apostles and attributes to him

[77] Jn. 16:6, 22.

a personality like his own. Certainly, his protection and help
will not be of the same kind as Christ's on earth was, but
both of them were equally sent and given by the Father and
both fulfill the same mission of love. Their mission consists
essentially in bringing the strength, joy, and consolation of
a presence; it is for this that they are paracletes. The purpose
of their mission is strongly emphasized: "to be with you for
all time," *hina ēi meth' hymōn eis ton aiōna.* Although he is
invisible, the new assistant will be always there for the disciples, remaining with them, and consequently always ready
to help them.

An analysis of the uses of the preposition "with," *meta,* in
the New Testament shows that it often has a theological
connotation, particularly when it refers to the disciples who
live in community with Jesus. They "are and remain with
him." [78] Their nearness to him is more than proximity and
devotion; it is a real working-with and participation, as the
texts show which associate the elect with the joy of the
Lord.[79] In another place, the presence of Emmanuel among
men means "God with us," *meth' hymōn ho theos* (Mt.
1:23), and Jesus described his presence several times with the
words, "I am with you," *meth' hymōn eimi,*[80] like a Bridegroom surrounded by his friends (Mt. 9:15), a phrase which
adds a note of tenderness. Actually, when God is "with"
someone, that person knows he is enveloped in love, protected by Providence, and lavished with blessings.[81] God's
presence can make conversions and work miracles,[82] yet it
is primarily an intimate presence which comforts the heart
and dissipates fear. "He who has sent me is with me; he has
not left me alone" (Jn. 8:29). "Not that I am really alone,
for the Father is with me." [83] Besides being an all-powerful
support, this communion, *koinōnia,* is a sharing by those who
love one another of everything they have. "My son, you

[78] Mk. 3:14; 5:18; Mt. 12:30; 26:69, 71; Lk. 22:28; Jn. 15:27.
[79] Mt. 8:11; 26:29; Lk. 23:43; Jn. 17:24.
[80] Jn. 13:33; 14:9; 16:4; 17:12. Cf. Mt. 28:20.
[81] Lk. 1:28; Acts 7:9; 10:38.   [82] Jn. 3:2; cf. Acts 14:27; 15:4.
[83] Jn. 16:32; Acts 18:10.

have always been with me, and all that is mine is yours" (Lk. 15:31). The Paraclete, gracious and definitive gift of God, will be to each disciple the pledge of the Father's love, a permanent and active divine presence, and the source of all the goods of salvation. "May the communion of the Holy Spirit be with you all" (2 Cor. 13:13). Jesus had pitched his tent among men only for a time and had to return to his Father (13:1), but the Holy Spirit, on the contrary, will remain forever "with them."

In calling the Paraclete "the spirit of truth," Jesus was making it clear to Jewish ears that his assistance would be permanent and durable, because in Hebrew *'émét*, "truth," is derived from the root *'âman*, "to be stable," which is used, among other things, of the foundation of a building. The Lord wanted to explain how privileged the disciples were in receiving such a gift. He asked the Father to give it to them alone, for themselves, because he does not pray for the world (17:9), which is incapable of receiving his Spirit (Rom. 8:9). The final clause, therefore, accentuates the idea of presence and immanent possession. "As for you, you will know him because he will make his permanent stay with you (*par' hymin*) and in you" (14:17). Like the other New Testament writers, St. John usually uses *para* with the genitive and never with the accusative. Here, however, he uses the dative, which means "near" a person or "at his house." It suggests a more or less immediate proximity [84] and being "at home" (1 Cor. 16:2). It was currently used with verbs of hospitality and sojourn, therefore; a person stays with the one who invites or receives him.[85] The implication goes beyond the idea of remaining permanently in a place and extends to constant presence, active relations, and real communion. Therefore, "while I am lingering in your midst," *par' hymin menōn*, of John 14:25 describes not only Christ's presence on earth, but also his office of giver of revelation to the

---

[84] Lk. 9:47; Mt. 22:25; 28:15; Col. 4:16; Apoc. 2:13.
[85] Jn. 1:39; 4:40; cf. Lk. 11:37; Acts 9:43; 10:6; 18:3; 21:8, 16; 2 Tim. 4:13.

disciples, the office which will be continued by the Paraclete (v. 17). The Lord taught what he had seen in the
bosom of the Father, *para tōi patri* (8:38). When the Father
and the Son come to make their dwelling in the soul of the
disciple (14:23), they come to be active there and make
him beautiful with their gifts. The phrase, *par hymin menei,*
"he will remain with you" (14:17), suggests the assistance
of the *para-klētos,* the Advocate (v. 16). The first description, "He will be with you" (v. 16), is strengthened by the
second, "He will remain with you" (v. 17). He will always
stay with you, as near you as possible, in order to help you.

    There is still more to come. Finally, "He will be in you,"
en hymin estai. There is no need to explain the usage of *en*
with the dative to convey the idea of place, but it should be
noted that it implies both accompaniment and possession—
an inhabitation is a having. The usage is a technical locution
of the Christian life and divine realities. "To be in Christ"
and "to be in the Spirit" (Rom. 8:9) are definitions of
Christian being, of the unique way of existing in union and
community with Christ. It is a question not only of immanence but also of vital relationship. The believer responds
by seizing and making his own the word, the charity, the
joy, the life which the Father and the Son communicate to
him.[86] Consequently, to say that the Holy Spirit "is in" the
disciples suggests a living, interior presence in the most profound communion, like the union by which the Father lives
in Christ and Christ in God—by their relations of knowledge and love—and both Father and Christ are united with
the Paraclete in his dwelling in souls.[87] This permanent and
intimate union is the result and fruit of the faithful *agape*
of the disciples (vv. 15–16). We may legitimately conclude,
then, that it is by love that the three divine Persons live and
remain in the soul (cf. v. 21). Love for one another creates
the union between the soul and the Trinity; in fact, a certain degree of fervor in charity is probably required of the

[86] 5:38, 42; 6:53; 15:7, 11; 17:26; 2 Jn. 2.
[87] 10:38; 14:10, 11, 20; 15:5; 17:21, 23; 1 Jn. 2:27; 4:4; 4:16.

disciple. Certainly, only a sincere love which has already proved itself in obedience to the will of Christ can merit the presence and asssitance of the *Dulcis hospes animae*.

Verses 18–21: "Yet a little while, and the world sees me no longer, but you will see me, because I live, and you, too, shall live. On that day you will come to understand that I am in the Father, and you are in me, and I in you. He who accepts my commandments and keeps them—he is the one that loves me. And he that loves me will, in turn, be loved by my Father; and I will love him, and will manifest myself to him."

Verses 18–21 begin with the spontaneous cry from the heart, "I will not leave you orphans," without a Father, without a friend, without help, all alone. Jesus' words brought a new consolation to the grief of parting. Indeed, they almost seem intended to soften or cover over the substitution of the "other" Defender who has been promised (v. 16) for the Master they love. The Apostles were completely given to Jesus himself. He was the one whose presence they desired; he had just appealed to their love for him (v. 15). He assured them that he would return to them even more living and real than before (v. 19). Because the coming of the Holy Spirit would bring them a comprehension of the faith, they would see at last his exact relation to God, the relation of the Son to the Father (1:14), and hence the essential immanence and unity of nature of the two Persons. They would understand, too, that they possessed the presence of the Lord within themselves through their participation in his own life. Undoubtedly, their relationship to Christ would be different and completely spiritual, but he would not leave them, as they would come to understand when they truly experienced his living in them and his making them live. *Agape* "realizes" God's active presence. It creates an awareness of the divine presence, a non-speculative "experience" of the invisible, which is analogous to taste (1 Pet. 2:3). The undeniable certitude of the experience gives strength and joy. "You will see," *theōreite*, and "you will know," *gnōsesthe*.

The announcement of their seeing and knowing is so absolute as to be disconcerting; it required an explanation. Therefore Jesus clarified the nature of the manifestation by restating its condition, and his description makes the experience more comprehensible. The first love of the disciples is parallel to the love of the Father and the Son from which the "manifestation" of Jesus comes. "Seeing" and "knowing" are functions of *agape*. They are on the same plane with it; the manifestation of Christ is a manifestation of love. Just as the interior charity of the disciples shows itself in exterior observance of the commandments, so the invisible charity of the Father and Jesus manifests itself to the disciples by bringing about a presence. "He who accepts my commandments and keeps them—he is the one who loves me" (v. 21). Verse 15, "If you love me, you will keep my commandments," presented *agape* as the source of fidelity and the condition for receiving the Paraclete. Here, v. 21 gives a universally applicable definition of authentic *agape* as necessarily including obedience. The proposition begins, "He who accepts my commandments and keeps them." In the Greek, "accepts" and "keeps" are both participles joined under one article *ho*. The phrase seems to be a Semitic redundancy expressing a superlative, used to bring out the integrity of a fidelity that will neither falter nor grow weary. Such is "the one who loves me." "The one," *ekeinos*, is emphatic in the Greek (cf. 1:8, 18): "He is the only one who loves me." "He who accepts my commandments," *ho echōn*, and "he who loves me," *ho agapōn me*, are synonymous. The only love for him which Jesus can recognize as valid is the *agape* which accepts his spirit and conforms itself to his will. Fidelity is the criterion of love's sincerity.[88]

The disciple, whose entire moral conduct is the dissemination of *agape,* is loved by the Father. "He who loves me will be loved by my Father." The second part of the verse begins

[88] 2 Cor. 8:11; Philip. 3:12; 1 Jn. 3:18–19.

immediately with the same words which had closed the first part, "he who loves me." This immediate repetition shows that the Father's charity is aroused by the disciple's loving fidelity to Jesus. Dare we say that God is grateful to those who love his Son? At least, there is reciprocity: he who loves will be loved, *agapōn—agapēthēsetai*. The new love will no longer be the merciful love which God has for all men (3:16), but a motivated love of delight and intimacy, like the love of the Father for the Son (Mt. 3:17). Everyone who adheres to Jesus Christ and proves his love for the Son becomes the beloved of the Father.

"And I will love him." It might seem that at the proof of the disciples' love for him, Jesus would have immediately mentioned his own love for them, but the respect he felt for his Father—who is greater than he (14:28)—led him to name the Father first. He did only what he had seen the Father do, and he based his own actions on the Father's.[89] Reposing in the Father's bosom (1:18) and seeing the Father's *agape* for his disciples, Jesus was united with them by a new or stronger tie. He loved them more because God loves them tenderly; not that his love increased (13:1), but its manifestations became more generous and more consoling. A love that is living and total is not changing when it expresses itself in infinitely varied ways as it responds to the actions and responses of the beloved. Only its gestures are new, and they seem each time to be expressing a new love, new at least in its having taken on a nuance it did not have before.

The new form of Christ's *agape* and the proof of its increase is precisely that he will manifest himself personally to his loving disciple: "and I will manifest myself to him." Everything had led up to this intimate revelation. To arrive at the exact meaning of the verb "to manifest," *emphanizō*, is difficult. St. John uses it only in these two verses, 21–22. It is derived from *phainō* and had the original meaning "to make visible, to show." However, it is used in the Bible in

---

[89] Jn. 5:19, 30; cf. 3:11, 32; 6:38; 8:38; 10:25, 37–38; etc.

several senses, both religious and profane. The variation in
its uses explains, for instance, why Jude misunderstood
what Jesus meant (v. 22). One of its meanings is "to lay
open publicly with nothing concealed or veiled" (Is. 3:9).
Moses's double request that God reveal himself to him (Ex.
33:13, 18) would suggest that *emphanizō* in John 14:21
refers to an exterior revelation, an epiphany or parousia of
Christ, like that of the risen saints of Jerusalem who "appeared to many" after the crucifixion (Mt. 27:53). That
was a manifestation of specters, however, like the ghosts in
Wisd. 17:4, and, besides, Moses never had any idea of seeing
Yahweh with his own eyes. The manifestation he asked was
one made through signs which would translate or prove
Yahweh's presence. In this sense, the smoke manifested that
the camp was in flames (1 Mac. 4:20) and the gift of manna
showed God's sweetness to his children by adapting itself
to the desires of those who ate it (Wisd. 16:1). The predominant meaning of *emphanizō* is "to make known" or "to
inform," as when an effect reveals its cause (Wisd. 18:18) or
an action its motive (Heb. 11:14). An *emphanismos* is an
"indication" (2 Mac. 3:9) or a piece of information. "To
make known" is the usual meaning of *emphanizō* in the
Acts of the Apostles, the inscriptions, and the papyri. Someone brings a person up to date on an affair, presents a cause
to a magistrate before whom he is pleading,[90] or expresses a
desire (2 Mac. 11:29).

In other words, what Christ promised the apostles was
to make them see ("you will see me," v. 19) the effect of
his presence, not to appear visibly before them. Hebrews
9:24 and Wisdom 1:2 are relevant here. In the first text the
high Priest enters heaven and "now presents himself," *em-
phanisthēnai*, in the presence of God on our behalf. Wisdom
says, "God lets himself be found. . . . He manifests himself
to those who do not refuse him their faith." Clearly, the
revelation is completely interior and, consequently, indi-

[90] Acts 23:15, 22; 24:1; 25:2, 15; cf. 2 Mach. 3:7; *P. Tebt.* 3:905, 4;
P. Hal. 1:33, etc.

vidual. It is a *presentation,* not in flesh and blood as at the
resurrection (Lk. 24:39; Jn. 20:27), but still under a form
that can be grasped, the result of Christ's coming. "I am
coming back to you" (v. 18). Jesus comes back; he is there;
he "produces" or presents himself. How? By the spiritual
revelation explained by the three uses of the verb *agapan* in
the verse. Charity makes the Christian know and feel the
presence of Christ. Each loving believer experiences Christ's
love for him. In the active communion which mutual love
creates, the invisible itself is grasped and made near; there
is contact. The illumination is of a spiritual order, and the
vision suggested in verse 19 is "vision" in the Hebrew sense
of the term, neither physical sight or speculative knowledge,
but knowledge of the heart. "I will manifest myself" means
that the apostle, because of charity, will have an intimate,
warm, and comforting certitude of Christ's presence.

This kind of revelation, which they had never before
experienced, confused the apostles, who were still thinking
in terms of a brilliant manifestation of the glorious Messia-
King entering upon his reign (6:15). For the fourth time,
one of the apostles, who did not understand, interrupted the
Lord (13:37; 14:5, 8). Jude had grasped that the Savior's
coming is reserved to his own and that it implies certain
conditions, but he wondered why there was a restriction
put on messianic publicity or promulgation. "And what is
the reason, Master, why you intend to manifest yourself to
us and not to the world?" (14:22). As usual,[91] Jesus did not
reply directly to the question. He reaffirmed his teaching
and summarized it forcefully, for if the disciples understood
his manifestation clearly, it would become obvious to them
that unbelievers would be incapable of benefiting from it.

"Anyone who loves me will keep my word, and my Father will love him and we will come to him and make our
home with him" (v. 23). A comparison with v. 21 suggests
several interesting things: 1) The *agape* of the disciples,
which was mentioned after the observance of the command-

[91] Lk. 12:41; 13:23; Jn. 21:22.

ments in v. 21, is now at the head of the sentence in the most prominent position; love is the condition for the coming. 2) Instead of the general formula, "If you love me" (v. 15), explained by "he who accepts my commandments and keeps them—he is the one who loves me" (v. 21), v. 23 has, "Anyone who loves me," a wording which implies that the possession of charity is an individual, personal thing. It strengthens the subjective character of the requirement of love and restricts Jesus' manifestation to the disciple who loves (cf. 1:12). 3) The substitution in verse 23 of "word" for "commandments" softens the juridical aspect of obedience and emphasizes loving fidelity instead (cf. Apoc. 3:20: "If anyone listens to my voice"). 4) Christ's *agape* is not mentioned in verse 23, and the love of the Father is expressed by an active verb, "My Father will love him," rather than by a passive one as in verse 21. The Father's initiative in giving is stressed, as it was in his gift of the Holy Spirit (v. 16). 5) Finally, and most important—this is the original contribution of the verse—Christ will not return alone. He will come with the Father on terms of perfect equality. "We shall come together and we shall not come in passing but to make our home." Since this sojourn is the same as the sojourn of the Paraclete—"the Paraclete will make his permanent stay with you" (v. 17), the indwelling of the Holy Trinity must begin the moment the soul has proved the fidelity of its love.

In the Old Testament, Yahweh was thought to dwell in the midst of his people and to reside in the Tabernacle.[92] Here he does much more. His presence is a presence of love, no longer in a sanctuary, but now in a soul. The three divine Persons fashion for themselves a permanent home, as it were, within the disciple, similar to their home in heaven (14:2). Their presence is so real, so immediate and manifest, that the soul recognizes its guests and tastes the joy of their love. Jude had not asked so much. "For he asked about the mani-

[92] Ex. 25:8; 29:45; Lev. 26:11–12; Zach. 2:9.

festation of Christ and he heard about love and a dwelling place" (St. Augustine).

Verse 24 completes the answer to Jude's question. When the Master said, "I will love him and manifest myself to him" (v. 21), Jude picked up only the last detail and asked, "And why do you intend to manifest yourself to us and not to the world?" (v. 22). After having emphasized the dependence of his coming on his disciples' love for him, Jesus had only to conclude: If I restrict my manifestation, it is because the world does not fulfill the conditions for perceiving it. The world does not love me, since it does not accept my message. Thus, at the end of his life, the Lord divided men into two groups according to their greater or lesser closeness to God. The discrimination is based on their having or not having *agape:* "he who loves me" (v. 21); "he who does not love me" (v. 24). Men give or refuse charity to the person of the incarnate Word, the mediator. They approach the Father or remain far from him according to whether or not they love Christ, receive his revelation, and obey his precepts. "For love separates saints from the world" (St. Thomas).

The final clause, "And the word which you have heard is not mine but the Father's" [93] amounts to a condemnation of the alien and stupid world (cf. 1 Cor. 2:14): it does not love. Christ's statement points up the seriousness of the refusal to obey and give a loving welcome to God's accredited Ambassador. The negative form of the verse reiterates the theme of the entire pericope—the unique importance of *agape*, the virtue of union with God. Without charity, man remains riveted to earth, delivered over to himself. With *agape*, he receives the visit of God the Father, the Son, and the Holy Spirit, and lives in permanent communion with them.

[93] Jn. 7:16; 8:26; 12:49.

23. The joy of Christian charity

You heard me say to you: "I am going home and I am coming back to you! If *you loved* me, you would rejoice that I am going to the Father, because the Father is greater than I (Jn. 14:28).

Chapter 14 of St. John is the chapter of formal farewell. Jesus had just announced his departure to his apostles, and he wanted to strengthen them against grief and discouragement. "Do not let your heart be troubled" (vv. 1, 27). *Agape* would be the true source of their consolation.[94] As the conversation drew to a close, the Master summarized their reasons for having confidence—"I have told you this"; the perfect tense, *lelaleka,* indicates a conclusion (v. 25)—and then gave them his peace (v. 27). He even asked his disciples to rejoice over his return to heaven.

"You heard me say to you: 'I am going home and I am coming back to you' " (v. 28), and you know that my going to the Father is the condition of my return and permanent abiding in your souls (vv. 21–23). That should console you in your grief over our separation. I will not leave you orphans (v. 18). Trust me (14:1). Try to understand what my return to the Father means to me. Instead of thinking of yourselves and the apparent solitude in which I am leaving you, you would feel glad that I am going if you loved me deeply and disinterestedly for myself and not just for yourselves. The verb in the protasis, "If you loved me," *ei egapate me,* is in the imperfect, indicating a condition contrary-to-fact in the present, an unfulfilled condition. In fact, there is a shade of reproach in the sentence: If you loved me as you should love me. . . . Jesus' words were primarily an appeal to the intelligence of the heart and to a new and different manifestation of the disciples' love. Their sorrow and grief at the idea that their Master was going to leave

[94] *Agapan* occurs ten times in vv. 15–31, the same number as *agape* occurs in 1 Cor. 13:1–14:1.

them proved that they did truly care about him. Jesus did not doubt their faithful charity, to which he had just made such great promises (vv. 15, 21, 23). However, he invited them to a growth in love or a new nuance of love, to a love so perfect that it would become one with its object and flower into joy (cf. 16:22). The *agape* of v. 28 is deeply tender love. It is no longer obedience to the commandments, but instead has become profound union with the person whom they most cherish and who shares his own happiness with them. Consequently, verse 28 is the Lord's ultimate teaching about charity. He asked his own—whom he loved with great delicacy and fervor (13:1)—to show him, in their turn, the *velle bonum* which would characterize a love entirely given to him. One might gloss: If it truly is charity you feel for me, you should be happy; your happiness would prove that your love is real.

Jesus was returning to the Father. His return had two aspects: he was leaving this sad world which had weighed so heavily on him, and he was going to his true homeland where he would be reunited with his Father and receive the glory and beatitude that are rightfully his (Jn. 17:5). True friends could not help rejoicing to know that he whom they loved would be exalted and completely happy. They would not merely consent to the separation which would assure his happiness, but they would actually prefer to sacrifice themselves so that he could receive the fullness of joy. This perfectly pure love is *agape* and, because Christ in heaven is always perfectly happy, authentic Christian charity necessarily makes the disciples permanently and perfectly happy too. It gives them a foretaste here below of heavenly beatitude (15:11; 17:13).

The final clause, *"hoti* the Father is greater than I," is difficult to understand, especially when *hoti* is taken to mean "because," as most commentators take it. Why should the apostles rejoice because the Father is greater and supreme? Jesus was speaking here not as the Son of the Father, but as a man. Sent by the Father (3:17; 17:3), he receives everything from the Father (3:35; cf. 1 Cor. 15:28), and, first of all, his glory (17:5; Philip. 2:9–10); he is not greater than the Father who sent him.[95] Jesus seems to be emphasizing his new mode of existence in heaven in terms of his "passage." We would say he will exist "near the Most-High," "the God of Our Lord Jesus Christ, the Father of glory" (Eph. 1:17). As St. John Chrysostom has remarked,[96] Jesus' words, "I am going to one who is greater than I," refer to the monotheistic faith of the apostles; they appeal to his disciples' confidence in unfailing Providence.[97] The disciples can and must rejoice, for Jesus is going to rejoin his Father, the great Father who will shower him with power, glory, and joy. Throughout the chapter the Lord had insisted on the *agape* which his own owed to him. Now he directs their thoughts to the Father who surrounds him with his delight [98] and whose love is his happiness (v. 31). If you love me, rejoice because the Father loves me and showers me with gifts. The disciples' love for Jesus flows into the stream of Jesus' love for God.

24. Jesus' death, a proof of his charity for the Father

But that the world may know that *I love* the Father and am acting strictly according to the Father's instructions, rise; we must be on our way (Jn. 14:31).

There is general agreement among scholars about the purpose for which Jesus made his sacrifice. He immolated

---

[95] Jn. 13:16; cf. 1 Cor. 3:23; 11:3.

[96] "What is the true meaning of this text? The disciples were not sufficiently instructed about the resurrection and did not have a correct idea about Christ. And how could they have a correct idea since they did not even know that he would rise from the dead? But they had a very high idea of the Father. If you fear for me . . . rejoice at least in hearing that I go to the Father . . . It is from the Father, whose greatness I proclaim, that I send you consolation."

[97] Jn. 14:1: *pisteuete eis ton theon.*

[98] Jn. 15:9: *sicut dilexit me Pater . . .*

himself to the Father's will and went to death in order to prove his love for the Father. However, there are many ways of constructing St. John's sentence. The Greek reads *all'hina gnōi ho kosmos hoti agapō ton patera, kai kathōs eneteilato moi ho pater, houtōs poiō egeiresthe, agōmen enteuthen.*

Many interpreters consider the opening proposition elliptical and join it to the preceding proposition, supplying a verb like "I desire," "this is happening," or "I am acting like this" to govern the "that," *hina.* The sense would be, "The Prince of this world comes to deliver a last attack on me. And yet he has no power against me. If I agree to confront him, I do so that the world may learn my fidelity to the mission the Father has confided to me." Other interpreters, instead of supplying a verb, ignore the "and" (*kai* before *kathōs*) in the middle of the sentence and make the first clause depend on the verb "I am acting," *houtōs poiō.* This reading has the advantage of respecting the link between the two propositions and giving full emphasis to the words, "and exactly as . . . so," *kai kathōs . . . houtōs.* However, it does not explain the meaning of Christ's conduct, so that it becomes necessary to gloss: I go to my death . . . so that the world may know. . . . It seems preferable, therefore, to consider the whole verse the expression of a single thought. "That," *hina,* which is almost an imperative, depends on the two verbs "rise" and "we must be on our way," *egeiresthe, agōmen:* Because the world must learn the love I have for my Father and my obedience to his will, we can stay here no longer. We must set out for Gethsemani.

Whatever the interpretation of the verse, it is clear that Jesus intended his voluntary death to be a revelation to the whole world. There is a strong contrast between the intimacy of the little group gathered privately in the Cenacle (cf. 12:36) and the disclosure to be made to the universe present and to come. Christ could no longer remain united with his disciples in private; it was time to mount the cross. Those who are really open will understand from this that

Jesus was wholly given to his Father and that he continued to show his love for his Father in the most crucial circumstances, even to the point of immolating himself for the Father's glory. His death, which proved his supreme love for men (15:13, cf. 13:1), is now presented as a testimony to his love for God.[99] Christ's *agape* for his Father is evidently a real attachment and a true affection, but with the religious nuance which *agape* has in the Septuagint of adoration, consecration and faithful service. Jesus is the only man who ever perfectly fulfilled the precept, "Love the Lord your God with your whole heart, with your whole soul and with your whole mind" (Mt. 22:37).

Not that the Father took pleasure in the martyrdom of his only Son, of course, but he had decreed that redemption would come through the blood shed on Calvary (Jn. 3:16), and Jesus' *agape* is essentially union of wills. Christ willingly accepted the saving mission which God confided to him. His obedience is measured by his love. His love is absolute; his obedience is total. His demonstration of *agape* by his voluntary death (cf. 10:18) makes his sacrifice an irrefutable testimony, a "martyrdom." The apostles would at last understand the intimate union between heroic obedience and authentic charity which the Lord had inculcated into them (14:15, 21, 23–24) and of which he would always be their model. The final confidence which he made to his own (15:15) was made to reveal what lay deepest in his heart, what he had never yet told them: the fervent devotion which unites him to God and which is the secret of his every action. I do exactly as my Father commands me. No doubt the twelve profoundly meditated on Jesus' revelation, and it must have inspired their spirituality of *mimēsis*

[99] All the commentators note that this is the only time Jesus declares his love for his Father. However, 15:10, "I have kept my Father's commandments and abide in his love" implied the reciprocity of Jesus' love in the declaration of his communion with the Father in charity. These two texts, which are not commented on by A. Nygren, are decisive in favor of a mounting, disinterested charity, one that is not egocentric like *erōs*.

of Jesus Christ. Actually, though, the first to be convinced
of the perfection of Jesus' loving submission to God were
the centurion and the good thief.

Jesus gave the signal to depart. "Rise; we must be on our
way." He freely delivered himself to the snare which Judas
had laid for him in the garden and, through it, to the hatred
of Satan. With complete knowledge of what it would mean,
he calmly took the initiative in their meeting. The emphasis
is on the spontaneity of the Lord who offered himself to
death out of love and obedience and on the strength of his
effective charity which did not know hesitation or fear. He
submitted himself to the will of the Father, but his immolation was a freely made gift (10:11). His resolution was
truly taken in triumph; he was sure of his victory (16:33).
This verse has the same importance, therefore, as 13:1, which
opened St. John's account of the passion, since it gives the
real meaning of Christ's immolation. Both verses reveal
Jesus' supereminent charity, which proved itself in death.

25–29. Having revealed to his disciples that both he and they are objects of the Father's love, Christ asks that divine charity be infused in their hearts

22 The glory you have bestowed on me I have bestowed on
them, that they may be one as we are one,—23 I in them and
you in me. Thus their oneness will be perfected. The world must
come to acknowledge that I am your ambassador, and that *you
love* them as *you love* me. 24 O Father! I will that those whom
you have entrusted to me shall be at my side where I am: I
want them to behold my glory, the glory you bestowed on me,
that *you loved* me before the world was founded. 25 Just Father!
The world does not know you, but I know you, and thus these
men have come to know that I am your ambassador. 26 I have
made known to them your name, and will continue to make it
known. May the *love* with which *you love* me dwell in them
and I in them (Jn. 17:23, 24, 26).

Before his sacrifice, Jesus, the high Priest, prayed aloud to his Father. He included his disciples in his prayer. Most commentators see three objects: Jesus prayed for himself (vv. 1–8), for the eleven (vv. 9–19), and for the generations to come who would receive the faith through their ministry (v. 20). The dearest wish of the revealer of the Father and founder of the Church was that his disciples should be united in believing and possessing the charity which God bears his Son and extends to his Son's disciples (vv. 20–26). Although it is possible to discern his wish through an attentive reading of the pericope, no one need flatter himself that he understands the verses adequately. For one thing, the union of Christians, when it is conceived of a type of the unity of the divine Persons and even as inserted into their union, necessarily remains mysterious. For another, St. John's vocabulary is highly specialized, and his elliptical formulations easily admit of a variety of interpretations.

Verses 22–23 form a single sentence (M. J. Lagrange) which repeats in exactly parallel literary construction the request made in vv. 20–21. The repetition and parallelism reveal how important Christ's prayer was to him. As far as he could, he had done everything to prepare and establish the unity he desired. He asked God for its fulfillment and consummation not only that it might produce all its fruits, but also because it would be meaningless unless it reproduced the communion of love which unites the Father and the Son in all their works.

The vocabulary and theology of v. 22 present two problems: to determine the nature of the "glory" which Jesus received from the Father and communicated to the disciples, and to determine in what way this "glory," *doxa,* is the foundation and source of the unity of the apostles. Obviously, it cannot be the essential glory which the Word possesses as equal to the Father and which cannot be communicated to any creature (Is. 42:8; 48:11), yet it must refer to some divine gift which is proper to Christ but can also be transmitted to others. It is certainly not immortality, the power of performing miracles, the glory of the resurrection, or even God's love for Jesus. "Glory" is probably the divine sonship which is the special gift of the Word incarnate to believers (1:12); it must be identified, consequently, with sanctifying grace, which exists precisely to assimilate us to God, to unite us to him (2 Cor. 3:18).

Perhaps it is not prudent, however, to determine rigorously from the beginning the content of the *doxa* which is common to Jesus and to all his own. *Doxa* includes a participation in God's nature or in one of his attributes which can be perceived by men.[100] It is an intervention of power [101] as well as of light (Eph. 5:14). The context suggests that *doxa* should be taken in its usual sense of richness, prosperity and opulence. It is a treasure made up of all the supernatural gifts proper to the Savior's humanity. He came to earth to bring it to believers. "And of his fullness we have all received a share" (Jn. 1:16). The New Testament attributes to Christ a personal glory which he himself asserted (17:24), and his disciples saw and proclaimed.[102] It is a reflection of the glory of the Father (Heb. 1:3), which shines on Christ's face (2 Cor. 4:4, 6). Its best description is in Jn. 1:14: The glory of the Word incarnate is the glory which an only Son receives from his Father. Consequently, "the glory you have bestowed on me" (17:22) is above all the presence and life of the Father in the Son, the personal union of God and Jesus—"you in me," *su en emoi*, as Jesus said a moment later (cf. 14:20)—which the apostles could perceive. "He who sees me sees the Father" (Jn. 14:9).

The gift which Jesus has transmitted to men is God himself (17:3, 6–8). Christ the Revealer has made his Father known (14:26), for, being in the bosom of the Father (1:18), he displayed the Father in his own person and in his entire life. In the Septuagint *doxa* unites the ideas of

[100] Ex. 33:12–23; Is. 40:5; Jn. 1:14; 2:11.
[101] Mk. 8:38; 9:1; 13:26; Rom. 6:4; Col. 1:11.
[102] Lk. 9:26; 24:26; Jn. 2:11; James 2:1.

glory, *kabod,* and habitation or presence, *shekinah.* Thus Christ's glory is the habitation of the fullness of the divinity in his humanity (Col. 2:9). Through his supremely effective mediation, the divinity can shine on men and enrich them with its fullness. In other words, the Lord was saying that he has communicated the revelation of his kinship with his Father to the disciples. He has given them the divine life itself, particularly grace and truth (1:14, 17), along with all the weight of the riches included in God's diffusive *agape* (17:23–24). The work which Christ the Revealer performed in making the mystery known (v. 26) and giving believers power to participate vitally in it was a work of enlightenment transmitted and mediated by his very person in virtue of his union with the Father.

Consequently, it becomes clear that the *doxa* which is communicated to believers not only unites them with one another—"that they may be one"—but also establishes them in communication with the Father and the Son in a relationship as close and personal as the mutual indwelling of God and Christ—"as we are one." Participation in the glory which the Father gives the Son is nothing other than participation in the unity of the Father and the Son.

Verse 23 is emphatic in stating the nature and result of the glorious union. The union of Christ and God is more than the model or principle of the union among Christians; it is its constitutive element. *Doxa* is the divine presence or indwelling communicated and even given by Christ. Consequently, it becomes an immanent, reciprocal relationship of union like the union of the Father and the Son. "I in them and you in me" (14:10, 20). Since the Christ in whom the Father lives—and this is his glory—exists in the believers, the Father lives in them also. From the moment the gift of Christ's *doxa* is made, all are one with the Father through Jesus (Col. 2:10).

One cannot exist in Christ without entering into relationship with the Father, because the two are one. The words, "thus they will be perfected into oneness," *hina ōsin teteleio-*

menoi eis hen (17:23), refers to the transcendent unity of God and Jesus. The verb *teleioun*, which occurs most often in the New Testament in St. John and the Epistle to the Hebrews, means not only "to accomplish" but also "to bring to perfection, to reach the goal," *telos*. Its second meaning is emphasized in these verses by the words "into oneness," *eis hen*, which imply that "perfected" refers to the accomplishment of an ideal. The accomplished perfection shares the divine pattern: "as we are one," *kathōs hēmeis hen*. Jesus communicates his glory, which is the presence of God, to his disciples in order to unite them to the Father as intimately as he himself is united to him, or at least to unite them in the same way in a progressive and even more manifest union.

The final, "that the world may know," *hina ginōskēi ho kosmos*, takes up the element of light and manifestation which had been passed over in the insistence placed on God's indwelling presence in Christ and his disciples. Just as Jesus had made known the glory of the Father living in him, so his disciples will glorify him in their turn. Their unity is transcendent; it cannot be humanly explained. It will make its author known to the world; it will show the world the authenticity of the mission of Jesus, or, more precisely, the exact relation of Christ to the Father. The Father sends his Son into the world to save it (3:17; cf. 9:7). He is true (8:26); he gives testimony of him whom he sends (5:37; 8:18); he remains with him constantly (8:29). For his part, Jesus leads men to understand the words of the Father who sent him (3:34), and his works testify that his mission is divine (5:36). To obtain eternal life one must believe that Jesus Christ is the representative of the Father (16:30; 17:3, 8, 21); one must see his glory, that is, discern God in the Son. The Evangelist uses the verb *ginōskō* here instead of *pisteuō* (v. 21) to emphasize the kind of knowledge that is characteristic of faith. There is much more to it than simple adherence to the revelation that Christ is divine. Faith implies an understanding of God's personal relation with his

apostle, and first of all the understanding that God has
become visible in Christ.

To be convinced that God sent his Son to save sinners
is to be persuaded that God himself wanted to reconcile
the world through Christ (2 Cor. 5:19) and, consequently,
that he loves men (3:16–18). It means, finally, that the sending of Jesus is the manifestation of the *agape* of the Father—
"in order that the world may know that . . . you have
loved them." This is the summit of St. John's Gospel and of
all revelation. The Old Testament tells enough about the
love of God to convince men that it exists, but it required
the sending of the Son to enable men to grasp it and realize
it as it really is—no longer God's generous kindness lavishing
his elect with gifts but now the gift of his only Son and the
presence of the Father and the Son together in their souls.
Christian faith is characterized by the perception of this
glory. The disciples know that Christ lives in them and that
through him they are in communion with the Father. As
St. John's first Epistle would later state, the Christian arrives at faith through the proof of love, but here Jesus was
aware that his mission was essentially a manifestation and
demonstration of the love of the Father. Not only does his
mission proceed from love, but also Christ in his own person
is the channel and instrument of our receiving God's love.

"The world must come to acknowledge that I am your
ambassador, and that you love them as you love me" (17:23).
The qualification, "as you love me," is overwhelming, because it associates the only Son with the sinner in one and
the same love. This association is infinitely useful in determining the nature of *agape*. There are not two loves of divine
charity, one full of delight for the well-beloved Son, and
the other kind and condescendingly merciful toward men.
Although the degree of intimacy varies, it is clear that there
is only one charity, which extends both to Jesus and to his
disciples, precisely because Christ and his disciples are one,
like a vine with its branches or a body with all its members
(Eph. 1:6). It is proper, therefore, to attribute the marks of

the Father's *agape* for his Son (15:9) to his *agape* for Christians. His love for men is eternal (v. 24), generous (3:35), full of delight and intimacy (5:20; 10:17; cf. Mt. 3:17); it is the love of a Father who cherishes his adopted children (1 Jn. 3:1) just as he does his own Son. Christ gives believers a "power to become the children of God" (Jn. 1:12) in actual fact, and God actually engenders them by communicating his nature and life to them. "They were born of God" (Jn. 1:13). The Evangelist compares the gift-power of the new children of God with the filial *doxa* of the Word incarnate—"such a glory as befits the Father's only-begotten Son" (Jn. 1:14)—the glory which he received from the Father in order to communicate it (vv. 16–17) to men. *Doxa*, then, means the principal riches Christ referred to when he said, "The glory which you have bestowed on me I have bestowed on them" (17:22). It refers to adoptive sonship, expressed here in terms of love. Thus, the end of v. 23 corresponds exactly with the beginning of v. 22. Since Christ has obtained glory, the divine nature, and communicated it to God's new sons, the world recognizes in their enrichment the intervention of the only authorized mediator and sees the effusion of the Father's love reaching from the incarnate Word to those he engenders. Christ and his adopted sons are one because a single divine presence lives in them. The divine *agape* manifests itself precisely in the special relationship of authentic sonship.

"O Father! I will that those whom you have entrusted to me shall be at my side where I am: I want them to behold my glory, the glory you bestowed on me because you loved me before the world was founded. Just Father! The world does not know you, but I know you, and thus these men have come to know that I am your ambassador" (vv. 24–26). These verses are not only a continuation of the preceding verses "but also the conclusion of the entire prayer, with two invocations to the Father in the center of the prayer. Christ continues to pray for all the faithful, but the goal has be-

come eternal life" (J. J. Lagrange). The repetition of the invocation "Father" (vv. 24–25) shows the growing urgency
with which Jesus addressed God as he approached the end.
The urgency is even more marked in the change from the
verb "I ask," *erōtō* (vv. 9, 15, 20; 14:16; 16:26) to "I will,"
thelō (v. 24). Jesus had constantly asserted that he was not doing his own will but the will of the Father; [103] at Gethsemani,
too, he distinguished between his human will and God's
will.[104] At this moment of the Last Supper, however, when
the Savior had consecrated himself to the will of the Father
even to the point of giving up his life, as J. H. Bernard has
observed, he had identified himself with God's will (5:21;
15:7) so completely that he could legitimately say, "*I* will."
This is the only time he used *thelō* in speaking to God. It
does not express a desire, but rather his certitude that he was
in complete accord with the will of the Father. He was exercising his own authority, *exousia* (17:2). Christ put forth his
rights as King and Priest, who had received mandate and
power for the sake of the salvation of men. In offering
himself to death, he expressed his final desire. He formulated
his last will and testament and deposited it in the hands of
the Father. His last will was for the beatitude of his
own. . . .

The delicacy of the expression is admirable; the disciples
appear as a gift which God has given to his Son. The Son
is responsible for them, and he is authorized, therefore, to
ask the Father for the happiness of these men who belong to
both of them together. However, Jesus had consecrated his
entire life to his disciples. He was going to die for them.
He was so attached to them (13:1) that he presented his
request as the desire of his love: May death itself not separate me from my own; may we remain united forever
(13:36; 14:3). Where I am and where I will soon be, with
you, I want them to be with me too. In the eternal presence
of heaven, which is less a place than a living relationship,

---

[103] Jn. 4:34; 5:30; 6:38–40.
[104] Mk. 14:36, *ou ti egō thelō alla ti su.*

the disciples will contemplate the glory of Christ. Their *doxa* will become more than the glory they had discerned in the humanity of the Savior with their eyes of flesh, *theasthai* (1:14); it will become the glory they had seen momentarily revealed at the transfiguration, *horan* (Lk. 9:32). It is the splendor of the incarnate Son, shining through his human nature. It is the fullness of the divinity; it is the happiness which the eternal *logos* has with his Father. At the very least, *doxa* refers to a vision which is both intellectual—it discovers the Son as he is (1 Jn. 3:2), united to his Father (Jn. 12:45)—and formally religious in the sense that "to see his glory" is not primarily to contemplate his glory but to reflect and assimilate it (cf. 2 Cor. 3:18), to share and enjoy it. The Christian can contemplate such an object only by being vitally brought into the mystery of the life of the Trinity, by being in some way initiated and associated in the nature and eternal generation of the Son. "Glory" is precisely the beatific vision, the true transfiguration of the Christian, who can be where the glorified Christ is only by having himself become glorified.

In spite of the agreement of the vast majority of commentators that *hoti ēgapēsas me* in v. 24 should be given a causal sense and be translated "because you love me," we prefer, with Godet and Bernard, to consider the particle epexegetical or explanatory. Jesus did not intend to explain why he possesses glory or the reason behind the Father's gift, but to specify in what his glory consists or to express one of its aspects. He is the Father's infinite delight. The disciples would see and, in their love for the Master, would rejoice in God's complete and unchanging *agape* for his Son. The reference may be to the Holy Spirit in person, for the love which unites the Father and the Son long precedes creation. There is a very marked advance here over v. 23, where the world *believed* in the Father's love for Jesus. Here the elect are beatified in contemplating their living love. God's eternal *agape*—manifest, seen, praised—is the glory of the Son. His glory is filial, hence the invocation "Father" at the beginning

of the prayer and the force of the "I will." Jesus commented
on the words "where I am," *hopou eimi egō*, and referred to
his preceding request, "And now, Father, glorify me in your
bosom with the glory I possessed in your bosom before the
world existed" (17:5; cf. 16:28). He asked this splendor and
beatitude not only for himself but also for his own—"that
they may be where I am" (17:24)—who will be transported
with joy by seeing the love in which the Father envelops his
beloved Son (Col. 1:13).

Verses 25–26: "Just Father! The world does not know
you, but I know you, and thus these men have come to know
that I am your ambassador. I have made known to them your
name, and will continue to make it known. May the love
with which you love me dwell in them and I in them."
The conclusion may be considered the justification of the
request or the exposition of the reason it deserved to be
heard. It summarizes the whole prayer and refers particularly
to vv. 3–4: "And this is the sum of eternal life—their knowing you, the only true God, and your ambassador Jesus
Christ. I have glorified you on earth by completing the work
you gave me to do." The Savior's work was primarily an
apostolate of light and knowledge. He had revealed the name
of the Father—not only the person of the true God, but also
the secrets of his life (cf. 15:15), especially his love, solicitude, and generosity toward men. Only he who is in the
bosom of the Father could have unveiled and explained the
mystery of the Trinity and persuaded men that they are
loved by God. The qualification, "I know you," is not simply a parenthetical remark. It points up the competence of
Jesus in making the revelation (Mt. 11:27), especially since
what is revealed is not a piece of purely objective, speculative information, but a permanent union of life, knowledge,
and love with the Father.[105] Jesus communicates the knowledge of God to men in precisely this religious way and in the
same way he will continue his revelation and gift.

[105] Jn. 7:29; 8:55; 10:15.

Actually, the world did not want to receive the glory, presence and life of God, which Jesus offers to all men. Rejecting the mediator, it became unable to know the one who had sent him. The disciples, in receiving the Son (1:12) and giving him their faith (16:31), found in him the living, personal revelation of the Father (14:9–11). Their reward was magnificent—he loved them. "May the love with which you love me dwell in them." Jesus had already assured them, "Of his own accord the Father loves you dearly, because you are settled in your love for me and in your conviction that I come from the Father" (16:27). He went on to explain that conveying to them the gift of the Father's love was the crown of his entire work on earth (*hina*) and that the love he conveyed was nothing other than the reflection and prolongation of the Father's charity for his Son. Furthermore, the Father's *agape* is not just a benevolence which envelops and protects the disciples. It is a love which is in them and will always remain in them. The emphasis in the verse is on the words "love in them," which were developed in Jn. 14:23 and Rom. 5:5, where it is made clear that *agape* is not so much a quality or a divine gift, however completely appropriated by the believers, as it is the loving presence of the Father. The union of the disciple with God is a union of charity.

There is something else even more moving in these verses. If Jesus asked this grace of graces for his own, it was because he loved them intensely (13:1). The last word of his prayer expressed his heart's desire, his consolation in the face of death: "May I too dwell in them." The Lord was about to go away and he was saying goodbye, yet he knew that he would remain present in the souls of his own by the eucharist and by the mutual, active charity which would increase until it reached fulfillment in glory: I in them in absolute fidelity and intimacy. It is remarkable that in so spiritual and theocentric a theology as that of the fourth Gospel, Christ's last prayer should be so human and tender a desire—not to be separated from those he loves—and that the final result of the relationship of love between the Father and Son should work to the benefit of man. It is not said that men must love God, but that God and Jesus will never stop loving men. The earlier verses of the chapter suggest that for St. John *agape* is a link constituting the lover and the beloved in a union so close that it must be described as a mutual indwelling, *einai en* (vv. 21, 23, 26). In verse 26 the accent rests completely on the eternity of love. By its nature *agape* is stable, and here *agape* belongs to God, who does not change —*Ego sum Deus et non mutor*—(Mal. 3:6). Moreover, an eternal and immutable love was being discussed, the love the Father bears his Son from before the creation of the world. In addition, in attributing to the Father the initiative and, as it were, the responsibility of their relationship in love with the disciples, Jesus is guaranteeing the permanent indefectibility of their union. However strong men may be, they are never beyond the possibility of failure, and they experience real anguish in engaging themselves in a promise of eternal fidelity. Yet, "though we be faithless, he remains faithful, since he cannot disown himself" (2 Tim. 2:13). The sure guarantee for the Christian of strong, determined hope (cf. *tharseite*, Jn. 16:33) is God's love for him, which rests upon him in the inner presence of the Savior: "Christ in you, your hope of glory" (Col. 1:27).

One cannot imagine greater depth, serenity, or disinterestedness in those moments before Jesus' martyrdom, which, chosen out of love (15:13), was his *Amen* to his work. The mediator who "made known the Father's name," who revealed that God is love and that his love is entirely directed to his Son, obtained a participation for his disciples in their love. They are at last introduced into the intimacy of the divine Persons, into an abiding with the Father and the Son in a relationship of knowledge and love.

CHAPTER III

Philein, Philos, and Agapan
in the Johannine Writings

THE USES OF *agapan* which have already been analyzed have all had a similar religious meaning. There are several other less clear uses of *agapan*—most of them profane—which remain to be elucidated and compared with St. John's rare uses of the verb *philein*.[1] It must be determined whether the two verbs are synonymous.

At first reading, Jn. 5:20, "the Father loves, *philei*, the Son," appears to be exactly parallel to Jn. 3:35, "The Father loves, *agapai*, the Son," but the context reveals why the Evangelist intentionally varied the verbs. Jn. 3:35 refers to the Father's generous and respectful love for his Son, which is the reason for his giving Christ all power; the verb *agapan* must be used if this idea is to be conveyed. In Jn. 5:20, however, the Jews had just reproached Jesus for making himself equal to God. The Master answered that he took no initiative whatsoever but acted and judged in all things like his Father, for his Father loves him and "shows him all he does." The Father has no secrets from the Son, who shares his inmost

---

[1] The verb *philein* occurs ten times in the Fourth Gospel and twice in the Apocalypse, once (Apoc. 3:19) as a quotation of Prv. 3:2 which the prophet has Christ say. As for *philos*, it is used six times in the Gospel and once in 3 Jn. 15. On the ten uses of *agapētos* in 1 and 3 Jn.; cf. C. Spicq, *Agape in the New Testament*, vol. II, pp. 431 ff.

thoughts and intentions. The intimacy of God's love for Christ is stressed here. The Father trusts his incarnate Son. He tells him all his secrets and everything he does. He treats him as a friend. *Philein* here has exactly the same meaning as *philos* had in Jn. 15:13–15: "No one can give a greater proof of his love than by laying down his life for his friends, *philos.* You are my friends, *philos,* provided you do what I command you. . . . I have called you friends, *philos,* because I have made known to you all that I have heard from my Father" (cf. supra, pp. 43–44). This is not the religious, reflective love of a superior for an inferior, but the spontaneous abandon of two persons united in a mutual love which has made them equals. This kind of love is perfectly expressed by *philein,* and the idea is reinforced by the perfect symmetry between the words "see," *blepēi* and "show," *deiknysin,* on the one hand, and "nothing," *ouden,* and "everything," *panta,* on the other: "The Son can do *nothing* on his own initiative; he can do only what he *sees* the Father do" (Jn. 5:19–20) and "The Father loves the Son and *shows* him *everything* he himself is doing" (Jn. 5:20). The Father's showing corresponds to the Son's seeing. Jesus does nothing he has not seen his Father do, and the Father discloses absolutely everything to his Son. There could be no exchange more complete nor intimacy more absolute than this fruit of the permanent union of thought and heart (*philei* in the present).

2. In the same way, "Of his own accord the Father loves you, *philei,* because you are settled in your love for me" (Jn. 16:27), appears very close to "He that loves, *agapan,* me will, in turn, be loved, *agapēthēsetai,* by my Father" (Jn. 14:21b). In both cases Jesus stated that the Father loved the disciples because they loved his Son, and *agapan* and *philein* are very close in meaning. To consider them identical, however, would be to disregard several nuances which the Evangelist wished to suggest. Jn. 14:21b is a general proposition defining the disciple as "he that loves me," *ho de agapōn me,*

which is the same as "he who keeps the commandments." [2]
The religious *agape* ascending from disciple to Master is very
different from the sensible, emotional warmth which the
eleven had come to feel for Jesus in their permanent contact
with him from day to day since he had first called them to
himself. In Jn. 16:27, the relationship is expressed anthropo-
morphically in terms of friendship, of tenderness strictly
limited to the little group of the Son's *socii*. *Agape* is always
manifest, with effects which can be seen by everyone
(17:23), but here the affection is private and the shared
thoughts intimate (cf. 21:15–17). Only Jesus could reveal
this nuance of the love in his Father's heart. Finally, to show
the Father's love as being motivated by man's having loved
first would contradict the essential notion of Johannine
agape. God loves first; the charity of man is pure response.
The Evangelist could not use the verb *agapan* to express the
contingent aspect of divine affection. Only *philein* can express the notion of reciprocity in God. The disciples' *philia*,
which is an almost fraternal love for Jesus, arouses the
Father's *philia*, which is a tender, paternal attachment.

3. A similar psychological note, this time in a pejorative context, is sounded in Jn. 15:19: "If you were children of the
world, the world would love, *an ephilei*, its own." Jesus was
accounting for the hatred which would follow his disciples
as it had followed him. It was a necessary hatred. The world
cannot love you, because you are strangers to it. *Philein* expresses an egotistical attachment, *philautia*, passion in the
widest sense, whose nature it is to be able to love only what
resembles it or is its possession.

4. In the aphorism of evangelical morality, "He who loves,
philōn, his life destroys it," [3] the verb *philein* means the primary, instinctive love which each man has for himself. It is

---

[2] 14:21a; 23–24; 15.
[3] Jn. 12:25. The expression of this same thought in Mt. 10:39;
16:25; Lk. 14:26; 17:33 does not contain the verb *philein*.

aimed, basically, at the preservation and enrichment of human existence, whereas the love required for salvation is a choice and preference given to the highest good, to God. The distinction between the blind love guided by instinct and the judicious, rational love of classical *agape* is very clear here.

Lazarus

To evaluate the alternating uses of *philein* and *agapan* in the story of Lazarus' resurrection is a very delicate task. According to St. John, Jesus raised his friend Lazarus because he loved him, yet the precise nuance of his affection is difficult to capture.

Martha and Mary sent a message to Christ "saying, 'Lord, he whom you love, *hon phileis*, is ill'" (Jn. 11:3). When he received the message, Jesus said that the illness would not be fatal but would promote the glory of God. St. John notes, "Now Jesus loved, *ēgapa*, Martha and her sister and Lazarus" (v. 5). Then the Master announced to his disciples, "Lazarus our friend, *ho philos hēmōn*, has fallen asleep" (v. 11). Finally, when Jesus gave in to his grief and began to weep, "The Jews remarked, 'Look how he loved him!'" *ide pōs ephilei* (v. 36).

A candid reading of the text reveals hardly any difference in the respective meanings of *philein, philos,* and *agapan*. It seems very probable that their variety is due either to St. John's desire to vary the style or simply to chance, since the two verbs were used without distinction in profane contexts in the first and second centuries and even in the Septuagint. However, St. John's language is usually quite precise, and a more attentive reading reveals several notable distinctions. First of all, the four expressions of love come from four different persons, and each expresses the speaker's personal conception of friendship.

In its delicacy and discretion, the message of the two sisters (v. 3) recalls the prayer of the Virgin Mary at Cana.[4] Their reference to Jesus' affection for Lazarus—"whom you

v. 3

---

[4] Jn. 2:3: "They have no wine."

love," *hon phileis*—could mean anything from simple liking to the deepest friendship. Here it is certainly an appeal to Jesus' warmest human compassion, respectfully corrected by the invocation, "Lord." The verb *philein* contains all their emotion and feeling, all their agony. "He whom you love" is more than a man who happens to be our brother and your disciple. He is someone you love—and we are so worried about him. At most, *agapan* could have suggested only the pathos of their tender love (cf. he whom my soul loves, *ēgapēsen*, Cant. 1:7).

When the Evangelist mentions the Master's affection for all the members of the family at Bethany, he uses the more usual verb of love, *agapan*, without giving it any special value. "Now Jesus loved, *ēgapa*, Martha and her sister and Lazarus" (v. 5). The imperfect tense links Jesus' present and permanent friendship with them to his earlier proving of his attachment over and over. The imperfect "he loved," *ēgapa*, echoes and strengthens the present "whom you love," *phileis* (v. 3). St. John implies that the request of the two sisters was well founded and that the Master understood at once the meaning of their appeal to his heart. St. John uses *agapan* here especially in order to explain why Jesus did not go immediately to his friend's bedside. Instead of following the impulse of his flesh and blood, he seems to have reflected and especially to have consulted his Father. Lazarus' illness was ordained to the glory of God (v. 4), and Christ's love, obedience, and dedication to his Father (cf. 5:19–20) came before his human tenderness for his friends. Consequently, *agapan* here has its specific meaning of judicious and reflective love which is supernatural and religious. Jesus loved Lazarus very tenderly and he loved him in relation to God. That is why he did not intervene immediately to save him from death—that would have been his human good—but instead waited until he could raise him from the tomb and so glorify God.

In calling Lazarus "our friend," *philos hemōn* (v. 11), the Lord was referring to the message of the two sisters (v.

3), but in associating the twelve in the friendship—"our friend"—he recalled the cordial, generous hospitality they had all received in Bethany. *Philos* loses something of intensity and intimacy as it gains in extension (cf. 3 Jn. 15).

Finally Jesus could not keep his feelings hidden any longer, and he broke into sobs. Those who saw him were deeply moved, too, and said, "How he loved, *ephilei*, him!" *Ephilei* has exactly the same meaning it had in v. 3, but here it should be translated as a perfect rather than an imperfect (cf. Rom. 6:17): "Look, how he loved him!" because the Jews thought Lazarus was forever dead. They had no inkling of the miracle that was about to happen. Far from being insensitive or incapable of compassion (cf. Heb. 4:15), Jesus loves in the most real sense of the term. His heart clings to the other and he feels in his body the sorrow of those he loves. It is legitimate to conclude that in Jn. 11 *agapan* and *philein* are almost synonymous. The nuances which *philia* has in this specific context are identical with those which *agape* always has on the human plane.

There are five references in St. John to "the disciple whom Jesus loved," and they vary in much the same way as the references to Lazarus do. At the Last Supper, "one of the disciples of Jesus lay resting in his bosom—the one whom Jesus loved," *hon ēgapa ho Iēsous* (Jn. 13:23). As he hung on the cross, "Jesus, seeing his mother and the disciple whom he loved, *hon ēgapa*, standing by, confided her to the disciple's care" (Jn. 19:26). On Easter morning Mary Magdalen saw that the stone had been moved from the entrance to the tomb, "so she ran and came to Simon Peter and to the other disciple, whom Jesus loved, *hon ephilei ho Iēsous*" (Jn. 20:2). At Christ's third appearance by the Lake of Tiberias, "the disciple whom Jesus loved, *hon ēgapa ho Iēsous*, said to Peter, 'It is the Lord' " (Jn. 21:7). A few minutes later, "Peter turned around and saw the disciple whom Jesus loved, *hon ēgapa ho Iēsous*, following them, the same one who at the supper had been resting against his bosom and had asked,

'Master, who is it that is going to betray you?' " (Jn. 21:20).

Even if the Evangelist intended to use the beloved disciple as a symbol of the perfect Christian and a type of the believer according to the Spirit, he was certainly speaking of a real person—a Palestinian Jew and an apostle, since only the twelve were at the Last Supper (Mk. 14:17; Lk. 22:14). The beloved disciple was probably John, son of Zebedee, close relative of Peter (cf. 18:15, 16), and of the Mother of Jesus. He belonged to the inner circle of disciples who were at the Transfiguration and the agony in the garden, and even within that circle he was especially and almost officially loved. Jesus' friendship for Lazarus was expressed in various ways by various persons, but St. John is always named in a stereotyped formula, "the disciple whom Jesus loved," *ho mathētēs hon ēgapa (ephilei) ho Iēsous*, a phrase which is used only in the narrative and never in direct address. Jn. 21:20 gives the impression that neither Jesus nor John himself created the expression but that it was current in the primitive Church, sometimes with *agapan*, sometimes with *philein*. It must have arisen because of the way Jesus treated the apostle who seemed to be especially close to him; the Lord gave John the privileged place at the Last Supper and, above all, he confided his mother to him.

Jesus loved "his own" in a very special way (Jn. 13:1). Besides, he felt especially fond of the rich young man,[5] and his friendship with Lazarus was common knowledge.[6] His *agape* for John was of the same kind as his friendship for Lazarus; it was *philia* rather than *agape* in the strict sense. He loved John tenderly and intimately (Jn. 13:23; 21:20), confidently and generously (Jn. 19:26). His affection was evidently returned, for John did not hesitate to ask the Lord apparently indiscreet questions which no one else dared ask (13:23). He began to follow Jesus and Peter without having been invited (21:20). He recognized the stranger on the lake shore by intuition—*ubi amor, ibi oculus* (St. Albert the

[5] Mk. 10:21; cf. *Agape in the New Testament* I, pp. 59 ff.
[6] *Supra*, pp. 89 ff.

Great). Finally, he expressed his humble, fervent gratitude for the Lord's love by describing himself by the expression the primitive communities were already beginning to use, "him whom the Master loved," or, rather, him whom the Master had constantly cherished. *Ephilei* and *ēgapa* are imperfects of custom or continuity; they refer to actions which are done over a long period of time, and especially to repeated actions which arise from a stable habit.

St. John was Jesus' intimate friend and favorite disciple. How and why? The question is traditional in the Church, and St. Thomas often answered it.[7] If it is decided on the basis of the reciprocity of friendship—*Ego diligentes me diligo*[8]—it would seem that Peter, who was questioned about loving the Lord more (21:15), should have been more loved by the Lord. Was the Lord's love for John perhaps an injustice? It may be that Peter loved Christ, but more in his members, so that Christ loved him more precisely under that aspect and confided the Church to him. John loved Christ himself in his own person, and Christ in return loved him more too and confided his mother to him. But if it is true that the person who is wished more good and given greater gifts is the more loved, then it is clear that there is no way of knowing which of the apostles loved the Lord more or which of them God loved more and has given greater glory in eternal life. In other words, Jesus' *agape*-predilection for John must be understood not on the plane of divine charity but on the plane of human affection instead. John was loved as Lazarus was loved. "John was loved more in the signs of familiarity which Jesus showed him" (St. Thomas).

As a matter of fact, the Evangelist never says that "Christ" or "the Lord" loved John but that "Jesus" did. It is Jesus' human heart which was captured by John. St. Thomas gives three reasons for Jesus' affection. The first is St. John's keen intelligence. Masters are more drawn to intelligent disciples,

[7] I p, q. 20, a. 4 ad 3m; III p, q. 45, a. 3 ad 4m; *In Mt.* 17:1; *In Jn.* 13:23 and especially 21:20.
[8] Prv. 8:17. Cf. *Prolégomènes*, p. 105.

and John, with his sublime wisdom, penetrated more deeply than the others into the mysteries of the divinity. Secondly, John was absolutely pure; he remained a virgin. Finally, he was still very young. Most persons are drawn to children and to the weak and feel naturally close to them. Christ loved John's youth (cf. Os. 11:1), already consecrated to the Lord.

The Word made flesh really experienced all the emotions and affections which he and his brothers in humanity share. His love took on a thousand nuances as it warmed to different persons. He felt a stronger liking for some whose special characteristics aroused his love and gifts in a particular way. He warmed to the candor of little children; to his unfortunate compatriots; to true believers like the centurion of Capharnaum; to faithful souls like the rich young man; to receptive, responsive friends like the family of Bethany; and to the impetuosity of the Sons of Thunder. Among them all, however, there was one who was different from the others— the young disciple who lived three years with him (1:14; 1 Jn. 1:1–2) and with whom he felt so many affinities. Jesus felt a love, *storgē*, for him that was as spontaneous as it was expressive. When St. John uses the verb *agapan*, with its religious resonances, to describe Jesus' affection, he does so because *agape* is the love of the incarnate Word, whose human heart was always in exact accord with his divine will.

Peter

Having seen the various meanings of *agapan* and *philein* in the passages just studied, we are now in a position to grasp the meaning of the final uses of the verbs in the solemn conversation which Jesus had with Peter immediately after their last meal. "After they had breakfasted, Jesus said to Simon Peter: 'Simon, son of John, do you love (*agapais*) me more than these others do?' 'Yes, Lord,' he replied, 'you know that I love (*philō*) you.' 'Then,' Jesus said to him, 'feed my lambs.' He asked him a second time: 'Simon, son of John, do you love (*agapais*) me?' 'Yes, Lord, you know that I love (*philō*) you.' 'Then,' he said to him, 'be a shepherd to my sheep.' For the third time he put the question to him: 'Simon,

son of John, do you love (*phileis*) me?' It grieved Peter that
he had asked him the third time, 'Do you love (*phileis*) me?'
and he replied, 'Lord, you know everything; you know that
I love (*philō*) you!' 'Then,' Jesus said to him, 'feed my
sheep'" (Jn. 21:15–17).

All the commentators from the time of St. Augustine have
agreed that the triple question of the Master is an allusion to
the triple denial of the disciple. Jesus' first question about
Peter's greater love discreetly recalls the Apostle's presumptuous claim: "I will give my life for you" (Jn. 13:37); "Even
if all the rest are shaken in their faith, I shall not be shaken
in mine" (Mk. 14:29; Mt. 26:33). After his denial, could
Peter repeat his oath of fidelity? Could he set himself apart
from the twelve and swear that he would never deny his
Master? His cowardice had taught him the extent of his
weakness, and he had no wish to protest his exceptionally
faithful and generous *agape*.

His new insight explains why he gave a response that is
humility itself. He said that he certainly did love his Master,
but he omitted "more than these others" from his answer. He
hardly dared put forth the sincerity of his statement as a
proof of his love, but preferred to rely on the Lord's knowledge instead. "You know that I love you." Finally, he intentionally substituted *philein* for *agapan;* he affirmed his
personal attachment as a man rather than the religious love
Jesus was asking.

Commentators are divided about the respective value of
the two verbs, but those who make them synonymous either
ignore the semantics of *agape* or minimize the importance of
the scene. It was not a private conversation or a moral lesson
given to a disciple, but the institution of Peter as head of the
Church, as its primate. The Lord was not asking him for the
affection of a friend, but for the religious love of *agape*
which constitutes the very life of the Church (17:26). Consequently, *agapan* refers, not to a love that is more rational
and voluntary than *philein*, but to love in the technical sense
it had in the Septuagint: religious attachment and consecra-

tion to God expressing itself on the moral plane by total fidelity and obedience in exclusive service of the Lord.[9] *Philia* simply does not convey the nuances which Jesus wished to convey to the turncoat. Jesus asked of Peter both charity and the virtue of religion, which expresses itself in devotion to the interests of the Lord. To fulfill the charge which was confided to him, Peter had to be consecrated body and soul to the service of his Master and "his own." The Apostle could not have misunderstood what the Lord's question meant. Just as the angel at the incarnation asked Mary to believe, so the founder of the Church asked his future vicar to profess his love and fidelity. He made his request in the very words whose meaning he had so insistently defined during the Last Supper. They form an exact parallel with Jn. 21:15–17: "If you love me you will keep my commandments. . . . He who accepts my commandments and keeps them, he is the one who loves me. . . . Anyone who loves me will keep my word. . . . He who does not love me does not keep my word." [10] Moreover, Jesus had suggested that authentic charity is not the same thing as instinctive liking, inclination, or passion; it is the desire to die for the beloved (Jn. 15:13). When Peter made his statement at the Last Supper, he did not in the least doubt his willingness "to die with" Christ, *synapothnēiskein* (Mk. 14:31; cf. 2 Tim. 2:11). How could he dare to say two days after his denial, "Yes, I love you with that kind of faithful and unfailing love —*agapō se*—unto death"?

Jesus wanted to test the sincerity and determination of Peter's attachment, so he asked a second time, "Do you love me, *agapais me?*" but this time he did not add "more than these others do." Peter answered in exactly the same words as before, but apparently with greater conviction and spirit. Touched by Peter's insistence, the Master repeated his ex-

[9] Jesus' last word on the charity of his own corresponds to the first mention of charity in the Bible (Ex. 20:6), where "to love" signifies "to keep the commandments" and "to serve." Cf. Deut. 6:5; 10:12, 20; *Prolégomènes*, pp. 88–98.

[10] Jn. 14:15, 21, 23, 24; cf. *supra*, pp. 55 ff.

pression, *"Phileis me"* (v. 17). Really? You still love me? I
can believe that you are a real friend? I can rely on your
word and trust your heart? According to the Evangelist, this
question filled Peter with sorrow. He was grieved to the
heart that Jesus had changed the wording of his question
when he asked it the third time and said, "Do you really love
me?" He had been attached to the Lord from the very first
day, and he could not bear the thought that Jesus doubted
the fervor and depth of his human affection, which was the
very thing that just a little while before had pushed him
to promise to die for his friend. It was a natural tenderness, perhaps, but it was also the authentic love of a man who
had given himself body and soul to his friend. Peter must
have had tears in his eyes as he answered, acutely aware of
his weakness and sorry for his faults, "Lord, you know it
better than I do."

That Jesus accepted Peter's friendship is proved by the
charge he laid on him after each one of Peter's answers:
"Feed my sheep; be the shepherd of the flock." The two
present imperatives, "feed" and "be the shepherd," *boske*
and *poimaine*, must apply to the future. In the same way,
agapais in the present should be understood with the volitive
nuance which is frequent in the Bible. "Do you wish to love
me?" (cf. Jn. 15:15) and more exactly, according to the
proper meaning of *agapan*, "Do you wish to manifest your
love to me, to prove your fidelity to me from now on, to
show you will be entirely at my service?" [11]

St. Peter was to offer proof of his devotion through his
pastorate. He showed his love for the Lord through his
ministry and work in helping those whom Jesus loves. There
could be no closer union between charity for Christ, charity
for neighbor, and even Christ's charity for his disciples. The
Fathers of the Church were right when they emphasized
the note of affection in the way the faithful are described
as "lambs," "little sheep," and with the possessive "my."
The flock remains the property of the "great shepherd of the

[11] Cf. Jn. 13:1; 15:14.

sheep" (Heb. 13:20). How could it not be infinitely precious
to him when he gave his life for it? He confided the flock
that he loved to Peter, and, consequently, as St. Ambrose
has so admirably expressed it, his vicar was instituted the
representative of his charity.[12] That is why feeding the
Lord's flock must always be preeminently a work of love.
St. Augustine says, "Feeding the Lord's flock should be a
duty of love. . . . Do the Lord's words, 'Do you love me?
Feed my sheep,' mean anything other than, 'If you love
me, do not think that you are the shepherd; but feed my
sheep as mine, not as yours; seek my glory in them, not
yours; my good, not yours; my profit and not yours." [13]

According to Mt. 9:36; 10:6; 18:10–14; Lk. 15:4–7, Jesus'
messianic work was to gather together his scattered and
lost sheep, a work which was to be continued by his apostles. Mt. 25:31–46 says that at the end of time Christ will
place his sheep at his right hand, those blessed of his Father
who have given proof of their fraternal love. Thus it may
be concluded that although the supreme Shepherd remains
the head of the flock, until the Parousia Peter is the shepherd
who will provide for all the needs of the sheep, especially
by keeping them in one sheep fold (Jn. 10:16; 11:52). The
fold is described as the place where charity is exercised,
so *agape* is the virtue proper to the shepherd just as it was to
the "Good Shepherd."

The revelation of "authentic charity" which Jesus had
made to the world through his death (15:14) and which
will continue to the end of time in the fraternal love of his
disciples (13:35) thereafter had its own institution. The
Church, led and directed by Peter, is, as it were, the sacrament of the *agape* of the Savior. It is the real presence of
the love with which the Father loves the Son, who has
"given" their love to believers so that they may be one as
and with the three divine persons. Christ the Revealer's
last teaching and final gesture on earth were meant to in-

[12] *In Lc.* X, 175 (PL 15:1942).
[13] St. Augustine, *In Jn.* XXI, 15–17 (PL 35:1967).

sure the eternal existence of the charity over which Peter
had the care and guardianship.

Two profane and technical meanings of "friend," as it is
used in the fourth Gospel, remain to be mentioned. The
Savior's union with the messianic community is compared
to a marriage, and John the Baptist, who prepared the alliance, calls himself "the friend of the Bridegroom" (Jn.
3:29). The Rabbis called this personage the *shoshbîn*. He
was an official who played an important role both before
and after the wedding celebration, exercising the offices
of the three Greek officials, *paranymphos*, the *nymphagōgos*,
and the *philos tou nymphiou*. He was more than the Greek
paranymph; he was simultaneously the chief witness at the
wedding, the best man, a confidential advisor, and the master of ceremonies. He was essentially the bridegroom's
representative and mediator.

Selected from among the bridegroom's companions, the
shoshbîn was his friend par excellence. After the engagement had been arranged, he served as intermediary between
the future husband and wife. He had to arrange all the
wedding feasts[14] and preside over them during the week
of the festivities. He organized and led the noisy procession
that went to get the bride and bring her to the groom.
Always present, he took care of everything. After checking
on the good order of the marriage chamber, he waited
outside the door to hear the joyful shout of the bridegroom
when he had verified the existence of the *signum virginita-
tis*. After the wedding, the friend of the bridegroom acted
as a mediator in any discussions and misunderstandings which
arose in the life of the newlyweds. Jn. 3:29 brings out the
role of John the Baptist in concluding the alliance between
the Messiah and the society of the elect, whom he had prepared by a bath of water (Eph. 5:26) that they might be
worthy of the union. It stresses the joy of the Precursor's
love. The friend rejoices at the Bridegroom's happiness.

[14] Cant. 5:1; 1 Mc. 9:39.

During the trial of Jesus, the Jews of the Sanhedrin threatened to denounce Pilate to the emperor if he persisted in acknowledging Jesus' innocence. "If you release this man, you are not a friend of Caesar. Anyone who declares himself a king renounces allegiance to Caesar" (Jn. 19:12). The phrase, "friend of Caesar," *philos tou Kaisaros*, could have any of three different meanings here. It could be a banal reminder of fidelity or a litotes to mean, "You will be an enemy of Caesar's if you do not condemn this pretender to royalty" (cf. Lk. 23:2). However, the legal context and especially the procurator's fright suggest that the phrase should be given its technical sense of *amicus Augusti*, as Wettstein has already noticed. The Romans had adopted this aulic title from the Seleucids and the Lagids. The friends of the emperor are, strictly speaking, his counselors or traveling companions. Pilate was not a dignitary or a high personage with influence at court, so he had received the honorary title, "friend of Caesar," because he was a knight and the procurator of Judea. The title has all the many connotations which official "friendship" for the prince carried at this period.

Elevation to the rank of "friend" was not conferred through specific nomination and conferring of letters patent, but it was always bestowed on senators and, after the reign of Augustus, often on legates and prefects as a reward for loyal service. Those who had been promoted to the rank liked to vaunt their guarantee of imperial favor and show off its prestigious symbol, a golden ring. In 27 A.D., when Tiberius retired to the Isle of Capri, the all-powerful prefect of the pretorian, Sejanus, immediately placed his men in the best administrative positions. Pilate was one of these men, and his reward was the governorship of the province of Judea. If he did not already belong to the equestrian order, he was raised to it immediately so that he would have the right to exercise his procuration. It is very likely that he received the coveted title, "friend of Caesar," *philos tou Kaisaros*, at the same time.

Pilate was the fifth procurator to administer the province. He owed everything to Sejanus, whose anti-Semitism he shared. Despite Pilate's political mistakes, he did not become uneasy until his protector was removed on October 18, 31. During his ten years in office, his implacable energy enabled him to subdue all efforts at rebellion at once, but he was aware that the Jews were working to destroy his reputation and that they sent many denunciations of him to Rome. Tiberius preferred not to change the magistrates on duty in the provinces, but one day he had heard enough. On the grounds of a complaint brought by the council of the Samaritans, the legate of Syria, Vitellius, relieved Pilate of his functions and ordered him to return to Rome. Tiberius had just died (March 16, 37) and Caligula sent the ex-procurator of Judea into exile, reporting Pilate's disgrace a few months later to Flaccus, governor of Egypt.

The full implications of the insidious threat of denunciation to the emperor (Jn. 19:12)—surely the maneuver of that clever politician, Caiphas—can be seen when the threat is placed in its historical and psychological context. It explains the statements of Mk. 15:15 and Lk. 23:24 that Pilate wanted to please the crowd. The inflexible procurator had been at the point of releasing Jesus. Violence does not seem to have moved him or even to have impressed him. He had seen such things often before. The thought of the emperor's disfavor alone was able to overcome his conviction of Christ's innocence and make him yield out of cowardice. "I find no fault in him" (Lk. 23:4, 14, 22). Pilate's entire career depended on imperial favor. A disgrace would mean the ruin of his ambitions, a compromised future, the confiscation of his fortune, the loss of his liberty, his exile, and possibly death. The Jews of the Sanhedrin touched their enemy at his most vulnerable point. In shouting, "You will no longer be a friend of Caesar if you release this man," they knew they would chill him with fright. As they said the words, they must have been staring at the ring which he wore as "friend of Caesar."

Pilate chose the friendship of Caesar. There can be no doubt that St. John wished to evoke the opposition between the two lords. The procurator had to decide between the Messia-King, crowned with thorns and clothed in purple (Jn. 19:5), and the bonds that connected him with the head of the empire. Was his heart sufficiently attached to the light (3:19–21) to listen to the voice of truth (19:37) which would have liberated him from his slavery to the Prince (8:32)? Neutrality was impossible.[15] Theologically speaking, there is a depreciative note in the word "friend" here —friend of the world or of the powerful. *Agape* alone chooses Christ to the detriment of self (2 Cor. 5:14).

[15] Mt. 10:37; 15:19 and especially Ja. 4:4.

CHAPTER IV

Agape in Saint John's Epistles

THE NOUN *agape* occurs only seven times in St. John's Gospel, but twenty-one times in his Epistles. The verb *agapan* is used thirty-seven times in his Gospel and almost as often—thirty-one times—in his Epistles. These figures suggest that a thorough study of charity in St. John's epistles will require an exhaustive commentary. However, St. John was always faithful to the meaning of charity which he had learned directly from the Lord, so we need only concentrate on those new and complementary elements in the epistles which definitively enrich the New Testament notion of *agape*.

1. Charity, the criterion of a true disciple

But whoever keeps God's word, truly that man's *love* for God is perfect (1 Jn. 2:5).

The Christian is defined by his communion and dwelling with God, which have many components: knowledge, possession of the light, *agape*, observance of the commandments. In this text the emphasis is on *agape*, which has the same meaning it had in Jn. 14:15, 21, 23–24. True love proves itself by obedience, and by the fidelity in observing the commandments which is the sign and proof of the *agape tou theou,* of truly divine and Christian charity. *Agape* in this text seems to be an original entity. It is the love with which God loves himself, from which he lives, and which he bears toward his creatures. He communicates his love by giving it to his creatures, who live from it in their turn. It enables them not only to love both God and their neighbors but also to live in a particular way even to the smallest details of their lives, to live in conformity with God's word or orders and in accord with his will. Thus every disciple is characterized by the possession of charity, the love that is both total and specific.

"Truly that man's love for God is perfect." The verb "is perfect," *teteleiōtai,* a perfect passive, could refer to an ideal of perfection: in the faithful and obedient disciple, charity arrives at its point of highest development; it reaches its fullness or maturity, since it bears fruit. The context suggests, however, that *agape* should be considered an unchanging greatness and an objective reality; it is the divine nature participated in to varying degrees (*en toutōi*) by the believers. The emphasis is on God's infusion of love or on the Christian's reception and possession of God's gift (cf. Eph. 3:17). The verb *teleioun* should therefore be given the sense of "to accomplish" and "to realize" with an existential nuance. In the obedient Christian, the unique, divine *agape* really exists in all its authenticity. It is truly and integrally accomplished only in him, especially in its effective dynamism. In other words, *agape* always implies manifestation and proof. The love of God implies the effective accomplishment of the divine will.

2. Fraternal love is always contemporary; it guarantees communion with God and preserves from sin

He who *loves* his brother abides in the light, and so he has no cause for stumbling. But he who hates his brother is in darkness and walks in it (1 Jn. 2:10).

There is no union with God possible apart from fidelity to the commandments (2:3–11) and particularly to the precept of love of neighbor (vv. 7–11) which sums up all the others. For the recipients of St. John's Epistle, this was an old commandment, *entolē palaia*.[1] They had learned it and accepted it from the moment of their conversion and first initiation into Christianity. It is nonetheless a new commandment, *entolē kainē*, too, since it was called new by the Lord himself (Jn. 13:34). It always remains contemporary because its imperative never loses its force and because it can always be applied to every circumstance of life.

St. James and St. Paul had called Christians "those who love God,"[2] and St. Paul had explained that in loving another one keeps the whole Law.[3] However, for St. John the expression, "he who loves," *ho agapōn*, when it has no specified object, is a definition of apostle and of the authentic believer who is born of God. It is the opposite of "he who does not love" and does not know God.[4] *Agape* is not only a fundamental virtue but also a state. To love—both God and one's brothers—[5] presupposes that we are begotten by God and that God's seed lives in us; we manifest his love, live it, and act because of it. "He who loves" is of a different race from "he who does not love." Born of the devil, the non-lover is a liar who lives in death.[6] 1 Jn. 2:9–11 opposes the world of light to the world of darkness; the former is characterized by love, and the latter by love's absence, hatred. That is why St. John does not give neighbors or enemies as the object of love, but rather brothers, all those who belong to the same world, God's children who, in Christ, are united to their Father in heaven.

To love in this way is "to live in the light," "to be in communion with God (v. 6), who is light" (1:5). It is just as accurate to speak of being a true believer (cf. Jn. 12:46). The verb "abides," *menei*, is in the present tense and corresponds to "he who loves," *ho agapōn*, to emphasize the per-

[1] 2:7–8 (*hapax Jo*).   [2] James 1:12; 2:5, 8; 1 Cor. 2:9; Eph. 6:24.
[3] Rom. 13:8.   [4] 1 Jn. 3:14; 4:7–8.   [5] 1 Jn. 4:21; 5:1.
[6] 1 Jn. 3:10, 14; 4:20.

manence of the Christian's union with God through knowledge and love. The second part of the verse stresses the
security which comes from the unchangeableness of the union. In the light of perfect security, there can be no "scandal" or trap to make us stumble. We are guaranteed against
possible falls. To live without sin, we need only keep ourselves in the union of *agape*. More precisely, the light into
which we are plunged illumines the way and makes us see
clearly and walk straight ahead without danger of stumbling
over an obstacle or a trap. Conversely, he who does not love
his brother, and therefore exists and walks in darkness (*estin,
peripatei;* cf. Jn. 12:35), is sure to lose his way or stumble.
It may be concluded that *agape* prudently and effectively
orients the entire moral life under the light of God, as St.
Paul had already explained in 1 Cor. 13:4–7.

3–5. Divine charity and attachment to the world are incompatible

Do not *love* the world or what the world has to offer. If
anyone loves the world, the *love* of the Father does not exist in
him, because all that the world has to offer is the cravings that
arise from our fallen nature, the cravings that arise from what
we see and a vain display in one's mode of love. These come not
from the Father, but from the world (1 Jn. 2:15).

The command, "Do not love," is addressed to all members
of the family of God, to the "little children"—young and
old—who know their Father and live in communion with
him. They have conquered the Evil One (2:12–14) and consequently they live in radical separation from the evil
"world" whose prince he is (Jn. 12:31). In a pejorative and
concrete sense, "the world," *ho kosmos,* refers to pagan society or civilization with its idolatry and vices, to every world
order or social and political system which ignores God and
gives free rein to corruption (James 1:27). It is synonymous
with *ho aiōn,* the "world," characterized by darkness and

perversity (Gal. 1:4; Eph. 2:2), which has its own wisdom
(1 Cor. 1:6, 21; 3:19) and its own god (2 Cor. 4:4).

It is an obvious fact and one of the most constant teachings of Christian catechesis that the world of God and his
children is in radical opposition to the world of the devil
and his subjects. Therefore, "love" in "do not love," *mē
agapate*, must be understood as attachment in the strict sense
—full of esteem, appreciation, and especially of the religious
values of respect and service. In the second proposition, "if
anyone loves," *ean tis agapai*, however, the feeling seems to
be desire and preference, as in 2 Tim. 4:10, since *agape* is
immediately explained by the perverse desire, *epithymia*, of
the *cosmos*. Love of world and love of the Father [7] are in-
compatible. A person who loves this world and has given
himself to its pleasures cannot have the Father's love within
him. The Father's love is first of all God's own charity by
which he loves his children—the Father does not give his love
to a divided heart—and it is also the possession of the divine
charity which lives in the believers' hearts and makes them
Christian. *Agape* is much more than a virtue; it is a life and,
as it were, a new nature. It is the link which makes men belong to the divine world. We belong either to God or to
this world, depending on the object and quality of our loves.

The evil world is characterized by all kinds of sinful desires. Only those who are of the world and belong to the
world can give themselves over to these desires. Those who
are born of God and live in dependence on him, united to
him in mind and heart through *agape*, cannot become attached to anything radically different from him, because to
love is to conform oneself to the divine will (2:5) and love
what God loves. Begotten by God and having no other love
but the one he has received from God (4:7), the Christian
is radically incapable of loving what God does not love or
what does not make God present to him. The Father's love

---

[7] *Tou Patros* is not an objective genitive, as most of the commentators claim, but a subjective genitive (Jn. 5:42), or better, a "comprehensive" genitive (1 Jn. 4:16).

already has its determined objects, which his children can neither modify nor extend. As soon as they possess his love, they begin to cling to what is good (Rom. 12:9). It could not be more clearly stated that *agape* is a love of the beautiful and the good; it is entirely different from *erōs*.

6. Divine sonship is the overwhelming gift of the Father's love to believers

See what kind of *love* the Father has bestowed on us that we should be called his children, for that is what we are (1 Jn. 3:1).

God loved all men so much that he gave them his only Son (Jn. 3:16), and his love for Jesus' disciples was so great that he made them his own children, sharing his divine nature with him (1 Jn. 2:29). His gift is stupefying, and St. John could not conceal his emotion as he spoke directly to the religious sensitivity of his readers.

The verb "to see," *idein*, does not have its common meaning of "to see physically, to look at." [8] It means, rather, "to note, to verify" [9] signs or miracles,[10] for example, or "to discern, to reflect" and even "to understand." [11] Divine *agape* does not fall under man's senses. It is a spiritual reality which is nevertheless perceptible in its effects—for example, the *pneuma* (Jn. 3:18)—and which is the object of faith—"like one seeing the unseen" (Heb. 11:27). In this passage, the children of God are invited to reflect on their baptismal regeneration (Tit. 3:5), not only speculatively as one works back from an effect to its causes, but also with the heart, because it is a love to be appreciated, not just an object to be understood. In this sense, the Psalmist said, "Taste and see (*idete*) that the Lord is good" (Ps. 34:9; cf. 1 Pet. 2:3). Consequently, the "seeing" is as much a religious experience

[8] Mt. 11:2; 17:8; 23:39.
[9] Mk. 12:34; Lk. 2:15; 24:39; Acts 26:16; Jn. 1:39, 46; 20:25, 27.
[10] Mt. 12:38; Lk. 19:37; 23:8; Jn. 4:48; 6:14.
[11] Lk. 9:47; 19:3; Acts 15:6.

as it is a grasping with the intellect. It is what a sympathetic and especially attentive regard sees when it beholds something which fills it with admiration. St. John's "see," *idete*, refers unmistakably to the astonished and joyful contemplation [12] which penetrates deep into the revelation of the mystery of God. It discerns the divine *agape* in the present and concrete fact that the believer is begotten the son of God.

The element of surprise and admiration is accentuated by the rather rare Hellenistic word *potapos*, "what kind of," which modifies "love." *Potapos* was nearly synonymous with *poios* and was used for both persons and things. In its six New Testament uses, *potapos* always refers to a type, to a distinct and even unusual category. Before the splendor of the Temple the disciples said to the Lord, "Look, Rabbi, what (*potapoi*) wonderful stones! What (*potapai*) buildings" (Mk. 13:1). The element of wonder is even clearer after the miracle of the calmed tempest when the people in the crowd asked one another, "What kind of (*potapos*) man is this?" in the sense of "Where does he come from?" The astonishment of the Blessed Virgin when she heard the completely unexpected salutation addressed to her by an invisible being can also be understood in this way. "But she was startled at what he said and wondered what (*potapos*) this greeting meant" (Lk. 1:29). She was trying not only to understand the words of the angel, *epi tōi logōi*, but also to place him: "Where does he come from?" The *Protoevangelium of St. James* understood her words in this sense (11:1): "She looked around her, to the right and to the left to see where this voice came from," *pothen hautē hē phōnē*. In our text, the word *potapos* seems to combine the three notions: *qualis, quantus, unde,* what kind of, how great, and whence. God's love for us is an exceptional, stupendously generous love which comes from heaven. Its nature must be divine.

Agape should be interpreted in its Christian sense. It is manifest, active, expressed love, but, more, it has its own

---

[12] Jn. 8:56; cf. Mt. 13:17; Lk. 17:22.

reality, existing in itself and communicable. It becomes a gift of the Father to believers. "See what kind of love the Father has bestowed, *dedōken,* on us that we should be called God's children, for that is what we are." The verb "bestowed," *dedōken,* emphasizes the gratuitousness and reality of the gift; the perfect tense shows that the gift is given once and for all. The communication of love is a communication of God's very nature (2 Pet. 1:4), since it results in the believers' becoming authentic children of God. The begetting to divine life, which all other New Testament texts link with faith, baptism, or the Holy Spirit, is attributed here to the Father's *potapē agapē,* his marvelous love which cherishes Christ's disciples as his own sons (Jn. 14:21).

In religious language, "to be named" and "to be" mean the same thing, because when God calls someone something or names him, he accomplishes what he states. Consequently, Christians who are called "children of God" are, in reality, just that. The seemingly redundant words, "for that is what we are," *kai esmen,* arise from the fervor of St. John's wonder and gratitude for the great truth. He wants to convince his reader that the great gift of God is not a doctrine that is taught, but a possession that is enjoyed by each person. "We are the ones who are God's children!" Lastly and especially, he wants to stress that this grace and dignity are being bestowed right now: "Today, this is our present state."

The forthright and graphic statement, "A child of God does not commit sin, because the divine seed remains in him" (1 Jn. 3:9), indicates that the divine sonship is to be taken in the most realistic sense. Christians are not God's children in any metaphorical or merely moral sense. It is not because God surrounds them with his attentive providence that he is their Father. Each of them is really newly begotten, reborn, sharing in the very life of God. In contemplation, faith recognizes the immense love expressed in the Christians' regeneration. Like St. Paul, St. John learned in the crucifixion of Jesus (Jn. 3:16; 13:1 ff.) the dimensions of the divine charity which surpasses all knowledge. Toward the end of

his life, Saint John discovered the same love in the fact of
the rebirth of the believer. The divine *agape*, which is always generous, appeared to him as tender and intimate.
Charity is union and even communion of being and life.
Finally the very fact of being a Christian, of having been begotten by God, is permanent proof that one is loved by the
Father. Each Christian possesses within himself a guarantee
of God's inexpressible charity. It is, as it were, inviscerated
in him.

7–14. Fraternal and effective charity, which is God's message and Christ's commandment, is the criterion of the disciple; it conditions his relations with God

10 Here is the sign which reveals who are God's children
and who are the devil's: Whoever fails to lead a holy life is no
child of God, neither is he who fails *to love* his brother. 11 This
is precisely the message which you have heard from the beginning—that we should *love* one another. 12 Be not like Cain who
was a child of the evil one and murdered his brother. Why did
he murder him? Because his own life was wicked, whereas his
brother's was holy. . . . 14 We know that we have passed from
death to life, because we *love* our brothers. He who does not
love abides in death. 15 Everyone who hates his brother is a
murderer, and you know that no murderer has eternal life abiding in him. 16 We know what *love* is from the fact that Jesus
Christ laid down his life for us. We, too, ought to lay down our
lives for our brothers. 17 How, then, can the *love* of God abide
in him who possesses worldly goods, and seeing his brother in
need, closes his heart to him? 18 Little children, let us not *love*
merely in word or with the tongue, but in deed and in truth.
19 By that we shall know that we are born of the truth, and
we shall calm our conscience in his presence, 20 no matter
what our conscience may reproach us with, because God is
greater than our conscience, and knows everything. 21 Beloved,
if our conscience does not reproach us, we have assurance in

God's presence. 22 We also receive from him whatever we ask, because we keep his commandments and do what is pleasing in his sight. 23 His commandment is this, that we should believe in the name of his Son, Jesus Christ, and *love* one another, as he commanded us. 24 He who keeps his commandments abides in God and God in him. It is the Spirit abiding in us who gives us the assurance that God abides in us (1 Jn. 3:10–11, 14, 16–18, 23).

This collection of somewhat disjointed considerations on fraternal charity is a meditation on "the Lord's new commandment" recorded in Jn. 13:34–35: to love one another as Christ loves us. This love is the criterion of the disciple. *Agape* is indeed a message, *aggelia* (1 Jn. 3:11) and a commandment, *entolē* (vv. 22–24). Its model and its nature are taught by the crucifixion of the Savior (v. 16), and any person who possesses *agape* is an authentic Christian. Jesus had said that everyone would recognize his disciples by their *agape*, and St. John was reminding the disciples of this criterion. Charity is a manifest sign, *en toutōi phanera* (v. 10), and an indisputable proof of discipleship, as well as a concrete and obvious fact. It is also a unique quality, a test which distinguishes true Christians from those who only bear the name. The Apostle knows only two classes of men: 1) "those who love," the totality of the faithful, *agapōmen* (vv. 11, 14, 18, 23), and individual exceptions, "he who does not love," *ho mē agapōn* (vv. 10, 14). St. John's use of the present tense and especially of the participle, which is equivalent to a noun (cf. *tēroumen, ho tērōn:* vv. 22–24), shows that loving is not an isolated act but rather a permanent quality, a habit, or even a religious condition or state. In each case, the emphasis is placed strongly on the manifestation of incessantly active charity. Charity proves itself, devotes itself, gives and sacrifices itself; it loves "in deed and in truth" (v. 18). By these very fruits it becomes an unquestionable criterion of divine sonship. The Christian is defined by love, or rather, by loving: *ho agapōn*. St. John incorporates the possession of charity into the whole of his theology. The person who loves his brothers is born of God or of truth (vv. 10–11), and he has passed from death to life (vv. 14–15); henceforth he belongs to the world of charity and is a stranger to the world of darkness which will hate him (v. 13). On the other hand, his filial relations with God are filled with joyful confidence. His heart is at peace; he has free access to his Father; his prayers are heard; he lives in the greatest intimacy with God, since he lives in God and God in him (vv. 19–23). Thus the authentic disciple is the one who has believed in Jesus the Son of God (v. 23), received the message of divine and fraternal love from the time of his baptism (v. 11) and put it into practice (v. 18) after the example of the Savior (v. 16) with the help of the Holy Spirit (v. 24). Consequently, the disciple is certain, *en toutōi*, that "eternal life lives in him." The entire Christian economy is centered on charity. To live, within the Church—for it is still a matter of loving *brothers*—is to love.

Verse 10 is probably the most important in the entire section, which it introduces perfectly in making *agape* the evident sign of discrimination of Christians and the criterion of divine sonship. It says: "Here is the sign which reveals who are God's children and who are the devil's: whoever fails to lead a holy life is no child of God, neither is he who fails to love his brother." To love is to be a son of God to the point of loving as God loves and because God loves. The Christian depends on God so completely that he cannot think or act other than as God thinks or acts. His dependence is like a law of nature stated by the Lord. "By their fruits you can tell them. Are grapes picked from thornbushes—or figs from thistles? In the same way as every good tree bears healthy fruit, so a sickly tree bears fruit that is bad. As a good tree cannot bear fruit that is bad, so a sickly tree cannot bear healthy fruit." [13] In actual fact, the relationship those who love have with God is the relationship of children with their Father. The manifestation of charity is precisely the expres-

---

[13] Mt. 7:16–18; cf. 12:33–34; Lk. 6:43–45.

sion of the divine nature possessed by the Christian. This fact presupposes that God himself is *agape* (1 Jn. 4:8), and hence that whoever loves his brother reveals that he is an authentic son of God, just as those who do not love him are children of the Evil One [14] or of the devil.

St. Paul believed that fraternal charity was the new justice and the full accomplishment of the Law (Rom. 13:9–10), as the Lord had expressly taught (Mt. 22:40). St. John recalled this elementary catechism to those who were surprised that the possession of *agape* should be a sufficient criterion of moral perfection and of the mysterious divine begetting. "This is precisely the message which you have heard from the beginning—that we should love one another" (v. 11). The Church transmitted the message, which came from God and was taught by Christ, to all converts at the time of their conversion. It is a nearly exact quotation of Jn. 13:34; 15:12, and it gives the precept which governed the neophyte's conduct. The man born of God need do nothing but give himself over to mutual love. His sonship is so apparent and exposes so active a presence of God that the jealousy and hatred it stirs up in the world (v. 13), which belongs entirely to the Evil One, should not be surprising (1 Jn. 2:13–16).

The world's hostility is all the more understandable in that the converts are runaways who have escaped from Satan's power (Heb. 2:14). When Christ "calls" a man to be his disciple, he takes him out of the world [15] to attach him to himself by faith and love; the believer "has passed from death to life" (Jn. 5:24). In this text, fraternal charity, the criterion of a true disciple, effects the transition from one universe to the other (1 Jn. 3:14). The verb *metabaino*, which is always used in its strict sense, "to pass from one place to another," [16] can also be used to mean a changing from one condition to another, as when Jesus passed from

[14] 1 Jn. 3:12; cf. Mt. 13:38; Acts 13:10; Jn. 8:44; 17:15.
[15] Jn. 13:18; 15:16, 18.
[16] Mt. 8:34; 11:1; 12:9; 15:29; 17:20; Lk. 10:7; cf. Acts 18:7.

this world to his Father (Jn. 13:1). With the exception of Christ, all men "live in death"; the only ones who escape it are those who become children of God and so obtain eternal life, which they possess forever (the verb *metabaino* is in the perfect). Death is separation from God; life is union with God. Conscious and active *agape* for one's neighbor is the infallible sign of having passed from death to life.

What is the love that is the same as divine life? Verse 16 defines it as pure gratuitousness and total gift of self. "We know what love is from the fact that Jesus Christ laid down his life for us. We, too, ought to lay down our lives for our brothers." That is what the example of Christ offering his life for men teaches us. His voluntary sacrifice is the expression of his true fraternal *agape*. Here again St. John is referring to the *ipsissima verba* of the Lord, who had presented his death as a manifestation of his love (Jn. 15:12–13). The essence of the living faith of the disciples will always be the association of Calvary and charity.[17] In this verse St. John refers to the Savior as *ekeinos* (cf. 2:6), "that person," with the stress less on his person than on his being the model, archetype, and teacher. The cross is an historical fact which reveals a mystery to believers, the mystery of the epiphany of *agape*. St. John does not insist on the manifestation; he simply calls the disciples to its contemplation. They have passed from death to life and they know that Christ loves them and that they have benefited by the shedding of his precious blood for them. The divine "message" which they received when they were converted (v. 11) was summed up in their redemption from sin through the purely gratuitous love of God's Son. They bound themselves, accordingly, to express their faith by a fraternal love as disinterested as his. St. John gives the simple reminder, "We, too, ought to lay down our lives for the brothers." The duty is both elementary in its logic and heroic in its execution. It follows on Christ's example and derives from the information, "he . . . we too," *ekeinos . . . kai hēmeis* (cf. 2:6). The disciple's

[17] 2 Cor. 5:14; Gal. 2:20; Eph. 5:25, etc.

authenticity lies in his *mimēsis* of his master's charity (Jn. 13:34–35).

All the commentators are amazed that after the demand for so total a gift, v. 17 proposes so banal an application: "How, then, can the love of God abide in him who possesses worldly goods, and, seeing his brother in need, closes his heart to him?" St. John's pedagogy is the same as the pedagogy the Lord used in the Sermon on the Mount; concrete examples are given to suggest a spirit. To explain what patient *agape* means, Jesus proposed submitting to blows or giving up one's tunic even though the only adequate effect of *agape* would be to undergo death. So too, to bring out *agape*'s selflessness and generosity, St. John presents the almost scholastic case of almsgiving serving as a test of sincere charity: to love is to give. However, the words in which St. John states his example stress primarily that charity is a pure and simple love capable of strong feeling and unrestrained spontaneity. The rich man is supposed to really look at the beggar, and his gaze, as in the case of the good Samaritan (Lk. 10:33), should immediately arouse his pity (Deut. 15:7). The rich man in this text, however, like the wicked man in Prov. 12:10, closes his heart and will not let it be moved. The verb *kleiō* is very strong. It means "to bolt or bar." St. John makes it even stronger by adding the strange qualifier, "to him," *ap' autou*, which describes the rich man's refusal of any movement of pity. He closes himself within himself so resolutely that the poor man can find no way to his heart—or to his money. The conclusion is admirable: "How, then, can the love of God abide in him?" The interrogative form emphasizes the impossibility of charity's existing in a heart which does not respond—it is the heart of a murderer (v. 15). There is surely no point in trying to determine whether "the love of God" refers to God's love for the wicked Christian or the wicked Christian's love for God. It is certainly true that God cannot love those who do not love their brothers; to want to love God without at the same time having fraternal charity is an idle dream (4:20). How-

ever, here "the love of God" refers to the divine charity as
such (4:16), to the reality which makes one a child of God.
The Christian receives it from the Father, possesses it forever, and uses it as Christ himself did. St. John does not hesitate to associate the heart of the Christian (literally, "entrails," *ta splagchna*) and the love of God, *hē agapē tou
theou*. He lets it be understood that if a Christian voluntarily
and seriously lacks compassion, the divine love no longer
dwells in his soul. In any case, true *agape*, the most spiritual
of loves, makes the sensibility of the child of God extremely
delicate, so that he immediately responds to the misfortune
of a brother. Responsiveness is not only a psychological consequence of the infusion of divine charity into a flesh-and-
blood being but also a moral demand. The disciple of Jesus
Christ is merciful, *eusplagchnos* (Eph. 4:32; 1 Pet. 3:8). An
insensitive person is not a Christian.

Thus St. John uses a very tender expression in the next
verse. "Little children, let us not love merely in word or
with the tongue, but in deed and in truth." He is asking his
readers to take the demands of charity very seriously. Charity is an efficient love. The double explanation, both negative and positive, "not in word or with the tongue, but in
deed and in truth," accentuates the realism of the prescribed
gift. St. James, too, had denounced the hypocrisy of the rich
who try to feed the poor with kind words (James 2:15–16),
but here the emphasis is even more serious, since "to love
in truth" is to love as Christ crucified has loved us (v. 16).
All almsgiving, all service, and all kind acts are modeled on
the Savior's total gift of self. They are accomplished with
the same charity and the same authenticity of love as inspired Christ on the cross. The Lord and his disciples are
one.

"By that we shall know that we are born of the truth, and
we shall calm our conscience in his presence" (v. 19). An
effective love, devotion, and service of our neighbor assure
our peace of conscience just as they make manifest that we
are children of God (v. 10), or, as it is expressed here, "of

truth." The "love which accomplishes," like the love of God
and Christ from which it proceeds, is the "love without pre-
tence" which St. Paul and St. Peter talk about. The insistence
of the three apostles on the sincerity of the fraternal love
which proves itself in actions says a great deal about its un-
equaled importance, but, even so, only St. John makes it the
criterion of divine sonship. It is impossible to love in this
way except through God; that is why we can be so sure of
his love for us and our communion with him. We do not
try to be a law unto ourselves or to calm our more or less
well-founded scruples, but in the presence of God, through
his light, objectively, we know that we are justified.

Nevertheless, every man is a sinner, and a just man is the
first person to recognize the fact (1:8–9). How can we feel
reassured, under the eyes of God, when our consciences reproach us with so many failures? St. John answers: If our
conscience condemns us for anything (*hō ti ean*, with the
present subjunctive), we can still be sure we are true children of God because of the exercise of fraternal charity,
"for God is greater than our consciences and he knows all"
(v. 20). Why is God's greatness the basis of our certitude?
St. John said earlier that our assurance of pardon rests on
God's fidelity and justice (1:9). Here he bases it, instead, on
God's infallible knowledge of hearts: "He knows everything" (cf. Heb. 4:12–13; Acts 1:24). A heart filled with remorse is neither the final nor the competent judge (1 Cor.
4:4–5; cf. 8:2–3). Only divine judgment is infallible. In
every single case, there is an appeal to the transcendence of
God and, very specifically, to the transcendence of his love.
"God is greater than our heart." He loves in a way that is
not like the way we love. His charity, which is acutely aware
of our misery and ignorance (Lk. 23:34), is an infinite
mercy which is permanently extended to all his children
who want to love him and who love their brothers in deed
and in truth. St. John's statement is an application of the
beatitudes of the merciful and the peacemakers (Mt. 5:7, 9)
and of the parable of the judgment (25:31–46). It is based on

soteriological optimism: "If God is for us, who is against us?" (Rom. 8:31); and on the axiom: "Charity wins forgiveness for many sins" (1 Pet. 4:8). It derives especially from the fundamental principle of the New Covenant: justice is a grace that comes, not from man, but from the pure gift of God. St. John bases the peace of soul enjoyed by God's children on the magnanimity of the heart of their Father. The monks of Qumran called this "the immensity of his love." It will be not without value to quote here this hymn which expresses reflections like St. John's.

Verily I know that righteousness lies not with man, nor perfection of conduct with mortals. Only with God on High are all works of righteousness; and ne'er can the way of man be stablished save by the spirit which God has fashioned for him to bring unto perfection the life of mortal man; that all his works may know how mighty is his power, how plenteous his love to all who do his will.

When I called to mind all my guilty deeds and the perfidy of my sins—when wicked men opposed thy covenant, and froward men thy word—trembling seized hold on me and quaking, all my bones were a-quiver; my heart became like wax melting before a fire, my knees were like to water pouring over a steep; and I said, "Because of my transgressions I have been abandoned, that thy covenant holds not with me."

But then, when I remembered the strength of thy hand and thy multitudinous mercies, I rose again and stood upright, and my spirit was fortified to stand against affliction; for I was stayed by thy grace and by thine abundant love. For thou wilt wipe out all sin and in thy bounty it lies to purify man from guilt.[18]

It is even more helpful to quote Osee 11:8-9, where we see that the divine transcendence implies an infinite mercy entirely out of proportion with what human heart and mind can grasp. "How could I give you up, O Ephraim, or deliver you up, O Israel? How could I treat you as an Adama, or make you like Seboim? My heart is overwhelmed, my pity is stirred. I will not give vent to my blazing anger, I will not

[18] IV, 29-37. *The Dead Sea Scriptures in English translation*, ed. T. Gaster (Doubleday: N.Y., 1956), pp. 145-146.

destroy Ephraim again; *for I am God and not man*, the Holy One present among you; I will not let the flames consume you."

A child-like heart (v. 10), freed from fear—"our heart no longer reproaches us" [19]—recaptures all its freedom and daring to speak to its Father. With complete confidence and boldness, the charitable person converses with God and expresses his desires to his Father (v. 22). All his prayers are immediately heard, as the two verbs in the present, "we ask, we receive," *aitōmen, lambanomen*, indicate. There are no formal supplications, but only the simple, direct requests, *aitein*, which a child makes to his Father, knowing very well that he will be heard. Jesus had promised his apostles that their prayers would be infallible [20] if they lived in him by being united to him in fidelity to his precepts. In this text he is concerned with the precept of fraternal love. The person who loves his brother lives with God in intimate communion, *koinōnia*, and among his joys, he has the joy of seeing his requests fulfilled precisely because his active *agape* is the most agreeable of all works in the Father's eyes. The same charity which reassures the heart and helps one's neighbor has free access to God from whom it obtains everything. How could the God who is love refuse anything at all to a request of love?

Verses 23–24 conclude that God asks of his children (v. 10) both faith in his incarnate Son (4:2; Jn. 16:27) and mutual love as he promulgated it (13:34; 15:12) by his ambassador. We must always love and we must never cease believing in Christ. These two acts are permanent, and the second one depends on the first. To give one's faith to the Son of God is to learn from him to live in charity, to bind oneself explicitly to love one's brothers, and to manifest this love to them "in Christ." The new religion is defined both by the object of its faith—Jesus is God's son—and by the

[19] 1 Jn. 3:21; cf. Acts 24:16.
[20] Jn. 14:13–14; 15:7, 16; 16:23–26.

everyday life of the disciples—the Christian is the person who loves his brothers in the Church.

Thus the child of God is assured of an extremely intimate, reciprocal communion with his Father: "He who keeps his commandments abides in God and God in him" (v. 24). Words cannot explain this; only love will understand. The transcendent God "who is greater than our heart" (v. 20) dwells within us. There is not only reciprocal union between God and the Christian but also interaction between them, because *agape* is just as active in its relations with God as with its brothers. Finally, the Christian is brought vitally into the unity of the Holy Trinity, as Jesus desired (Jn. 17:21–23), and that is surely why St. John makes the Holy Spirit intervene here. Prodigious though the assimilation to God is, it is knowable as well as real (1 Jn. 4:13). The Spirit, who sounds God's depths and resides in God's children as in a temple, makes them sure that God is present and is their Father.[21] Our knowledge of his fatherly presence is the consoling certitude and supreme fruit of fraternal *agape*, the résumé and center of the Christian life. "We know. . . ."

Jesus had made the new morality consist in the observance of the two commandments of love of God and love of neighbor (Mt. 22:40). St. John summarizes it in one commandment: believe in the crucified Son of God and love your brothers (1 Jn. 3:23). According to the Lord, fidelity in obedience assured eternal life; for St. John, fidelity wins access to God to "remain in his love." More precisely, St. John developed the connection between *agape* and eternal life. He summed up revelation in the completely new message of fraternal love (v. 11), since Christ has taught us what it is to love with charity (v. 16). Also, St. John identified love with life (v. 14); whoever does not love his neighbor is dead (v. 15). By learning to love, the believer is born to the present and eternal life which is the very life of God. The man who loves, *ho agapōn*, is the child of God, *teknon*

---

[21] Rom. 8:14–16; cf. 1 Cor. 12:7; 2 Cor. 13:13; 2 Tim. 1:12.

tou theou (v. 10). The Christian loves as God and Christ love, with the same divine love, which he possesses and which "lives" in him. His life is his love. The children of the devil or Evil One live in death and hate their brothers, but the children of God are alive. Because they are divinely alive, they necessarily manifest their charity to their brothers (vv. 18–19).

The relationship of origin and causality between God and love is so exclusive and direct that if a man loves with charity, it can be concluded that he is born of God. No one can love with charity if he does not have the divine life within him. *Agape* is so much the criterion of divine birth that it is impossible to doubt the permanence of God's love in us if we love our neighbor. Just as Cain's hatred proved that he was a "child of the Evil One" (v. 12), so an authentic fraternal love, tenderly and generously expressed, assures us that we are "children of the truth." Love and hatred are signs of heredity and belonging; they are the only unmistakable criteria of descent.

Doubtless, the Christian remains a sinner, and his conscience reproaches him with many faults (v. 20); but God, "who is greater than our heart," will pardon his failings if he lets himself be so moved by his neighbor's sorrows that he helps him effectively. Hardness of heart is the only failing which provokes the severity of the Sovereign Judge. In other words, the quality of our fraternal relations determines the quality of our relations with God. God accepts as faithful the Christian who observes "what is pleasing to him" (v. 22) —the "commandment" of fraternal love (vv. 23–24)—for he sees fraternal love as the sign of conformity of wills between his child and himself.

The Christian is conscious of this disposition of God's heart—"we know" (vv. 14, 16, 19, 24)—and he can and must approach God without fear, [22] and even remain in his presence with simplicity and daring (v. 19). He does not hesitate to formulate whatever request he wishes to make,

[22] V. 21. Rom. 5:1; 2 Cor. 3:4.

and his request is immediately granted. The charitable person has accomplished what God loves above all else.[23] The Father can refuse nothing to one who has revealed himself his authentic child. Above all, distances are truly abolished. God and the person who loves his brothers form but one: "God in him" (v. 24). Fraternal charity, the pledge of eternal life in the synoptic Gospels, has become the guarantee of divine indwelling and of the most direct, intimate relations of love between God and the Christian. The Holy Spirit, the supreme gift, permits us to be aware of God's presence. "It is the Spirit abiding in us who gives us the assurance that God abides in us" (v. 24).

15–19. The exercise of the divine gift of fraternal charity implies that one is begotten by God and lives in communion with him

Beloved, let us *love* one another, because *love* is from God, and everyone that *loves* is a child of God and knows God. He who does not *love* does not know God, because God is *love* (1 Jn. 4:7–8).

After developing some thoughts on the Holy Spirit and on faith in the incarnate Christ (4:1–6), St. John returned to the theme of fraternal charity.[24] For the third time, he formulated the exhortation, "We must love one another" (1 Jn. 3:11, 23). The other times he was referring to the precept of Jesus, but here he goes further and suggests that fraternal love is not an arbitrary obligation, not simple fidelity to a commandment, and not a "spirit." It is an exigency of nature, for God is love. He has begotten Christians by communicating his own nature and life to them, so that his children are capable of loving as their heavenly Father loves. The disciple's charity is therefore the practice and proof of

[23] V. 22. Cf. Acts 4:19; 1 Tim. 2:3; 5:4; Heb. 13:21; 1 Pet. 3:4.
[24] 1 Jn. 4:7–21; cf. 3:11–24.

his sonship. This clear, profound idea is the supreme revelation of New Testament *agape*.

The development of the Apostle's thought follows naturally. We must love one another . . . love comes from God . . . whoever loves, loves because he is begotten by God . . . God is love. In linking *agape* with its source, St. John is considering it in its formal, universal meaning. Love of neighbor and love of God share the same nature. The Christian is defined as "one who loves," *ho agapōn*, because he loves in a particular way with a special, divine love which has a name that sets it apart from all other loves, no matter how tender, kind, and good. It is *agape*, and it comes from heaven. The first statement in v. 7 emphasizes charity's divine character. Charity is from God.

St. Paul had already explained that *agape* is infused into the hearts of Christians (Rom. 5:5), but he had not made it clear whether or not *agape* is simply one divine gift like any of the others, whether or not it is some particular grace or charism given for a certain time at a particular stage of justification. Actually, *agape* is intrinsically linked with the believer's rebirth; it is the essence of his divine sonship. We love because we are begotten by God. "Begetting" should be understood in the most realistic sense. In begetting us, God communicates his nature and life to us. Since "he who has been begotten by God," *ho gennētheis ek tou theou* (5:18), and "he who loves," *ho agapōn*, are equivalent descriptions of the Christian, it is clear that the child of God has received a faculty or power of loving which is inherent in the divine nature he has come to share. The basis of the obligation to love one another, then, is not laid in moral convenience or an ideal perfection, but in a vital movement which springs from our new nature. "Let us love *because* . . ." *Agape* is the fruit of the divine seed received at baptism (1 Jn. 3:9). Rom. 5:5 might be interpreted to mean that it is the Holy Spirit who loves in us, but St. John explains that the Christian himself is the lover, for he has become capable of loving divinely. He is qualified for love in the same way that he is qualified for the divine sonship (Jn. 1:12).

Most commentators understand the last part of the sentence, "Everyone that loves . . . knows God," in the light of 1 Jn. 2:3–5, "By this we can be sure that we know God, if we keep his commandments. . . . Whoever keeps God's word, truly that man's love for God is perfect." It is unquestionably true that faith completes and proves itself in obedience. "No one who sins . . . has known him" (1 Jn. 3:6). Nevertheless, in all these texts, St. John is presenting the sign (*en toutōi*) by which the person who really knows the Lord can be discerned; his moral works mark him as belonging to the Lord. In the present text, on the contrary, St. John is speaking on the theological level; God's own nature is disclosed to the person who lives by charity. It is not a question, obviously, of speculative knowledge. Biblical "knowledge" is an experiencing and grasping of the being that is known, and it is *agape*, the faculty of union, which gives the believer the possibility of entering into communion with God and knowing him. The verb in the present, "knows," *ginōskei*, corresponds to the present participle, *agapōn*, "he who loves." Knowledge of God that is both present and permanent always accompanies habitual fraternal love. Everything has its origin in the Christian's rebirth. The believer who has been begotten by God shares the divine life and has the power of loving and knowing divinely. He has a "habitus" of knowledge of the same kind as his aptitude for loving with charity. His knowledge of God is a son's knowledge of his Father, and of his Father precisely as loving.[25] Since "to know God" is eternal life,[26] and the knowing is not only impregnated with love but also conditioned by love,[27] it may be concluded that the charity received from God governs the essential religious attitude and keeps us in the divine *koinōnia* (1 Jn. 1:3, 6). To perceive God and remain united to him, we must love.

[25] Rom. 8:15; Gal. 4:6.   [26] Jn. 17:3; 20:31; cf. 1 Jn. 5:20.
[27] 1 Cor. 8:3; 13:12.

Thus the antithesis in v. 8a can be glossed, "He who does not love divinely does not know God intimately or truly." Assuredly, a keen intelligence can have correct and penetrating insights into God, his being, his nature, and his attributes, but if these are pure speculation, without charity, then they are not knowing "as we must know," with a personal relationship based on a living, loving experience. The intellect can understand words and define notions; only love touches reality. Affective realities are as unintelligible to the man who has no heart, *ho mē agapōn*, as colors are to the blind man. God is love, and without love how can anyone have the sense of divine love?

That is the first meaning of the statement, "God is love," *ho theos agapē estin*, which will be repeated in v. 16. The context (vv. 7–9 ff.) gives the designation special importance. The Christian must love because he is begotten by God and love comes from God. Love has a special affinity, then, with the nature and life of God. It may seem that St. John intends to give a definition of God in the Greek manner—God is pure act, *to on;* intelligence of the intelligence, *noēsis noēseōs;* beyond all being, *epekeina pasēs ousias*—but actually he is not defining God. For one thing, he had already said, "God is Spirit" (Jn. 4:24); "he was the light" (Jn. 1:9); "God is light" (1 Jn. 1:5): all expressions which stress essential properties of God. Further, in 1 Jn. 9, "God" has an article, *ho theos*, and *agapē* does not. Therefore, *agape* is not a noun, and it is incorrect to translate *ho theos agapē estin* as "Love is God." [28] This translation would make an idol of *agape*, as the Athenians did of *eros*, whose feast they celebrated the fourth of Munichion.[29]

The least that can be said is that there is love in God, that love belongs to God, and that the love which comes from God (v. 7) is located in him as in its overflowing source. To understand the precise meaning of St. John's phrase, the best

[28] As many German exegetes have done: *Gott ist die Liebe* (H. Scholz, *Eros und Caritas*, Halle, 1929, p. 54, etc.).

[29] L. Deubner, *Attische Feste*, Berlin, 1956, p. 215; cf. *Prolégomènes*, p. 10.

method is to discover its origin, as v. 9 suggests. "God's love was made manifest among us by the fact that God sent his only-begotten Son into the world that we might have life through him." St. John is not speculating on the divine nature, nor does he intend to give an adequate definition of God as he is in himself. He is presenting the fruit of his contemplation on the manifestation of God through history, above all in the person, life, and teaching of Christ (Mt. 11:27; Lk. 10:22), for "since the creation of the world his invisible attributes are clearly seen" (Rom. 1:20).

The living God of the Old Testament reveals himself not only as the all-powerful creator of the world, legislator, judge, king, and savior of his people, but also as goodness itself, bestowing gifts on his creature the universe, which he has made out of nothing (Gen. 1:28–30). Provident, merciful, and forgiving to those who repent, he helps his own in their distress. His covenant with Israel depends on the divine love and *héséd* (Jer. 3:12; Ps. 145:8); the history of the covenant reveals the extent of its privileged attributes. In the Sermon on the Mount, Jesus described his heavenly Father's charity as generous even to enemies and the ungrateful. The divine mercy toward sinners was Christ's first teaching,[30] and his whole kind, patient life closed with the gift of himself on the cross as ransom, which the first converts interpreted as the expression of the love of God for men (Rom. 5:8; 8:32, 39). In the same sense, St. Paul spoke of the love of God, *agapē tou theou* (Rom. 5:5; cf. Eph. 2:4) and the God of love, *theos tēs agapēs* (2 Cor. 13:11). God reveals what he is by what he does.

St. John was heir to these theological reflections. More than anyone else, he meditated on God's active love, never in the abstract but always in relation to Christ, because the Father and the Son are one (Jn. 10:30), and in seeing the Son one sees and knows the Father (8:19; 14:7, 9). Having really grasped all the charity which the heart of Christ manifested in his death (15:13), the "disciple whom Jesus loved"

[30] Mt. 5:43–48; 18:23–34; Lk. 15; Mk. 10:18.

concluded that a love identical with the love he discerned in the Word made flesh exists also in God. "Just as the Father loves me, so I love you" (Jn. 15:9–10). To be sure, Christ makes believers participate in the plenitude of grace and truth which he possesses as only Son, but *agape* remains his most constant and magnificent revelation. Expressions of divine love are so extreme, frequent, and forceful in the life and words of the Savior, that *agape* seems to be the Father's predominant attribute. It is certainly the most frequently mentioned and displayed in the New Testament.

This nuance of manifestation is correct in the expression, "God is love," *ho theos agapē estin*, in 1 Jn. 4:9. According to classical Greek and the Septuagint, *agapan* and *agape* always refer to a manifestation or an effective proof of love. St. John respects this meaning in his Gospel (3:16) and first Epistle (3:18), and it is the meaning of v. 9. Our verse might be glossed: Let us manifest our love for one another exteriorly, because effective love comes from God. Whoever proves his love is certain that he is born of God, that he knows God, and that he possesses God within himself. He who does not show charity does not know God nor does he possess him, for God is essentially the manifestation of love.

We must go even further. If love connotes God's entire activity and all his relations with his Son and with creatures, then love is part of God's nature. St. John does not say that God is "one who loves," *agapōn*, or "one who has loved," *agapēsas*, but rather that God is love, *agape*. Furthermore, he does not write that love is in God, but that God *is* love, a statement which amounts to a designation, if not to a definition of his being. It can be correctly understood only if *agape* is given the transcendent meaning of "beneficent fullness." It is just the opposite of *erōs*, which is desire and need. God is, in himself and from all eternity, pure gift and communication of self. This property is not distinct from his substance.[31] God is, in himself, love, not as if he possessed some abstract quality, but because he is entirely life, strength,

[31] Man has love; God is love.

and diffusive goodness communicating himself totally to his Son, pouring himself out to his Son with infinite delight. The sovereign good is by nature supremely generous. The Father, who is love perpetually in act, gives himself to the Son so completely that he expresses himself perfectly in him. The Son unites himself to the Father within the love that exists between them.

God cannot be defined, but the loving soul believes that love is in God by his very essence and understands that the bountiful charity which the Father manifests toward man is simply a prolongation and participation in his essential attribute. Finally, it experiences in the charity which is infused into it—"*agape* is from God"—something of the subsistent love which is God himself. From the effect of *agape* the loving soul can discover its cause; by participation, join its source; by living its life, discover its author. The mystique of fraternal charity consists in this: the Christian who loves his neighbor can have *agape* only if it is given to him by God, because *agape* is a participation in the one love with which God loves himself and men. Consequently, the lover knows and reaches God as love. Because he possesses something of the divine nature in himself (2 Pet. 1:4), he grasps it in its most characteristic quality: pure and constant gift. In other words, *agape* establishes a community of nature and life between the son and his divine Father. Through his experience of the lucid love that is *agape* the believer realizes what God is.

Nothing stronger could be said about the specific quality of Christian love, which is participation in God's love. Unlike all human affections, *agape,* which originates in heaven, has a truly divine nature. It belongs to the world of spirit, light, and true life. Only God and his children are able to love in this way. These verses are responsible for Christianity's being defined as a religion of love. The fraternal charity of Jesus Christ's disciples wells up spontaneously from their divine nature, just as the love of their Father does, and therefore fraternal charity is the clear proof of their divine son-

ship. Its model is the Father's love for his Son, a love of
delight and union. "Just as my Father loves me, so I love
you. . . . Love one another as I love you" (Jn. 15:9, 12).
"To love one another," *agapan allēlous*, characterizes Christian behavior primarily because it already defines the relationship between God and his Son.

20. The redemptive incarnation, a manifestation of divine charity

God's *love* was made manifest among us by the fact that God
sent his only-begotten Son into the world that we might have
life through him (1 Jn. 4:9). Cf. C. Spicq, *Agape in the New
Testament*, vol. II, pp. 391 ff.

21–27. Authentic charity is the charity with which God envelops the Christian; it requires Christians to exercise fraternal love, the guarantee of God's presence in the soul

Love consists not in our having *loved* God but in his having
loved us and his having sent his Son as a propitiation for our sins.
Beloved, if God so *loved* us, we in turn ought to *love* one
another. No one has ever seen God, yet if we *love* one another,
God abides in us and our *love* for him reaches perfection (1
Jn. 4:10–12).

The central dogma of St. John's theology is the mystery
of *agape*, which best expresses both God's nature and the
Christian condition. When God begets children, he necessarily makes them share his love, because he communicates
his own life to them in such a way that they cannot help
being completely loving to their brothers (vv. 7–8). Christ
revealed and communicated his Father's love to men (v. 9).
Verse 10 repeats the thought, meditating on it and deepen-
ing it. Verses 9 and 10 appear to be parallel. "In this does
agape consist," *en toutōi estin hē agapē* (v. 10), corresponds

to "in this was God's *agape* made manifest," *en toutōi
ephanerōthē hē agapē tou theou* (v. 9). The English translations of these verses emphasize the consistent biblical use
of *agape:* a manifest, proved, and demonstrated love (cf.
Jn. 15:13). God revealed that he is charity in three ways:
he sent his Son into the world; his only Son died; he purified us from our sins. These three great mysteries of our
salvation—incarnation, redemption, grace—sum up the Gospel. Like St. Paul, St. John understood that they were conceived and carried out by God's infinite love.[32]

The wording of v. 10 shows that St. John intends to
define *in what love consists;* he is concerned with the love,
the charity that belongs only to God and Christians. The
phrasing, a negative followed by a positive, "not in our
having loved God but in his having loved us," does not so
much contrast the two parties, God and men, in their relationship of love, as contrast the times of their respective
entrances into the communion of love. The Vulgate's translation expresses this well: *"Quoniam ipse prior dilexit nos."*
The Christian's love for God may well be long-established,
conscious, and stable (*ēgapēkamen* is in the perfect), but
more than that is required to reveal what authentic charity
is. It is always response to an earlier love; it is gratitude
and religion, an obligation based on a precept and determined in every way by the quality of the Person loved.
More profoundly, it is a second state of being, a participation in the charity of God himself. St. John very correctly
declares: this is love as it is in God (v. 8), who alone, in
manifesting himself, can reveal what true charity is and,
first of all, can reveal that its essential properties are priority,
initiative, and spontaneity. The Greeks had a saying that
love is more proper to the lover than to the beloved. God
must by nature love us first because of his infinite greatness
and the diffusive fullness of his love.

These considerations are not all, nor are they even the
essential ones. The manifestation of *agape* is accomplished

[32] Rom. 5:8–9; Eph. 2:4–5; Jn. 3:16; 1 Jn. 3:16.

in a prodigious act: God sent his Son to earth (cf. 1 Jn. 3:16) with the mission of dying to expiate our sins so that the very persons who had offended him might live with his own life (v. 9). In other words, divine love revealed itself under its highest form—spontaneous, disinterested mercy which comes as pure gift. Far from being aroused by the good qualities of those it loves, divine love spares nothing to make its objects lovable.[33] God's charity is not simple delight or benevolence but active and efficacious love. God sent his Son. He gave him to sinners, abandoning to death the person who is dearer to him than any other, *edōken* (Jn. 3:16). The redemptive incarnation reveals most clearly the immensity of the divine charity (cf. 13:1, *eis telos*) as well as its holiness, because charity purifies guilty men in order to unite them with itself.

The historical fact of creation says all this, even shouts it, to those who know how to listen. It makes us understand at last that there is no common measure between all the forms of human love, even the most noble and generous, and *agape*. Therefore the phrase, "in this does love consist," *en toutōi estin hē agapē*, must be understood in its most technical and specialized sense. St. John is not presenting a definition of what love is, or setting up a model or ideal of love. He is speaking of the reality itself, which belongs only to God and those to whom he gives it: charity. Without any doubt, men are capable of loving with devotion and exquisite delicacy; they are even willing to sacrifice themselves for those who are dear to them (cf. 1 Cor. 13:3), but they are incapable of loving *as* God loves. It is not a matter of greater or lesser quality or extension or of a difference in degree; the difference is in nature. *Agape* is completely different from anything human beings possess or can even imagine. Only God can love with such fullness, infinity, and power of giving, regardless of the attractiveness or lack of it in the person he loves. In contemplating the incarnation and death of the only Son, the believer feels that he cannot

[33] Rom. 5:8–9; Tit. 3:3–7.

"understand" (cf. Eph. 3:19); he is facing the most profound mystery of all. The final word is that God loves us *in this way* because he is love (v. 8), or, more precisely, because he is *charity*. He loves us this way because love is his nature.

St. John must have written with profound emotion when he said for the sixth and last time in the epistle, *Agapētoi*, "Beloved" (v. 11). Christians, you receive this infinite love. Do you really believe it? Do you understand it? The first part of the verse amounts to a repetition of what has preceded, but this time with a note of wonder arising from his contemplation. "If God *so* loved us . . ." in so prodigious, inexpressible a way, we must love one another in turn. Commentators have correctly seen a connection between the phrase, "If God so loved us," *ei houtōs ho theos ēgapēsen hēmas* (1 Jn. 4:11) and the phrase, "so marked has been God's love . . . that . . . ," *houtōs ēgapēsen . . . ōste* (Jn. 3:16). However, in the second text *houtōs* expresses the exactness of the facts and the authenticity of their inspiration by accentuating their veracity. Therefore, *houtōs* means "in this manner," and the thought is, "Consequently, if God has truly manifested his charity by such acts . . ." In the same sense, Yahweh declared, "Thus, *houtōs*, my mercy shall never leave you" (Is. 54:10), and Judas Maccabeus said, "He will do just as, *houtōs poiēsei*, shall be the will of heaven" (1 Ma. 3:60).

The context of 1 Jn. 4:11, on the other hand, requires that *houtōs* be given a qualitative value, "marvelously, in so excessive a way." This meaning is well attested in classical Greek and in the papyri. *Houtōs* reinforces the idea of the word it modifies; in pejorative uses it constitutes a euphemism. A certain Paul, who wrote to his brother reproaching him for bad conduct, said, "If I had known that you were going to lose your reputation and your fortune so (*houtōs*) ignominiously . . ." [34] Several abused and mistreated plaintiffs summed up the mistreatment they had received, "He

[34] *P. Fouad*, 85:1.

(she) left me in this state (*houtōs*)." [35] *Houtōs* also has the
favorable sense of "so intensely," as in Didymus' letter to
his brother Apollonios: "So strong (*houtōs*) is my desire
to greet you." [36] Ptolemy was tempted to interpret the
silence of his good friend Apollonios as a sign of neglect,
and he asked him to write regularly so he could know how
much Apollonios loved him. In the Septuagint, consequently, *houtōs* often has the notion of "so." [37] Sometimes
it was used to express things too shameful to be decently
described. For example, Potiphar's wife reported to her
husband, "Thus did your servant treat me" (Gen. 39:19).
Tamar resisted Amnon. "Do not violate me, for it is not
so (*houtōs*) done in Israel; do not this disgraceful folly"
(2 Sam. 13:12). Sometimes *houtōs* expresses the intensity [38]
of a feeling or the exceptional character of an event: Yahweh has done nothing like this (*houtōs*) for the other nations (Ps. 147:9). No one ever had riches so great as
Solomon's or possessed a throne as beautiful as his.[39] In the
New Testament, the crowd, marvelling at Christ's works,
exclaimed, "Never has the like been seen in Israel." [40] In
our text, *houtōs* must be understood in this sense of ex-
clamation and wonder: "in a way so real, effective, marvelous, and unheard of." God's love, expressed in the gift of
his Son, surpasses all that we can say or think.

As all the commentators have remarked, the expected
consequence of "If God so loved us" would be "let us then
love God," but instead St. John says, "we in turn ought
to love one another." For one thing, man's response to
God's love for him is a living faith.[41] More important, the
Christian's *redamatio* cannot have the characteristic priority,
gratuitousness, and spontaneity of pure *agape* (v. 10). The

---

[35] *P. Ent.* 73:8; 79:8; 82:7.
[36] *P. Karanis*, 494, 5; cf. *P. Antin.* 44:14.
[37] Is. 52:14; 55:9; 58:5; 2 Sam. 13:4.
[38] Ps. 42:2; Ps. 63:3; 4 Mach. 15:21; 17:5.
[39] 1 Kgs. 10:20; 2 Chr. 1:12; 9:19; cf. Neh. 8:17; Is. 63:1; 63:14; Sir. 46:3.
[40] Mt. 9:33; cf. Mk. 2:12; Jn. 7:46; Mk. 15:39; Eph. 5:33.
[41] Gal. 2:20; Jn. 20:31.

child of God can take the initiative in love only by proving
his love for his brothers or for a neighbor whom he may
dislike, and he can do so with an effective benevolence that
he cannot extend to the author of all good. Only by loving
his brothers can the disciple love *as* God loves (cf. Eph.
5:1–2), manifesting a charity which is source and fullness
as well as pure gift (1 Jn. 3:16). According to 1 Jn. 4:20,
it would seem that there is also a question of authenticity
here. We can never be sure whether our worship or service
of God really expresses love, but we do know that mercy
and devotion to neighbor arise from real *agape*. The least
that can be said is that the proof of our love for God is in
our exercise of fraternal love (4:21). But these details are
of little importance here. For St. John, a person who has
received the revelation of divine *agape*, who has understood
the extent of God's immense love in sacrificing his Son for
us, and who has personally benefited from his enormous
generosity is absolutely constrained to show himself equally
loving toward his brothers.

Verse 12 reads: "No one has ever seen God, yet if we
love one another, God abides in us and our love for him
reaches perfection." By adding a second element to what
was stated in v. 10, v. 12 completes the definition of *agape*.
Through charity, God is united to Christians, and Christians
are united to their brothers and thus to God. Our *koinōnia*
with God poses a difficulty. A neighbor is visible—"our
brother whom we see" (1 Jn. 4:20)—but God is invisible
because of his spiritual nature and transcendence. And yet,
"to see" him, to reach and possess him intimately is the
aspiration of every religious person, which will finally be
fully satisfied only in heaven (3:2; cf. Mt. 5:8; Jn. 17:24).
St. Paul had already taught this truth in presenting knowledge, the vision of God in glory, as the fruit and consequence of fraternal love (1 Cor. 13:8–12; cf. Heb. 12:14).
However, three considerations lead us to conclude that
Christians have even now, through charity, a communion
of being and life with God and that their reciprocal indwell-

ing makes true divine knowledge possible (cf. Jn. 14:17). These considerations are that God is *agape;* that his being Father proves to his sons that they share in the divine *agape* (v. 7); and that charity is a possession common to Father and sons. The Johannine formula, repeated in v. 16, rejects the notion held by gnosticism and the mystery religions that God can be grasped through man's efforts. Perfection does not lie in a supreme understanding of the divinity. Rather, communion with God is accomplished in love by a completely free gift. Fraternal charity, divinely infused into the soul of the Christian (3:1; 4:7–8), accomplishes the *koinōnia.* It is not we who live in God, but God who lives in us, since *agape,* the cause of our communion, comes from him. The two present tense verbs "if we love," *agpō-men,* and "God abides," *menei,* are presents of duration and correspond exactly to each other. As long as we possess and practice charity toward neighbor, God is there within us as the Lord himself promised (Jn. 14:23).

The conclusion, "the love of God reaches perfection, *hē agapē autou teteleiōmenē en hēmin estin,* can be understood in various ways. If "of God" is taken for a subjective genitive, "God's love," as would seem at a first reading to be correct, the sense would be that the love which God manifested to us by the sending and death of his Son bears fruit and reaches its perfection when Christians effectively love one another. Fraternal love would be the final outcome of the diffusion of charity which Christ transmitted to men. If, on the other hand, "of God" is an objective genitive, "love for God," then the meaning is that our love for God is perfect only if we love our brothers. The phrase would be a reference to the second commandment which is like to the first (Mt. 22:39; Mk. 12:31), to the unique theological love with its twofold object. It would imply the important truth that we grow in love of God through the practice of fraternal charity. Although it is correct in itself, it is not in harmony with the context; yet it should not be entirely excluded.

Once again, no sharp distinction between subjective and objective genitives should be made. "The love of God," *hē agapē autou*, represents a genitive of quality, "the love that is truly divine," already mentioned in 1 Jn. 3:17. Before being subjective or objective, love exists in itself as a distinct entity. It is possessed or shared by various persons and consequently has various manifestations, although it always keeps its own nature and essential laws. Perfect, authentic, full *agape* is described in 1 Jn. 4:10. God possesses it supereminently and essentially (v. 8). He communicates it to his children, whom it enables to love their brothers and to love him. Love creates the stable union among all those who share the same divine nature. When St. John says that *agape* "reaches perfection or fulfillment," he sees it in its plenitude, in its essential reality where there are no shadows or failings. What St. John calls "true love," we speak of as "charity in its pure state." This pericope attributes two apparently contradictory qualities to charity, as is often done with divine attributes. Charity is both static and dynamic: it is indwelling and gift, union and beneficence, delight and total sacrifice. The supreme teaching, however, is that by fraternal charity we are absolutely sure of possessing God in himself—whoever loves shares in *agape*, and God is *agape* —and thus of arriving at the summit of religious life.

"Let no one say: 'I do not know what I should love.' Let him love his brother and he will love the same love. For he knows the love by which he loves more than the brother whom he loves. And so, God can now become more known to him than his brother, actually more known because more present, more known because more within him, more known because more certain. Embrace love, God, and embrace God by love. It is love itself which unites all the good angels and all the servants of God by the bond of holiness, and unites us and them mutually with ourselves and makes us subject to Himself." [42]

[42] St. Augustine, *De Trinitate*, 8:8, 12. Trans. Stephen McKenna CSSR, *Fathers of the Church*, vol. 45, Catholic University Press, 1963.

28–30. *Agape,* the object of apostolic faith, and place of the reciprocal and vital meeting of the Christian with God

And we ourselves know and believe in God's enduring *love* among us. God is *love,* and he who abides in *love* abides in God and God in him (1 Jn. 4:16).

This verse, which forms a transition between the first and second parts of the pericope consecrated to the "charity which characterizes the children of the God who is love" (4:7; 5:3), is primarily the conclusion of the preceding development of the revelation of divine charity through the fact of Christ. We isolate it here in order to stress its unequalled value. Not only is it the doctrinal summit of the epistle, but also, in defining the adequate object of the Christian faith, it is a presentation of the new religion under its most specific aspect.

The especially emphatic "and we," *kai hēmeis,* refers primarily to the twelve, who had the privilege of knowing the Son when he appeared on earth and who were the first to give him their faith. They were eyewitnesses of the manifestation of the divine charity, and St. John insists on their absolute certitude. The knowledge he speaks of here is in no way speculative. It is the result of an historical and psychological experience, a grasping in which the heart played as important a role as intellectual insight. While they were with Christ, the apostles recognized the Word of life in the Master because they experienced his virtue and discerned his glory. By emphasizing the objectivity and security of their knowledge, the words, "we have believed," show the apostles' welcome and adherence to Christ. There may also be something of the notion of "profession of faith" in them (cf. *homologēsēi,* v. 15). The union of the two verbs, "to know" and "to believe," *ginōskein* and *pisteuein,* is a redundancy with the value of a superlative;

it is further reinforced by the use of the perfect tense. The certitude which the apostles once acquired has never been lost or even diminished—it is present and permanent; it is also total and absolute: "We are fully convinced and totally persuaded; we believe with all our souls." St. Peter expressed the same meaning and the same intense feeling in his profession of faith, using the same two verbs: "And we firmly believe and are fully convinced that you are the Holy One of God" (Jn. 6:69). He may have taken his inspiration from Isaia, whose affirmation is deliberately made with appeal and force. "You are my witnesses, says the Lord, my servants whom I have chosen to know and believe in me and understand that it is I" (Is. 43:10). This kind of knowledge is infallible, the knowledge of the first witnesses and pillars of the Church.

That which they know is *agape* in its classical and biblical sense of "manifestation of love" (cf. vv. 9–11), and especially in its Christian sense of divine love revealed and communicated to men: "God's enduring love among us." The phrase is difficult to translate from the Greek, *tēn agapēn hēn ho theos en hēmin*, because it unites the dynamic love which God possesses essentially and permanently with its concrete manifestation in our midst. Except for J. Bonsirven, all the commentators base their translations on the affinity between *eis* and *en* in the *koine* and read *en hēmin* as if it were *eis hēmas*, God's love *for* us. However, according to the first part of the verse and the whole context, especially vv. 9–10, the manifestation of divine love and the object of the apostles' faith was Christ the incarnate Redeemer. *En* must, therefore, have its local meaning of "in the midst of," a sense which is frequent in the Bible, especially when a group is concerned.[43] God's love was revealed when he sent his Son into the *kosmos* (v. 9), and the twelve discovered and acclaimed his living, tangible manifestation among us. "He lived among us" (Jn. 1:14).

From their long, close association with Christ the Apostles

[43] Jn. 1:10; 11:11; Lk. 22:26–27: *en hymin = en mesōi hymōn.*

concluded, as in v. 8, that "God is love made manifest." In the prologue of his Gospel, St. John stated that those who saw the incarnate Word contemplated the Father's *doxa* radiated by his Son (Jn. 1:14; cf. Heb. 1:3). In our text, he speaks of God's *agape* reflected in the life of his only Son (1 Jn. 4:9). Faith consists in discovering the presence and nature of God, who is *agape*, in the incarnate Word, in "God among us." The formal element in this knowledge is the discovery that God is love, and, precisely, love that expresses, communicates, and gives itself.

To believe the love which God extends among us means more than simply to confess Christ, the Savior who manifests God's love. It means also to welcome him, be united with him, and live from him—to incorporate oneself into the divine *agape* and, as the Apostle describes it, "to live in love." "He who abides in love abides in God and God in him." In Greek there is an article before the word "love." It has the value of a demonstrative and refers to the essential charity which God possesses and communicates to us in his Son. Charity is active in all the mysteries of the redemption and of grace to such an extent that "he who abides in love" is a definition of the Christian. A Christian is someone who adheres to the revelation Jesus has made of the true God and who takes his place in God's economy of salvation, faithful to his precepts (Jn. 15:9–10), especially to his precept of fraternal love (13:34–35). "In love" should not be given any complement which would limit its object or determine its mode. The words "he who abides in love" summarize the Christian attitude and life, just as "God's love among us" evokes both God as he is in himself and all his relations with men. The "existential" encounter of men with God is made "in love," as the conclusion explaining the reciprocity of communion makes clear: "He who abides in God and God in him." Mutual, permanent inhabitation is the very essence of religious life. St. John had considered the religious life earlier as the fruit of the *pneuma*, of faith, of fidelity to the precepts, and of the exercise of fraternal charity.[44] Here he defines it in its nature itself. *Agape* is more than bond and union. Since God is love, to abide in love is to abide—*caritas numquam excidit*—in God himself.

Agape cannot be thought of as a milieu or an atmosphere or even a virtue. The relations set up between the believer and God are personal, as the Master himself had stated, "May the love with which you love me dwell in them as I dwell in them myself" (Jn. 17:26). Perhaps the truly divine charity which permits the Son to live in the Christians is the Holy Spirit himself. However that may be, it is certain that charity brings about presence. For St. John, to love is to be *present* one to the other; then to be *for* the other, in function of the other; and, finally, to be one *in* the other. Since autonomous persons cannot be dissolved into one person, the reciprocal indwelling must be thought of as an assimilation of Christians to God. *Agape*, God's shared love, brings them into him and makes them like him.

It may be concluded that although it is impossible to see God here on earth, the disciples can nevertheless be sure they are united with him. If they believe in love and in Christ as the apostle and sacrament of the Father's love, they themselves will be assured of living in love.

31–41. Charity is incompatible with fear of God and hatred of neighbor

17 *Love* attains perfection with us, in that we have confidence against the day of judgment, because such as he is so also we are in this world. 18 There is no fear in *love;* rather perfect *love* drives out fear, because fear implies chastisement, and he who fears has not reached the perfection of *love.* 19 We exercise mutual *love* because he first *loved* us. 20 If anyone says, 'I *love* God,' yet hates his brother, he is a liar. Why? Because he who does not *love* his brother whom he sees, cannot *love* God whom he does not see. 21 Besides, we have received this commandment from God: He who *loves* God must *love* his brother also (1 Jn. 4:17–21).

[44] 1 Jn. 3:24; 4:12, 13, 15.

In verse 16 St. John had already established that charity is essentially communion with God. In verses 17–21 he brings out some of the fruits of charity, principally the feeling of security before God which only love can engender in a man's heart (v. 17). In practice, perfect security is not acquired immediately. It is the effect of perfect charity (v. 18, *teleia agapē*), of a consummated love strong enough to drive out fear. The wording, "This love has become perfect through our cooperation," *teteleiōtai hē agapē meth' hēmon*, is suggestive, in that the subject of the verb is "love" and not "the Christian." "Love" refers to the full, intense love which God has in himself and which he communicates to us. His love invades us, impels us (2 Cor. 5:14), and assumes more and more control over our faculties until it reaches its fullness in us. More exactly, it reaches its maximum of effectiveness "with us," when the faithful person gives over all his thoughts and feelings to the dominion of charity. In the vital communion where the believer "lives in God and God in him" (v. 16), each brings something of his own; each person brings his share of love. Man's share is always a greater or lesser participation in the charity he has received from God (v. 7). The supreme perfection of infused *agape* can be recognized by the bold confidence of heart it engenders in believers under even the most fearsome circumstances.

St. John speaks of the "judgment" which will close the great assizes at the Lord's Parousia. The terms "day," *hēmera;* "judgment," *krisis;* "fear," *phobos;* and even "confidence," *parrēsia*, were used in traditional Jewish and synoptic eschatology. The thought of appearing before the Lord's tribunal is terrifying,[45] for no one is above reproach (cf. 3:20) and a sentence of condemnation will allow no appeal. Yet charity brings about a living communion with God (4:16) and little by little eliminates troubled apprehension. The more charity grows, the more confidence and serenity

[45] Rom. 2:5; Apoc. 6:17; cf. Heb. 10:31; James 2:13.

increase. The Christian is not without reproach, but he is
without fear. The Lord had instilled this psychology in his
apostles at his farewell discourse.[46] "His own" had to be
reassured about the outcome of their sufferings in this world
and about their future in heaven. Therefore, after exhorting
believers to "full assurance at the time of the Parousia" (1 Jn.
2:28) because of their union with Christ, St. John says that
a feeling of security is the fruit of sovereign charity uniting
us to God (4:17). *Parrēsia* is a boldness full of liberty and
confidence, enabling a person to present himself without fear
before a superior, prosecutor, or questioner who can contradict him or accuse him. It is the signal privilege of Christians to be able to appear before the Sovereign Judge with
perfect assurance.

For "defendants" to have such a mentality is so extraordinary that it must be justified by some strong reason. The
reason St. John gives is so enigmatic that the manuscripts
have glossed it differently, and the commentators have given
different interpretations. The Greek reads *oti kathōs ekeinos
estin kai hēmeis esmen en tōi kosmōi toutōi*. Its literal translation is "because such as he is, so also we are in this world."
All the commentators agree that "he," *ekeinos*, refers to
Christ, the Lord and Judge at the Parousia (2:28; Jn. 5:22).
However, they complete "he is," *estin*, and "we are," *esmen*
by "in God," *en theōi*, or by "in love," *en tēi agapēi*, thus
considerably weakening the value of the two verbs in the
present. The clause is not about qualities and virtues or even
about states and modes of being in heaven and on earth, but
simply about *being*. The burden of the comparison rests on
the verb "to be." Just as he *is*, so we *are*. Who is he? He is
the object of the disciples' faith, Christ himself, precisely
the incarnate Son of God. Jesus is God and man. Similarly,
in this world, Christians are both men and gods. "You are
gods," *theoi este* (Jn. 10:34–35). Romans 8:29 had stated
that the children of God are "predestined to be conformed

---

[46] Jn. 14:1, 27.

to the image of his Son" and at the manifestation of Christ "they will appear with him in glory" (Col. 3:4). The Christian condition and structure are not visible here on earth, but "we know that when he appears, we shall be like him, because we shall see him just as he is" (1 Jn. 3:2). Consequently, the motive of our assurance on the day of judgment is our "Christian being" itself, our conformity to the Lord of glory, acquired when we were regenerated by God's nature at baptism.[47] We are as he is! Such a likeness is a legitimate basis for the strongest confidence, even on the Day of Judgment. Our confidence is all the more justified since it is not a question of being a more or less exact copy of a model, but rather of an "adoption" which is already accomplished and awaiting the full possession of its rights (Gal. 4:7), or, better, of an "assimilation" which will be completed in glory. No foundation more solid could be given to Christian hope than this one which completely eliminates any difference between the present and the future. Since they *are* other Christs, believers have only to *live*, to continue to be, and they will arrive successfully. We might add that the Christian is the most stable of beings (*esmen = manei;* v. 16). He is eternal like Jesus Christ who "is the same yesterday, today, and forever" (Heb. 13:8). At any rate, since our union–incorporation into Christ guarantees our access to heaven, we may gloss the opening words of v. 17, "Love attains perfection with us," by the words, "that love which Christ has among us," by Christ's presence among us and in us.

"There is no fear in love; rather perfect love drives out fear, because fear implies chastisement, and he who fears has not reached the perfection of love" (v. 18). Verses 18–19 explain the psychological relationship between *agape* and confidence, or, more specifically, they explain the initial assertion of v. 17, "Love attains perfection with us." The facts about the Christian conscience are the following. Objectively, the child of God, precisely because he is God's child,

[47] 1 Jn. 3:9; cf. Jn. 5:18.

cannot be condemned at God's tribunal, so he is confident.[48] Subjectively, however, since Adam and Eve, the
spontaneous reaction of man before God is that of a guilty
person who stands before his Judge (Gen. 3:8), dreading
his punishment: he is afraid (v. 18). St. John is affirming
the incompatibility of love and fear, or at least of the love
of charity which includes no fear at all. It would seem,
then, that the Christian who "lives in love" (v. 16) must
ipso facto be removed from all apprehension and filled with
confidence (v. 17). In reality, the solution is not so simple. A feeling of fear is inherent in every creature who
stands before God, in every sinner even though he is a
Christian, and in every defendant brought before a court.
The Christian convert knows that he has been begotten
by God and assimilated to Christ. He knows he is already
saved, but he cannot eliminate overnight his innate reaction of fear before the sovereign Judge, at least when he
thinks of the punishment he deserves. In other words, fear
is man's primary, spontaneous, and habitual attitude in such
a situation, and the infusion of divine charity cannot eliminate it all at once. The dominion of *agape* has to extend
itself gradually over the Christian's thoughts and feelings
until little by little it modifies all his responses. An evolution in his psychology will give the child of God a mentality conformable to his new state and to objective reality.
Consequently, he will pass from fear to confidence. Such
progress implies the great strength of love, which imposes
its dominion not only over the highest faculties but also
over the sensibilities. This is "*agape* which has attained
perfection with us" (v. 17a), *hē teleia agapē* (1 Jn. 4:18).
It is strong enough to drive out a fear that is completely
foreign to it. Since charity is union and communion with
God (v. 16), it engenders a respectful, confident boldness
in the relations of the child of God with his Father. Fear
would have the opposite effect; it separates, cuts off, and
withdraws. The two feelings cannot co-exist. Nevertheless,

[48] 1 Jn. 2:28; 4:17; cf. 5:14.

it seems preferable to understand the explanation, "because fear implies chastisement," in the light of the context. The strong assertion in the first part of the verse—"there is no fear in love"—is repeated in concrete form at the end —"he who fears has not reached the perfection of love." Fear is rejected for its inferior quality. It is a feeling aroused by the threat of punishment, a servile and egotistical reaction. Perfect charity cannot admit fear in those who are like Christ (v. 17) and who live in God. The lucid love of *agape* bases its confidence on these facts. How could it possibly admit a fear whose motives are opposed to its own?

Verse 19, "We exercise mutual love because he first loved us," confirms this truth. By opposing the motives of charity and fear, it explains why true Christians feel complete assurance. Unlike the fearful man who is not consumed in charity, the Apostle and his readers love because God loves them and they believe in his first and total love. God is charity, and when he has manifested his love to us and invited us to intimacy with him (v. 16), how can we not welcome his kindness? How can we not let our *redamatio* grow into complete confidence? We know that God's attachment and generosity will be permanent, because they arise from his own initiative; we have nothing to fear (cf. Rom. 8:37–39). We love with confidence because we know what love is when it is the love of God and Christ, and we know that we are sure of being loved. "We have believed in love" (v. 16). Finally, perfect charity is abandonment to the divine *agape*.

Verses 20–21: "If anyone says, 'I love God,' yet hates his brother, he is a liar. Why? Because he who does not love his brother whom he sees cannot love God whom he does not see. Besides, we have received this commandment from God: He who loves God must love his brother also." Surely such bold confidence in God's *agape* is presumptuous. The pretension of possessing "perfect love" may be only an illusion or a superficial emotion. St. John recalls,

therefore, the infallible criterion of authentic charity, its
two inseparable objects, God and neighbor.[49] It would be
impossible to exaggerate the importance of the declaration,
"I love God," *agapō ton theon*. It proves that *agape* ascends
from man to God. That it is made by an anonymous Christian implies that each believer must have learned it in his
elementary religious instruction and must have enunciated
it with conviction. However, as always when fundamental,
common realities are concerned, the meaning of this love
can easily be misunderstood. It will never become unneces-
sary to say again and again that whoever professes to love
God must also love his brother if he does not want to be
telling a lie; if he does not love his brother, he does not
love God. Such a Christian would be a liar in the same way
that "the man who says, 'I know him,' but does not keep his
commandments, is a liar, and the truth does not dwell in
him" (1 Jn. 2:4). St. John is not thinking in terms of capital
sin or even of serious sin, but rather of total exclusion from
salvation and communion with God. To be a liar is more
than to delude oneself either voluntarily or unconsciously;
it is to range oneself with Satan and against God. It is a
spiritual attitude with the two essential characteristics of
any sin—nothingness and illusion. The liar wounds that
integrity within himself which is the prerogative of the just.
St. John therefore brands the liar with the same strong
language which Jesus used to condemn the hypocritical
Pharisees. The great difference between the liar's relationships with God and those with his neighbor shows him to
be a "double-minded" person (James 1:8); the true child
of God must love both God and man with his whole soul
(Deut. 6:5).

St. John immediately proves the impossibility of exclud-
ing one's neighbor from charity. "Because he who does not
love his brother whom he sees cannot love God whom he
does not see" (v. 20b). Very strangely, most exegetes com-

[49] 4:20; cf. Mt. 25:40; 1 Jn. 3:10–11; 14–16.

ment that he who is incapable of accomplishing an easier thing cannot do a more difficult one. Anyone who has lived community life, whether conjugal or religious, knows that a human being is a thankless object of love. He has limitations and evident faults; he is basically evil (Lk. 11:13), whereas God, who is infinitely good and totally beautiful, is supremely lovable. The problem should be how one could not love love itself.

The difficulty clears itself up if we translate *agape* correctly. It means "to manifest love; to prove one's attachment." The Christian who does not show his neighbor respect or kindness has no other valid means of expressing his love for God (cf. 3:17 ff.; 4:12). Lacking effective fraternal love, he deprives himself of any authentic expression of his love for God. Moreover, St. John is applying here an argument of popular dialectic, the *qol wahômer* of the rabbis, which consisted in passing as easily from a less important category to a more important one (*e.g.* from men to God) as the reverse. It can be concluded, for example, that if all men are mortal, Socrates, being a man, is also mortal. Just as validly, in the popular dialectic, if Socrates is mortal, then all men are mortal. It is a question of logic, not psychology; they are not—as everyone knows—the same thing. In our text, the *a fortiori* consists in passing, not from the easier to the more difficult, but from the smaller to the greater, from the infinitesimal to the infinite.

We believe that the two expressions, "whom he sees" and "whom he does not see," must be interpreted in this sense. Although they have only a subsidiary value, they nevertheless suggest the disproportion between the two objects of love. The "invisible" God is transcendent and unable to be grasped. "Visible" man is near; he is permanently (the verbs are in the perfect) the object of respect and devotion. The liar, perhaps an ecstatic, claims to neglect his brother for the sake of concentrating his love on God alone—"I love God"—but the very nature of *agape* and of the divine economy (v. 21) is opposed to this dichotomy. The liar's sinful illusion lies in his assuming sentiments that are radically irreconcilable with objective, divine reality.

He "cannot love God." The word "cannot," *ou dynatai*, let us repeat, does not refer to a psychological impossibility, but rather to God's own refusal to be loved to the exclusion of other men. He had declared his refusal in the most categorical way, in a commandment (v. 21) transmitted by Christ and his apostles to all Christians, but St. John does not quote it here. He simply draws its conclusion: "He who loves God must love his brother also." The Lord has so prescribed, and the nature of *agape* requires it.

42–46. Criteria by which the child of God can recognize the authenticity of his love for his neighbor and for God

1 Everyone who believes that Jesus is the Christ is born of God. Everyone who *loves* the parent *loves* his child also. 2 We know by this sign that we *love* the children of God: when we *love* God and keep his commandments. 3 Yes, to *love* God means to keep his commandments. They are not burdensome (1 Jn. 5:1–3).

St. John completes his account of *agape* with a magnificent *inclusio* which repeats the theme of 4:7: charity and begetting by God. A very pure theological light permits him to unite, in terms of God's initial love (5:2), all his teachings on fraternal love and to define exhaustively both authentic *agape* (v. 3) and the total religious attitude of the Christian. The cycle of charity has two parts: God, Christ, and the children of God; and faith, love, and obedience to the precepts. Everything begins from faith and ends in the practice of the commandments, and everything rests on the reality of the Christian's begetting by the heavenly Father, who makes all his children brothers of one another and communicates to them the faculty of loving which they cannot help using if they are really born of him.

Essentially, the Christian is a man born of God, *ton gegennēmenon ex autou*. The Greek passive participle shows a quality acquired once and for all, maintaining its subject in permanent dependence on God. Unlike human generation (cf. Jn. 1:13), in which the sons, once they have been begotten and conceived, become autonomous persons independent of their parents, the child of God is always a person in-the-act-of-being-born; he never stops receiving his being and life from his Father. A child's relationship to his Father is one of love and filial respect (*ho agapōn ton theon;* 4:21). In speaking of "everyone who loves the parent," *pas ho agapōn ton gennēsanta,* St. John recalls filial piety, the attachment created by blood-ties which expresses a fundamental gratitude toward the person who has given being and life, the first goods which are the condition and point of departure for all others. How much more this is true when the creature regards his God, and the Christian his heavenly Father! The force of this law of nature increases immeasurably under the light of faith which understands to what an extent God is our first, permanent, total benefactor. The believer consciously and voluntarily attaches himself body and soul to the heavenly "Begetter" who dwells within him.

It is just as true that every noble love extends its affection and pleasure to everyone who is close to its beloved. Our friends' friends are our friends too. St. John's thought is profound in another way, also. It explains how the neighbor whom we love is united to God as a child is to his Father. There is, then, a profound similarity between child and Father (cf. Jn. 1:18). The Son resembles his Father because they both possess the same nature (Heb. 1:3), and not because they are alike as a copy is like its model. Something of the father exists in the child. Besides, in this case God continues to be personally present and to live in the Christian. *Agape*, a reflective love which is keenly

aware of the motives of its devotion, knows that it will
find God and reach him in everyone who "is born of him."
Therefore, it loves all Christians because of its love for
God. The faithful person, who knows that he is begotten
by God, knows that he has the same nature and benefits
from the same grace as his neighbor. Similarity is a cause of
love, and here it plays its most formal role. The children
of God are brothers in the most real sense, and the *agape*
which unites them is a *philadelphia*. Thus faith establishes
new relations among Christians and the law of loving God
and his children becomes rooted in the baptized person
(4:21).

"We know by this sign that we love the children of God;
when we love God and keep his commandments" (v. 2).
Verse 2 clarifies the meaning of *agapan* in v. 1; [50] *agapan* is
the manifestation and carrying out of love, as in v. 20. Verse
1 may be explained in this way: whoever venerates, ac-
claims, and adores God will also express his attachment for
the children of God. But nothing is more equivocal than
love, both in its tenderness and in its most absolute generosity. How is it possible to know whether the intimacy
and exchange among God's children within the Church
spring from authentic *agape*? Verse 2 gives the answer:
when (*hotan*) love is addressed first of all to God. If *hotan*
(= *hote an*) is taken as a synonym for *ean*, "if," the proposition may be understood as expressing a general condition.
Fraternal love is simply the expression of *agape* in a heart
directed to God and desiring to love its Lord and consecrate itself to his service. As soon as a person sincerely
loves God, he necessarily loves his brother. The extension
is part of the very nature of the love of God. However, in
the *koine*, *hotan* with the indicative present or future often
conveys chronological sequence. It refers to a particular action, especially if the action is repeated. The thought here

---

[50] Together with the majority of commentators and in conformity
with usage, we connect *en toutōi* with what follows (2:3; 4:9, 13, 17;
Jn. 13:35).

would be that each time we make an act of the love of God, we are sure of possessing the *agape* which unites us to our brothers. Whenever we love God, our love also includes love for his children. In accord with the Johannine usage of *hotan* with the indicative,[51] a proper translation would be that *at the very moment* when we manifest our charity for God, we have the assurance of loving our brothers with a supernatural love. There is nothing secret and hidden about the divine love; it exists only if we observe the commandments. Consequently, the believer who conforms himself to God's will knows by his very act of fidelity that his love for God is authentic. He has, *ipso facto*, the assurance that his fraternal love has the same divine nature. Few texts are as decisive as this one about the original, supernatural character of the love of neighbor in the Church of Jesus Christ. Only the "virtuous" person or, better, the "religious" person can have charity for his neighbor. *Agape* is entirely different from *philanthrōpia, erōs, storgē,* or *philia*. It exists only in a soul that is consecrated to God and belongs to him. It is part of the family heritage; it is the appanage of the children of God, who extend to their brothers the attachment which binds them to their Father.

"Yes, to love God means to keep his commandments. They are not burdensome" (v. 3). The first part of v. 3 merely repeats the definition of *agape* as given for the first time in Wisd. 6:18: "*Agape* is the observance of the law." It is repeated by the Lord (Jn. 14:15, 21, 23; 15:10), and finally taught by St. John (1 Jn. 2:3–6; 3:22–24; 5:2). It applies to love the basic axiom of the Gospel's moral teaching concerning works. It is not enough merely to listen to the teachings of the Master and believe them; his teachings must be put into practice (Mt. 7:24). In this case, action is all the more required because *agape,* by its nature, calls for exercise and exterior activity; charity for God is conformity of wills and, consequently, fidelity and obedience.

The final words of the New Testament about *agape* stress

[51] Jn. 7:27; Apoc. 4:9; 8:1.

its sincerity and effective fulfillment. In v. 3a the whole
moral life is conceived of as proof and deployment of love,
and in v. 3b, ease and liberty of soul in the strictest obedience are affirmed. "His commandments are not burdensome."
Jesus had denounced the Pharisees' onerous casuistry (Mt.
23:4; cf. Lk. 11:46) and declared that the burden he imposed
was light (Mt. 11:30). He repeated it to the community at
Thyatira: "I am laying on you no other burden" (Apoc.
2:24). His Church took care not to tyrannize the faithful
(2 Cor. 1:24) by laying heavy charges on them. By the end
of the first century, St. John was expressing the Christian
experience: The precepts of the Lord are not burdensome,
although their accomplishment undoubtedly demands effort,
and fidelity is ultimately a victory (v. 4; cf. Rom. 7:19, 23).
The Christian is not a slave acting against his will; he is a
child of God whose soul expands in the joy of love and
triumph. "Conquer evil by good" (Rom. 12:21). The precepts of God are not heavy, precisely because charity,
which receives them and carries them out, lightens their
weight so that they become easy to observe. At the same
time that *agape* is a precept, it is also divine force infused
into the soul of the believer. *Juvat qui jubet! Agape* is a duty
because it is an exigency of God's nature in us (4:8, 16), a
fact which sufficiently states the dynamism of this immanent
life whose pouring out and activity are necessarily causes
for joy.

47–48. Charity, an attachment that is both human and divine

The presbyter, to the Lady Elect, and to her children . . .
whom I *love* in truth (2 Jn. 1).
The presbyter, to Reverend and dear Gaius, whom I *love* in
truth (3 Jn. 1).

The titles of the recipients of St. John's letters are original
in the New Testament corpus. Whether the letters are addressed to the Church, the Lady Elect of God, the spouse of

Christ and mother of the faithful, or to the reverend and dear Gaius, the recipients are greeted with courtesy and honor, delicacy and respectful affection. Only St. John could say exactly what he intended to convey by his declaration of "love in truth," *agapō en alētheiai*. The modern equivalent, "sincerely" or "loyally," is surely insufficient. The verbal parallel in 1 Jn. 3:18, "Let us love in truth," *agapōmen en alētheiai*, meaning to love effectively, hardly applies here. "Truth," *alētheiai*, has no article before it, an omission which would suggest that St. John was writing to the Christians on the basis of their common possession of evangelical truth. St. Paul referred to this love as "love in Christ Jesus."

It seems preferable, then, to understand with Wescott, Brooke, and Dodd that St. John loves "in a true charity," an authentic *agape*, a holy love, if you will. This is the love which 1 Jn. 5:1–2 described as the bond among all the children of the one heavenly Father. It includes both respect and fervor, attachment and devotion, kindness and generosity. It has the notion of solidity, according to the biblical meaning of "truth": I love you profoundly. "Love in truth," then, is a love which is truly divine but humanly assimilated by the Apostle (*egō*). He loves the faithful "in God" (1 Jn. 4:21–5:1), and yet it is truly he who loves.

49. Charity and truth, criteria of the true disciples

Grace, peace, and mercy will be with us from God the Father and from Jesus Christ the Father's Son, in truth and *love* (2 Jn. 3).

It was customary for the salutation of an epistle to close with a wish for the gifts of salvation, but the addition of "in truth and love" is enigmatic. It seems to refer to objective religious truth, to the orthodox faith in the new revelation. *Agape* is the virtue of charity and, more precisely, of fraternal love. The gifts of God can be received and bear fruit only in authentic Christians who are characterized by the double note of truth and love. The divine love increases to overflowing in everyone who believes and loves.

50–51. The Christian life is to love

5 And now I beg you, Lady, let us *love* one another. This is not a new commandment that I write, but the one that we have had from the beginning. 6 Now *love* means that we live according to his commandments. The commandment, as you have heard from the beginning, is that you live in (love) (2 Jn. 5–6).

With great delicacy St. John exhorts the community to fraternal charity. He respectfully asks (*erōtō*, v. 5; cf. Jn. 17:15) that the precept of the Lord be applied. This is no new burden (1 Jn. 5:3), but the great commandment which they had learned and accepted at their initiation into Christianity.

One cannot withdraw from it, because *agape* proves itself in the observance of precepts (v. 6). Verse 5 and 1 Jn. 5:2 suggest that the charity he refers to is love of neighbor. According to 1 Jn. 5:3, it would be love for God. Wescott correctly unites the two meanings, but it is still preferable to do as Bonsirven does and identify *agape* with the very soul of the Christian life, participation in God's own charity (1 Jn. 4:7; Jn. 17:26) which belongs to all his children (5:1). This is the only interpretation which eliminates the apparent tautology of the conclusion: "The commandment is that you live in (love)." Authentic and religious *agape* reveals itself in fidelity to the totality of the Lord's commandments, but there is one precept apart, one essential and predominant precept to which all these others refer—love of neighbor: *hina agapōmen allēlous* (v. 5). St. John is repeating the teaching of his first Epistle. It is primarily by loving his brothers that the Christian proves that he loves God and is God's child. God's child is a loving person. All his life long, he manifests charity; his attention is concentrated almost exclusively on the precept of love. On this moral level *agape* is basically good will, which welcomes the authoritative divine will; it is a permanent effort to conform to God's will adequately in unchanging and effective fidelity.

52. Hospitality, a work of fraternal charity

They themselves spoke favorably in an assembly of the faithful about your *love* (3 Jn. 6).

Even when he did not know them personally (v. 5), Gaius had thoughtfully and generously taken care of Christians who were traveling. Moved by his hospitality, they gratefully sang his praises before the assembly of their local church. They were qualified witnesses because they had benefited personally from Gaius' charity, which they publicized as much as they could.

"Charity" here means all the services which Gaius performed for the travelers: lodging, meals, alms, etc. *Philoxenia*, hospitality, is *agapan*'s most classic sense, "to receive a guest cordially." It is no accident that Christian *agape*, despite all the riches of its new doctrinal content, retained its original, double nuance of cordiality and liberality. Moreover, when the travelers spoke forcefully about Gaius' love, they were doing more than expressing their surprise and praising his generosity and respect for them. In his welcome they had discerned an authentic charity, a divine love, and a model of Christian conduct. *Agape*, therefore, refers to both his generous gift and his disinterested love. Gaius was inspired by divine charity, which can always be discerned in noble actions like his.

CHAPTER V

Conclusion

THE doctrinal content of the texts have been brought out. It is now necessary to compare and harmonize their many teachings and to disengage the principal themes of St. John's thought on *agape*.[1] His writing is far removed from the Jerusalem *kerygma*, which was more or less eschatological, yet "the beloved disciple" is not only the theologian of charity; he is also and above all the witness of love. For him, as for St. Paul and the other apostles, Christ is the gift which God has made to humanity. St. John expresses the evangelical message in his own vocabulary. As his theology became more profound and his personal experience more intense, he summarized the entire mystery of salvation in the divine *agape*. The idea was not an innovation, for the revealed religion had always been presented as God's gratuitous gift and condescendence to men, but in Christ the meaning of his initiative and generous outpouring became clear. No one but the only-begotten Son was able to disclose the nature and secrets of his Father (Jn. 1:18). Only his confidants (15:15) can know that God is love or know what his love means. Everything is clear now that he has

[1] St. John uses the noun *agape* 30 times (7 times in the Gospel; 18 times in 1 Jn.; 3 times in 2 and 3 Jn.; twice in the Apoc.); the verb *agapan* 72 times (37 times in the Gospel; 28 times in 1 Jn.; 3 times in 2 and 3 Jn.; 4 times in the Apoc.); the verb *philein* 15 times (13 times in the Gospel; twice in the Apoc.).

157

come, and the believer is defined as a person who both knows what love is and clings to it (1 Jn. 4:16).

1. God and Jesus

According to the Synoptics, God revealed his love for Christ, a love of sovereign respect and delight, and Christ referred to his Father's signal love for him.[2] The declarations from heaven heard at the Jordan and Tabor are not mentioned by St. John. On the other hand, Jesus' awareness of God's love for him is constantly being represented, and the best expression of their reciprocal relation and union is *agape*.

When Jesus speaks of the divine love for him, he always presents it as the love of a Father for his Son—"the Father loves the Son"[3]—even when God's charity is addressed to the Christ-man. In these cases, the Savior proclaims that the Father is greater than he,[4] and the elements of the Father's love which are emphasized are kindness, intimacy,[5] and the generosity of his gift. "The Father loves the Son and has put all things at his disposal."[6] God manifests his charity by confiding his secrets to his ambassador and giving all power to him. *Agapan,* "to love," and *didonai,* "to give," are almost synonymous, because the generosity of the Father's gift is the expression of his love for his Son. The Father "honors" the Son: he holds him in special esteem; he respects him greatly; and his gifts are his way of giving authenticity to his message—"God the Father has set his seal of approval on him" (6:27; cf. 10:36)—and of proving his *agape* for his Son.

On Jesus' part, his charity for his Father is no less active or generous. It is expressed by a constant fidelity to the Father's will. In Christ's soul there is an exact equivalence between love for God and observance of God's commands.

---

[2] Mk. 12:6; Lk. 20:13.   [3] Jn. 3:35; 10:17; 15:9; 17:24, 26.
[4] Jn. 10:29; 14:28.   [5] Jn. 5:20; 17:23.   [6] Jn. 3:35; cf. 10:29.

"I treasure my Father's commandments and thus secure his love" (Jn. 15:10). His filial love manifests itself in obedience (*tērein tas entolas*). It inspires all his actions (17:6), especially his acceptance of the sacrifice of the cross. "The world must come to know that I love the Father and am acting strictly according to the Father's instructions" (14:31). Jesus' love reveals itself not only in a more or less passive, even though exact, fidelity, but also in a deep accord of wills and a sovereign spontaneity that extends even to total self-sacrifice. It is not so much that the Savior's deeds and actions correspond to the divine orders as it is that his soul thinks and loves as the Father himself thinks and loves. The precise point of their union is the salvation of men by the sacrifice on Calvary.

Christ is like a good shepherd who gives his life for the sheep God has entrusted to him.[7] His obedience is so courageous and so completely inspired by his love for the Father that the Father in his turn manifests even more openly the bond of love that unites him to the Son: "The Father loves me because I lay down my life" (Jn. 10:17). The Father's *agape* includes gratitude for Jesus' love of him, and their love for one another is seen to be permanent, active, and reciprocal. Christ and God never cease loving one another, telling their love to one another, and proving it to one another. Each initiative of one is met by a response of the other. Their relationship is an exchange in which total love is expressed in every sort of way. The Father loves Jesus and lavishes gifts upon him. Jesus loves the Father and glorifies him.[8] The Father is again thankful for what his Son does for him (12:28; 13:31). Jesus, aware of his Father's love, takes pleasure and rejoices in it (15:11; 17:25–26). His joy springs from his knowledge of the Father's delight. It supremely honors the Father. In all truth, Jesus can summarize his spiritual life in these words: "I remain in his *agape*" (Jn. 15:10). This degree of love cannot be God's love for one of his creatures, even the one chosen above all (Lk. 9:35); it must

---

[7] Jn. 6:37, 39; 17:6, 12, 24.   [8] Jn. 7:18; 8:49–50; 14:13; 17:4.

be the unchanging love which unites two divine Persons in a beatifying delight. Jesus relates the love his Father bears him now to the charity with which he has surrounded him from all eternity, before the incarnation and even before the creation. "You loved me before the world was founded" (17:24; cf. v. 26). In this context, the Father's *agape* is presented as a source of beatitude, since closeness and communion between two persons who love one another bring beatitude, especially if their union is not only a bond but also a mutual indwelling. "The Father and I are one" (10:30). "You in me . . . as you love me" (17:23).

2. Jesus and his disciples

The Master's tender, deep friendship for Martha, Mary, and Lazarus was the admiration of the Jews.[9] He made no attempt to hide his predilection for St. John, a predilection which was at the same time both human tenderness and supernatural attachment.[10] The twelve were especially singled out (15:16), and the Master seemed to have a special affection for Peter (21:15–17). In other words, the *agape* of the incarnate Word took on a thousand different shades which St. John was given the grace to discover and reveal to the world. The "beloved disciple," who rested his head on Jesus' breast during the Last Supper, shows himself uniquely informed of the secrets of the heart which he had heard beat, and he came to understand that Christ is divine love incarnate. More exactly, the only Son came to make the love of the Father present in the world. He incarnated the charity of God which rests on him for all eternity, and he died in order to transmit it to us (17:26). His mission and sacrifice were commanded by the manifestation and communication of the divine *agape*.

St. Paul considered the Savior's whole life an epiphany of God's kindness and "philanthropy" (Tit. 3:4). St. John

[9] Jn. 11:3, 5, 11, 36.   [10] Jn. 13:23; 19:26–27; 20:2; 21:2, 4, 7.

summarizes it as a deployment of *agape*. "The feast of the Passover was approaching, and Jesus knew that his time for passing from this world to his Father had arrived. He had always loved his own who were in the world, and he loved them to the end" (13:1), that is, he loved them totally. Having shown his love for his disciples all his life long, Jesus gave them the greatest proof of his love during his last hours when he made his supreme confidences to them, entrusting the eucharist to them and, especially, sacrificing himself for them. St. John's description is singularly suggestive of the dimensions of the Savior's charity. He defined Jesus' soul by his charity for the Father and then went on to say that his charity extends to the disciples at the same time. Jesus' love for his disciples has several principal characteristics. It is

a) *A declared love,* affirmed and reaffirmed and always proved. The Lord wants to convince the disciples of his love for them—"I love you" [11]—and he associates his love with the Father's love for him and for men.[12]

b) *A love of respect,* for the Savior's whole mission is ordained to those whom the Father confides to him (Jn. 17:6, 9) and whom the Father draws to his Son (6:44). This accounts for the value we have in Christ's eyes and for the attention with which he receives us (6:37; 10:29).

c) *A delicate, extremely solicitous love,* which wants to exclude all anxiety and fear from the hearts of those he loves (14:1). It communicates his peace and joy to them [13] and exhorts them to absolute trust.[14]

d) *A love of predilection,* because he chose his disciples with a first and gratuitous choice. "I have chosen you" (15:16) as a shepherd who knows his sheep and calls each one by name (10:3, 14).

e) *An intimate love.* "His own" are his familiars, *tous idious,* or even his friends, *hymeis philoi mou este,* whom he initiates into the mystery of the life of the Trinity (15:14–15). Knowing what a trial isolation is, he wants to shield his

---

[11] Jn. 13:34; 15:9, 12.
[13] Jn. 14:27; 15:11; 16:22.

[12] Jn. 8:42; 14:23–24; 16:27.
[14] Jn. 16:26–33; cf. 4:10; 14:13.

disciples from experiencing it and he brings about an intimate, mutual presence in spite of physical separation. The presence will be their "abode in love" (15:4–9) as they await the final reunion in the house of the Father.[15] This communion is the supreme wish of Christ's charity. "I in them!"

f) *A merciful and generous love.* Jesus did not come to judge; his entire mission was to save man from darkness, sin, and death. When he offered living water to those who thirst (6:35; 7:37), he wanted to communicate to them a superabundance of the divine life (10:10; 17:2) and a participation in his glory and his beatitude (17:23–24). Mediator of the divine charity, the Son transmits what he has received from the Father, all that fills him interiorly, his *plērōma* (1:16). Furthermore, he is the way, the truth, the life, the resurrection, and the light (14:6). His gifts are identical with his Person (6:35) so that when he gives himself, he gives all things (1 Jn. 5:11). Can it be said that Christ transmits even greater riches, *meizona toutōn* (14:12)? He will send you "another advocate to be with you for all time to come" (14:15).

g) *A gift-giving love.* "He loved them to the end." Christ manifested his charity to his own from the moment of his first call of them by the lake. He loved them all through the life they lived together intimately like nomads sharing the same tent,[16] and his love culminated in his immolation on Calvary. His sacrifice is a decisive proof of his love and a gesture which shows how great a love it is. Having always loved his own, the Savior ended his life by sacrificing himself for them. This is supreme charity. "No one can give a greater proof of his love than by laying down his life for his friends" (15:13).

The apostles could not help understanding the meaning of such declarations and especially of such actions. They saw the Master's whole ministry as a manifestation of charity and his death as the decisive revelation of his love. "We

[15] Jn. 14:2–3; 16:22; 17:24.　　[16] Jn. 1:14; 1 Jn. 1:1–3.

know what love is from the fact that Jesus Christ laid down his life for us" (1 Jn. 3:16). According to the Lord's own declaration, his *agape* is identical with his Father's. Jesus loves his own with the same absoluteness and the same delicacy with which God loves his Son. "Just as the Father loves me, so I love you" (15:9). In revealing his own charity, Christ especially wants to make his Father's love known. "I have made known to them your name, and will continue to make it known, so that the love with which you love me may dwell in them." [17] In and through Christ, men can see what God's *agape* is. This is St. John's Gospel.

3. God and the world

It cannot be too often repeated that the essence of the faith of the primitive Church lay in its seeing the life and death of Jesus as a signal manifestation of God's love for men. The incarnation and death on the cross are an epiphany of the Father's *agape*. The captivity Epistles and especially the Pastorals had already taught this lesson,[18] but St. John makes it explicit and repeats it frequently. "So marked, indeed, has been God's love for the world that he gave his only-begotten Son; everyone who believes in him is not to perish, but to have eternal life" (Jn. 3:16). "God's love was made manifest among us by the fact that God sent his only-begotten Son into the world that we might have life through him" (1 Jn. 4:9). This is the summit of "revelation" and the center of the Christian religion. The coming of Christ to earth, his life, and his death on the cross are historical facts, and believers discover a mystery in these particular events. They contemplate the "glory" of the Son-made-flesh, who reflects his Father's divine nature (1:14), and they understand that Christ's gift begins in the divine charity and is ordained to procure them eternal life, participation in God's own life. In the Sermon on the Mount Jesus had proposed

[17] Jn. 17:26; cf. 15:16; 14:7, 9, 11.
[18] Tit. 3:4; cf. *Agape in the New Testament*, vol. II, pp. 396 ff.

his Father's kindness as an example to his disciples. Because
he loves all men, even thankless ones, God generously gives
them all they need for the life of the body. The angels had
praised the heavenly *eudokia* which proposed salvation for
men and reconciliation of sinners with God (Lk. 2:14). The
Virgin Mary and Zachary sang the mercy of the Almighty.[19]
After Christ returned to his Father, the apostles meditated
upon his teachings and his stay among them. They concluded that the Savior had been sent because of the divine
mercy, and they also understood the nature and extent of his
agape. Their knowledge of charity grew as their faith in the
person of Christ grew.

Christ is more than an ambassador, more than a revealer
full of grace and truth, more than the Messiah, more even
than a Savior who sacrifices himself personally. He is God's
only Son. "Everyone who believes that Jesus is the Christ
is born of God" (1 Jn. 5:1). His only-begotten Son is the
person whom God honors and cherishes above all others.
That the Father has turned him over to sinners in order to
bring them to a part in his own life is proof of an infinite
love which no human imagination could ever have conceived. The price of the gift reveals the depth of his *agape*.
It is almost unthinkable that God would love creatures so
much, especially creatures who had offended him. "The
world must come to acknowledge that I am your ambassador, and that you love them as you love me" (17:23).
Faith enlightens us on precisely this point: "God's love was
made manifest among us by this fact" (1 Jn. 4:9). Such love
can scarcely be imagined, let alone put into words, so each
Christian is invited to meditate on it. "See what kind of love
the Father has bestowed on us" (1 Jn. 3:1). "*Thus* has God
loved us" (4:11), with this prodigious generosity. The beloved Son, crucified for us, reveals how much God loves us
and what his love, *agape*, is. "This love consists not in our
having loved God but in his having loved us and having sent
his Son as a propitiation for our sins." [20]

[19] Lk. 1:50, 54, 72, 78.   [20] 1 Jn. 4:10.

4. God is love

For St. John, what distinguishes believers from other men is their understanding of the mystery of Jesus. It is not only a matter of proclaiming the authenticity of the Messiah and the lordship of the Son of God, of adhering to the efficacy of his death, of awaiting his return in glory, but also of relating all these saving deeds to the love which conceived and directed them, of reading in the person and life of Jesus the divine charity they express. God, who is pure spirit (Jn. 4:24), is by his very nature invisible. No one has ever seen him (1 Jn. 4:12), but he becomes present in Christ, and we can see the Father through the Son (Jn. 14:9). In the charity which Jesus manifested for us, we reach the love of God himself. The strong conviction the apostles felt about Jesus' manifestation is expressed with the force of a clear discovery. "We ourselves know and believe in God's enduring love at work among us. God is love" (1 Jn. 4:16). In the religion of Jesus Christ, to know God is not simply to perceive his omnipotence, holiness, or justice, but to grasp that he is love (v. 8).

Deus charitas est! The import of the assertion in St. John's first Epistle must be understood in terms of its genesis. It is not a statement made by the Lord or a dogmatic declaration unrelated to history, but the outcome of St. John's contemplation of the life and death of Christ and of Jesus' relations with God. The more the Christian meditates on what the Savior did and on his teachings about charity, the more he discovers that Christ is first and foremost the revealer of God, not like the prophets who proclaimed what the Spirit suggested to them, but as the only Son who rests permanently on the Father's bosom and explains and makes known the mysteries of his intimate life with God (Jn. 1:18). Whether we consider God's relations with Jesus and men or the relations of the Son of God with his Father and "his own," *agape* is the summary and exhaustive explanation of everything.

First of all, *agape* is a gift—"See what kind of love the Father has given us" (1 Jn. 3:1)—and it can come only from God. "Love takes its origin in God" (1 Jn. 4:7). However, this charity as virtue is only an infinitesimal part of the divine attribute. Faith discovers an adequate object in the love God possesses in his own right in the person of his incarnate Son, "God's love among us" (1 Jn. 4:16). Jesus appears as love personified, and through him the Christian can truly know what love in God is. If Christ is all love, then his Father is all love too. The following two verses must be juxtaposed. "We know what love is from the fact that Jesus Christ laid down his life for us" (1 Jn. 3:16) and "God's love was made manifest among us by the fact that God sent his only-begotten Son into the world" (1 Jn. 4:9). There is so complete an identity between Christ's love and the Father's love that we can conclude from one to the other. It is more than a matter of manifestations and marks of love, as if God and Jesus were acting with one and the same heart. The relationship between the Father and his only Son springs from a reciprocal, permanent, and eternal charity (Jn. 17:23–24). Everything that Christ has revealed about the intimate life of God is summarized in its being an exchange made within the mutual relationship of knowledge and love between God and his Son. The union of the two persons seems to be accomplished in *agape*.[21] Thus one arrives at conceiving of a substantial charity which is God (1 Jn. 4:10). Love is of the same nature as God.

These remarks indicate that when St. John wrote "God is love," he intended first of all to furnish the explicative principle of the economy of salvation—in this he agrees with St. Paul[22]—and to take into account the personal relations which unite the Father to the Son within a single glory. Their *agape* is primarily the active manifestation of love. This is no definition of the God of philosophers, specified by aseity, but a valid designation of the essence of the living God. Love is more than an attribute of God; according to

[21] Jn. 17:22–23, 26.   [22] Eph. 2:4 ff.; Col. 1:19 ff.

the supreme revelation of the New Covenant, it is his own name. Love expresses God's nature and consequently all his other attributes—justice, patience, strength, etc. Above all else, God is love. *Agape* is not something *of* God. It is God himself, his substance; God is incapable of not loving.

Here we are face to face with a great mystery. Biblical theology cannot make it any more explicit, but the declaration, "God is love," says what is most proper to God and what he desires us to know about him. He has shown that he is love, and he wants to be recognized as he is. If we may dare to say so, charity is the property of his nature which means the most to him. St. John saw it as his most specific quality, as Jesus had implied in his teaching on "the Father who is in heaven." The Holy Spirit made St. John understand that charity is an active love; it is a fullness overflowing in kindness, whose movements are their own determination and justification, like a spring that overflows into the stream which it feeds. God is life, so his immanent love is completely spontaneous and communicative. He is light (1 Jn. 1:5) because his love is spiritual and clear. *Agape* expresses all of this. Like a sun that illuminates and radiates, like a spring that flows and fecundates, God is pure charity which loves by expressing and giving itself. His communication and sharing of himself are his nature and, therefore, the law of his life.

5. Divine sonship, the work and gift of the Father's *agape*

God loves men so much that he sacrificed his Son for them, and his charity does not remain external in the form of helpful providence which would first surround men with good things and finally assure their happiness. Instead it gives them eternal life (Jn. 3:16), which must be understood as the life of God himself rather than as a life that death cannot reach. In the depths of his being, the Christian possesses the life with which God himself lives. More profoundly still, out of love God begets believers by communicating his own nature to them. Of sinners, he makes children capable of entering into intimacy with him. "See what kind of love the Father has bestowed on us that we should be called his children, for that is what we are." [23] The words, "for that is what we are," *kai esmen*, exclude any watereddown or softened interpretation of the expression "children of God." It is not a metaphor, honorific title or affectionate name, as if God had for us a love like a father's love for his sons or as if only he treated us like sons. God actually is our father just as truly as our human fathers are, who begot us and transmitted their own lives to us. This is so true that according to St. John, the Christian is called "he who has been begotten by God." [24] Indeed, according to the mode of begetting of living things, "the life-germ implanted by God abides in him" (1 Jn. 3:9).

Anyone who is surprised or doubtful about this should reread St. Paul's teaching on the new birth (Tit. 3:5) and Jesus' conversation with Nicodemus in which the Master used the analogy of human birth to explain birth according to the spirit (Jn. 3:3–9). The new or divine begetting is just as real as the first begetting in the mother's womb, and Christians can truly consider themselves "of the race of God" (Acts 17:28). In fact, strictly speaking, begetting by the spirit is more true and authentic than human begetting. For one thing, human fathers are intermediaries who can only transmit a life that is not their own property (Eph. 3:14–15); for another, a human child is autonomous from the moment he comes into the world. Once the umbilical cord is cut, his dependence on his parents becomes only moral. The child of God, on the contrary, is forever being born. He is permanently being begotten, as the perfect tense of the verb *gennan* shows.[25] He is always being born; he is

---

[23] 1 Jn. 3:1; cf. vv. 2, 10; 5:2.
[24] 1 Jn. 3:3–10; cf. 2:29; 4:7; 5:1, 4, 18; Jn. 1:12.
[25] 1 Jn. 2:29; 3:9; 4:7; 5:1, 4; Jn. 3:6, 8.

always receiving direct participation in God's nature and
life. For St. Paul, the Christian is a person who "is in Christ
Jesus"; for St. John, the Christian is a person who "is from
God" [26] or "is from the Father" (1 Jn. 2:16).

Theologians identify the truly divine nature communicated to believers with sanctifying grace. Jesus called it
"glory." "The glory you have bestowed on me I have bestowed on them, that they may be one as we are one—I in
them and you in me. Thus their oneness will be perfected.
The world must come to acknowledge . . . that you love
them as you love me" (Jn. 17:22–23). Since the basic nature
of the heavenly Father is *agape* and since, strictly speaking,
a begetter transmits his own nature in begetting, God's children will clearly be persons who are essentially loving. The
divine glory or the divine nature in which we participate,
thanks to Christ, includes, first and foremost, entitative possession of the Father's love which also belongs to all his sons.
"May the love with which you love me dwell in them as I
dwell in them myself" (Jn. 17:26). This explains why and
how the children of the God who is love can be recognized
by their capacity to love. For St. John, the words *ek tou
theou*, "to be (born) of God," mean to belong to God and
to resemble him, as well as to take one's origin from him (1
Jn. 2:16). Someone who is especially patient, consoling, or
easily angered is sometimes referred to as "a son of" patience,
consolation, or anger. In the same way, the description "son
of God" suggests not only that a person is born of God but
also that he depends on the heavenly Father and possesses
the same qualities that his Father has. If God is love, "those
who are of God" are also love, and not accidentally, but by
nature. Furthermore, the child acts like his father. At birth
he is furnished with both his nature and his faculties, which
exercise themselves in activities. Authentic children of God
can be recognized by the charitable quality of their activities.

This doctrine must be kept in mind for an understanding

[26] 1 Jn. 4:2–3; cf. 3:10; 4:6; 3 Jn. 11; Jn. 8:47.

of the Johannine definition: "Everyone that loves is a child
of God" (1 Jn. 4:7), which follows the assertion, "Love
takes its origin in God." Charity is the criterion of sonship,
and, consequently, of the disciple. There is no more basic
teaching in the New Testament. Like St. Paul, St. John does
call the Christian "one who believes," *ho pisteuōn*, but he
conceives of him principally as "one who loves," *ho agapōn*.[27] The present participle indicates both incessant activity and a condition of stability—sometimes very much
emphasized, as "he who abides in love," *ho menōn en tēi
agapēi* (1 Jn. 4:16). The child of God is, as it were, always
in the act of loving, like his heavenly Father. At least, he
has a permanent disposition to love, and he is prompt to
manifest his charity. Love is his life, because love is his being.
Just as it can be stated categorically that "he who does not
love abides in death" (1 Jn. 3:14b), so it is equally true to
say that he who loves has passed from death to life (3:14a)
and lives in the light (2:10), in participation in the divine
life.

6. What is *agape?*

Having seen that for St. John a disciple is one who possesses divine love and lives from it, it is possible to examine
the nature of the divine love and determine its characteristics.
According to the Synoptics, God was the model for a love
which is respectful, kind and tender in its manifestations
toward neighbor. St. Paul is faithful to this meaning, but the
central place he gives to *agape,* the bond of perfection, in
his development of Christian theology forces him to enrich
its content. He says that the love of God conceived and accomplished the whole economy of salvation. Along with the
crucified Christ, God is "he who has loved us" (Rom. 8:37;
Gal. 2:20). Charity inseparably unites the Father and the
Son in their relationship with redeemed men (2 Cor. 13:13).

[27] 1 Jn. 4:21; 5:1; cf. Jn. 14:21.

St. Paul's words in Rom. 8:39, "God's love for us, which is in Christ Jesus our Lord," can be considered the point of departure for St. John's speculation on Christ, the redeemer and giver of the divine charity to believers. Furthermore, St. Paul had the merit of exalting *agape* as the essence of the Christian life. To have charity is everything; not to have it is to be reduced to nothing (1 Cor. 13). All morality is summed up in charity (Rom. 13:10). This, too, prepares for St. John's repeated assertions of the unrivaled importance of fraternal love.

Moreover, St. Paul prays unceasingly to God to make *agape* increase and abound in the disciples' hearts, and he writes that *agape* is constantly diffused in them by the Holy Spirit (Rom. 5:5). St. John insists on this point even more, and makes *agape* more than a simple gift of God, even if the greatest one, and more than a grace; it is participation in the divine nature. For St. Paul, the Christian is an adopted son of God, *huios tou theou*, whose soul is endowed with the qualities and titles appropriate to his new state, particularly with the right to his inheritance. For St. John, the Christian is a child, *teknon*, begotten by the heavenly Father. The Father is charity. When he communicates his nature and life to his child, he transmits something of the *agape* which is proper to him. The supernatural, divine character of Christian love could not be more clearly stated. Taken literally, many Pauline texts might seem to indicate that charity is a moral virtue, because the emphasis in them is on *agape*'s practical efficiency, "the labor of love," *ho kopos tēs agapēs* (1 Thess. 1:3). In St. John, however, the theological character of *agape* is always evident. Because of its origin *agape* is different from all human attachments. "Love is from God" (1 Jn. 4:7). Its origin is its specific character. God alone has charity. He alone loves in this way. On this earth, only those whom he begets possess this love and only they can love as God loves.

Pauline *agape* is a force, an extremely active *dynamis*; Johannine *agape* is above all a nature, considered sometimes as transcendent, sometimes as immanent, precisely because it is both divine and incarnate. It can be said that the Christian (*ho agapōn*) is in a stable condition because he possesses charity. He remains in a state which testifies to his spiritual authenticity. In a way, the love he has received surpasses him. It is greater than his own heart, and he is bound to *agape* and must plunge himself into it. At any rate, charity is the bond which unites the believer to God. It is the child of God's permanent participation in the nature and life of his Father.

This conception takes into account the expressions proper to St. John. He says that the charity of God or of the Father remains in the Christian (1 Jn. 3:17; cf. 2:15) and is rooted in him (Jn. 5:42). He defines the disciple as a man who abides in the love (1 Jn. 4:16) which God or Christ have for him (Jn. 15:9–10). Charity is a mutual attachment, therefore, between perfectly real and living persons; it is the love proper to God and revealed by Christ. It is divine and is given first, taking the initiative in every communication and gift (1 Jn. 4:10, 19). The disciple welcomes its declarations and manifestations. He believes in love (4:16), and his firm, stable adherence makes him live and remain in charity, live and remain in God. "He who abides in love abides in God and God in him" (1 Jn. 4:16; cf. v. 12). This way of expressing the link between God and the believer is original with St. John, and it is noteworthy that he already insisted on it so strongly when he had only just discovered it. Nevertheless, the indwelling was self-evident once it was realized that *agape* is a nature common to God and to his children. Charity is characterized, therefore, by the depth of its attachment. The whole person loves and is directed toward the beloved.

Charity is more than a simple relationship of delight. It draws together persons who love one another to the point of realizing a presence. The immediacy of the nearness is spiritual, of course, since it is a question of God and the soul, but it is also in a certain sense local, since St. John calls it a mutual indwelling and even an existence of one within the other. It is the common psychology of love that the beloved haunts the spirit and heart of the lover, and *vice versa. Ubi thesaurus tuus, ibi et cor tuum.* . . . However, the presence of a memory or an affection is purely psychological, whereas charity brings God, Christ, and the believer together, uniting them in their very being rather than by extrinsic relation. *Agape* is the place, the home, where the Father, the Son, and all believers meet (1 Jn. 5:1, 2, 18) because they all possess the same nature. It is not enough, then, to say that charity assures the mutual intimacy of the lover and the beloved, or even that it makes them present to one another. There is more than contact; there is communication of being and life, and it is on this level that we must understand the reciprocal indwelling which *agape* causes.

St. John's first epistle emphasizes so strongly the relationship between Christian charity and the new birth (1 Jn. 3:1; 4:7; 5:1) that we are led to conceive charity as a family love. God loves as Father. Christians love him as his children, and they love one another as brothers (1 Jn. 3:16). We are bound to love Christ and Christians because "everyone who loves the parent loves his child also" (1 Jn. 5:1). If we have God for a Father, we cannot help loving his Son (Jn. 8:42). In other words, God's *agape* for his only-begotten Son and for his children is of the same nature and founded on a fundamental similarity. "You love them as you love me." [28] The glory proper to the Father is received by Jesus and communicated to the disciples (Jn. 17:22, 24). The counterproof, "He who does not love his brother is no child of God" (1 Jn. 3:10), is as absolute as the proof, "We know by this sign that we love the children of God; when we love God." [29] *Agape* is a familial affection, an immense kindness which can contain a great deal of tenderness. This helps us to understand better why it has an innate tendency to unity (Jn. 17:23). Father, Son, and brothers are to form only one; the whole economy of salvation is ordained to this ideal (Jn.

[28] Jn. 17:23; cf. v. 26. [29] 1 Jn. 5:2.

12:52), precisely because it is governed by the Father's charity.

Progress Progress in the Christian life is progress in love, and it is marked by an ever closer union. No matter how strong the assimilation of his new child to him is at baptism, it can always be intensified, since it is conditioned by an increased awareness of God's love for us. The more the Christian knows the Father's *agape*, the more he becomes attached to Christ who manifests it to him, and the more the Father and Son draw near, uniting themselves more closely to him. "He who accepts my commandments and keeps them—he is the one that loves me. And he that loves me will, in turn, be loved by my Father; and I will love him, and will manifest myself to him. . . . My Father will love him, and we shall visit him and make our home with him" (Jn. 14:21, 23). The love which at first seemed so static appears here as singularly active. The highest faculties have come into play. For spiritual beings, to be is to live and to act. Therefore, to live in love is not an ideal of repose; it is rather to know God, direct the affection of the heart to him, and to prove one's fidelity. For his part, Christ manifests himself, *emphanisō*, and comes with the Father, *eleusometha;* together they bring about an active presence, *monēn poiēsometha*. The disciple cannot be unaware of their coming and permanent dwelling within him, because he lives in the light.[30] Since *agape* is a lucid love, it is very much aware of God and of all its relations with him. One of St. John's most original contributions to the theology of charity is his reiterated affirmation of the new vision. "Everyone that loves . . . knows God" (1 Jn. 4:7); "we ourselves know and believe in God's enduring love at work among us" (v. 16); "we know . . . because we love" (3:14); "by this we shall know" (v. 19); "by this we know . . . when we love God" (1 Jn. 5:2).

The knowledge intrinsically linked to charity comes from experience, from an intimate grasping based on the communion of nature and life established with God. The Chris-

[30] 1 Jn. 2:10; cf. v. 27.

tian is converted when he sees God's charity revealed. In the beginning, he sees a proof of God's love in the person of Christ, and as he grows, he acquires a clearer awareness of the Father's love. His supreme wish is not so much the Parousia or entrance into heaven as it is the consummation in unity (Jn. 17:22–23) and finally, the sight of the glory, *doxa*, and love, *agape*, that the Father has given the Son before the creation of the world (v. 24). The union and presence which he experiences will be completed in the contemplation of the Trinitarian life he shares. *Agape* will have become perfect when the manifestation is total (cf. 1 Jn. 3:2).

This doctrine is apparent in the texts only if *agapan-agapē* keeps its classical and biblical nuance of manifestation of love. More than any other New Testament writer, St. John shows charity as a love which reveals and proves itself. We have seen how enlightening this meaning was for an understanding of the divine "nature." "God is love," *ho theos agapē estin*, must be understood primarily in terms of the fact of Christ and of the economy of salvation, the epiphany of the *agape* of God. God is manifest and generous love. He makes no secret of his love for his Son and for men. St. Paul traced everything to God's paternity (Eph. 3:14), but for St. John, God is an overflowing and communicative love, a fullness poured out—*Bonum diffusivum sui*—and consequently the source of all love and all good. Thus the "greater love," *meizona agapēn*, of Jn. 15:13 is the most convincing proof of love and its decisive manifestation. Jesus' death is the most expressive act of his charity (cf. 13:1).

Furthermore, the Savior multiplies his declarations of love;[31] he requires the apostles' declarations in turn (Jn. 21:15–17), and he wants the proclamations to be confirmed by deeds.[32] Just as the incarnation is for believers a manifestation of the Father's charity (1 Jn. 4:9), so they will recognize one another as God's authentic children through the exercise of fraternal charity (3:10). The activity of this love will be an unmistakable sign by which even unbelievers

---

[31] Jn. 13:34; 15:9, 15.   [32] Jn. 14:15, 21, 23.

can always identify Christ's disciples (Jn. 13:35). Charity is spiritual, yet it draws attention to itself; it is invisible, yet it is radiant; it is intimate affection, yet it acts openly; it is recognizable in its works (1 Jn. 3:16). In definitions, *agape* must be understood in its traditional sense of manifest love. For example, *en toutōi estin hē agapē* is usually translated, "Love consists in this" (1 Jn. 4:10, 16), but the correct sense is, "The manifestation of love consists in this: God sends his Son as a propitiation for our sins."

Just as God proves his love and just as charity is necessarily efficient and effective, so St. John "defines" the Christian's *agape* (1 Jn. 5:3; 2 Jn. 6) by the proof of his love for God: the manifestation of charity is the observance of the precepts. Like St. Paul, he insists as much on the efficiency of the divine charity as on the disciples' works as characteristic of their love. To have charity is to keep the word of God (1 Jn. 2:5). To love God is to put his commandments into practice (5:2); the proof of *agape* is the keeping of the commandments (v. 3). "To walk in truth," "to walk according to his precepts," "to walk in love" (2 Jn. 4–6; cf. v. 3) all mean the same thing. The entire moral life, which is fidelity to the divine will, is the blossoming of charity. A person shows his attachment to God by obeying him, and the activities of *agape* constitute perfect obedience because the divine precept *par excellence* prescribes love. "His commandment is this, that we should believe in the name of his Son, Jesus Christ, and love one another, as he commanded us" (1 Jn. 3:23).

St. John did not invent this notion of charity. He learned it from the Master and then declared it in his own words: "We know what love is from the fact that Jesus Christ laid down his life for us. We, too, ought to lay down our lives for our brothers" (1 Jn. 3:16). Christ's example reveals how extremely active and efficient *agape* is. Jesus had commanded several times, "Love one another, as I have loved you" (Jn. 13:34; 15:12). He himself is the model of total devotion, carried even to the sacrifice of the cross. More clearly still,

the Lord had defined, "Anyone who loves me with charity
will keep my word. . . . Anyone who does not love me
does not keep my word" (Jn. 14:23). This is the same as
saying, "He who has my commandments and keeps them
—he is the one that loves me with charity" (v. 21), and "If
you love me, you will keep my commandments" (v. 15).

   Charity and fidelity are one and the same thing, as the
Old Testament consistently taught. Given the emphasis
placed on the values of delight and union in Johannine
agape, however, fidelity is no longer so much a matter of
obedience pure and simple or of strictly material submission
as it is of accepted dependence and agreement of wills. The
disciple fulfills the prescriptions of God and Christ out of
love; more exactly, he adopts their will and conforms to it.
"We keep his commandments and do what is pleasing in
his sight" (1 Jn. 3:22). *Agape,* authentic love, is exact in fidelity and prompt and fervent in welcoming the Father's will,
which it takes so completely to itself that God's will actually
becomes the believer's own will. That is why *agape* never
feels that its precepts are heavy (5:3). Jesus was referring
to the depth of this spontaneous adherence and conformity
when he said, "If you observe my commandments you will
remain in my love, just as I have observed my Father's
commandments and I remain in his love" (Jn. 15:10). St.
John echoes, "He who keeps his commandments abides in
God and God in him" (1 Jn. 3:23), and, "To love God
means to keep his commandments" (1 Jn. 5:3).

   Our piety should be essentially filial, and Jesus is its perfect model. "As he is, so we are" (14:17; cf. 2:6). The
children of God love not only because God has commanded
them to and because his Son has given them the example of
love, but also because as children of the Father and sharers
in his loving nature, they are incapable of having feelings
and desires different from his. When they love with infused
agape, their love has the essentially effective quality of divine
love. It manifests itself, dedicates itself, sacrifices itself and
proves itself in every way. For a Christian, loving is never

<u>anything other than manifesting what he really is</u> (1 Jn. 3:10), just as God's *agape* manifests him in himself.

It is now possible to understand the strength of the exhortation, "Little children, let us love not merely in word or with the tongue but in deed and in truth" (3:18). It would be monstrous for God's children to pretend to love if their actions were to belie the sincerity of their words (cf. 4:20). In any case, it would be contradictory to the nature of effective, convincing *agape*. True charity conforms to the effectively beneficent, generous, divine model (4:11), as St. John emphasizes in the stereotyped expression, "In this is love."

In conclusion, we must sum up St. John's very complex notion of *agape*. *Agape* is an overflowing fullness which springs from the very being of the lover and expresses him adequately. Completely spontaneous and gratuitous, it is a love of holiness and beauty which expresses itself in esteem and sovereign respect, in delight and kindness. Sometimes it vibrates with compassion at the sight of another's misery (1 Jn. 3:17); sometimes it rejoices in the happiness of its beloved (Jn. 14:28). It is so closely united with its beloved that it remains always in his presence. Its communion is the most intimate possible because it is reciprocal indwelling. We possess within ourselves the person whom we love and he exists in us. Mutual indwelling is possible because *agape* is God himself. His children remain in him (1 Jn. 4:16), and the loving and beloved brothers are united in the Father's charity which they share (Jn. 15:9). On this level, St. John explains, there is no true charity unless one loves God. "We know by this sign that we love the children of God: when we love God" (1 Jn. 5:2). In other words, charity is something completely different from tender *storgē* or the most perfect *philia*, although it includes the highest values of both these loves (cf. Jn. 11:3, 5, 11, 36), particularly the confiding of secrets to a friend (15:14–15) and the gentle, generous welcome reserved to guests (3 Jn. 6). As in the Septuagint, the Synoptics, and St. Paul, *agape* in

St. John is extremely active, powerful, and generous. It communicates the most precious thing it has; [33] it gives of its best (1 Jn. 4:10). It tends to sacrifice itself for the beloved (Jn. 15:13). Charity is belonging to another (1 Jn. 2:15), and it demands unchanging fidelity. When it is a matter of man's love for God or Christ, charity is equivalent to consecration (Jn. 21:15–17). At least, that is its ideal, for St. John's expressions, like our Lord's in the Sermon on the Mount, show that man, magnificently endowed with divine charity as he is (Jn. 17:26), tries to love his best but can never fully realize the infinite delight and gift that such a love includes by its very nature. "Whoever keeps God's word, truly that man's love for God is perfect" (1 Jn. 2:5).

7. Fraternal love

From the very beginning God had asked his people to love one another (Lev. 19:18). In the Sermon on the Mount Jesus extended charity even to enemies (Mt. 5:44–48), and in his Farewell Discourse he made fraternal *agape* his own precept: "This is my commandment: love one another" (Jn. 15:12). He called it a new precept: "A new commandment I give you: love one another" (13:34). He was referring to the love which his own must actively bear one another and which characterizes them as his disciples: "You are my friends, provided you do what I command you" (15:14). They are to love as Christ has loved them, as Jn. 13:34 and 15:12 emphasize. These texts show how the precept can be called completely new and absolutely proper to Christ. "As I love you, so I want you, too, to love one another" (Jn. 13:34). Thus, simple philanthropy, tenderness, and the kind of devotion which people ordinarily feel and practice are not what he was referring to. The Master was consciously introducing into this world an original love which was unknown until he himself lived it.

[33] Jn. 3:34–35; cf. Lk. 15:31.

He immediately explained how he understands and manifests his love: "No one can give a greater proof of his love than by laying down his life for his friends" (15:13). Love is therefore gift of self and desire for the happiness of one's friends which is so profound that one is even willing to sacrifice oneself for them. Examples of this kind of generosity exist outside Christianity (Rom. 5:7), however, and the Lord goes even further. "Just as the Father loves me, so I love you" (Jn. 15:9). Consequently, there can no longer be a question of human attachment alone; Christ's love is also divine love. To love as Christ loves is to love both religiously and humanly, to share in God's own love and to extend it to others. That is what makes Christian *agape* specific and new. Its origin and nature are heavenly, and it has the power to unite all God's children within the Church. Clearly, then, *agape* has something of the infinite about it and, clearly, it tends to immolation. Because it is divine, it is without measure. Christ alone has shown its perfect realization.

To love as Christ loves is not a more or less optional counsel or simply one precept among many. It is the last testament and supreme will of the Lord and Master who was actively fulfilling what he ordained for others (13:13–14). Love is the spirit of his Church and the soul of the new covenant which he sealed with his blood. Therefore Christ kept only fraternal love, as he defined it, as the criterion of authentic discipleship; he identified love with the Christian life itself. Jesus practiced all the virtues and prescribed them for his own, but only *agape* is specific because *agape* makes Christianity what it is. "By this token all the world must know that you are my disciples—if you have the love of charity for one another" (Jn. 13:35). Love that is a token must be active and manifest, able to play the role of witness and proof. It must be love so special that it cannot possibly be confused with any counterfeit. It must be an attachment so broad, constant and patient that even strangers can see in it the fulfillment of the command of Christ. They must see Christ's way of loving and even his presence and the presence of his Father in the disciples' community and communion. "I in them and you in me, that their unity may be perfect, so that the world will recognize that you sent me and that you love them as you love me" (17:23). *Agape* is the "mark" of the visible church, because no one can possess this love unless he has been chosen and loved by God, who transmits it to him in his beloved Son present with his Father, by love, in the midst of his own (Jn. 14:23).

St. John had meditated for a long time on the testament of the Lord, and the essence of his Epistles seems to comment: "This is all I command you: love one another" (Jn. 15:17). Referring to the very first catechesis which each convert received, he wrote: "This is precisely the message which you have heard from the beginning—that we should love one another" (1 Jn. 3:11). His reference to the early stages of initiation into Christianity seems to imply that the convert's commitment was made first of all to the reciprocal love within the Church. In any case, St. John does not consider love simply a wish or precept of Christ, but rather the will of God himself: "This is his (God's) commandment" (1 Jn. 3:23). The Christian life is summed up in faith in Christ and fraternal love, *en alētheiai kai agapēi* (2 Jn. 3). It would be impossible to give greater fullness to *agape* or to associate it more happily with the Witness-Revealer who prescribed it.

This is not just a general juxtaposition of dogma and morality in which the faithful are characterized by their confession of the incarnate Son of God and by their loving conduct. For St. John, the proper object of faith is the divine charity: "to believe in the love that God has manifested among us" (1 Jn. 4:16; cf. v. 10) in the person of his Son. He is the epiphany of the Father's *agape*, so that fraternal love finds its model in the love Christ has for his own. Fraternal love is verified in him: "the truth is in him" (2:8). Jesus had said: "Love one another as I love you. No one can give a greater proof of his love than by laying down his life for his friends" (Jn. 15:12–13), and the disciple comments: "We know what love is from the fact that Jesus Christ laid down his life for us. We, too, ought to lay down our lives for our brothers" (1 Jn. 3:16; cf. 4:11). "We ought," *opheilomen,* implies more than the necessity of conforming to a model; it refers to the obligation of the debt of gratitude. Having received so great a gift of love, how could we in our turn not love and surround our brothers with the same kind of generosity?

On the human plane, it is fitting that a superior person be able to rise to difficult circumstances. An honorable and noble-hearted person tries to share with others any benefits he has received. The Lord, who was severe to the slave who had been acquitted of his debts and then was intransigent toward his own debtors (Mt. 18:23–34), went on to say, "In the same way my heavenly Father will treat you if you do not each forgive your brother from your heart" (v. 35). St. John was not taking his position on the plane of human decency, however. He was intrinsically linking charity received from God with charity toward neighbor, and this connection is his most personal contribution to the theology of *agape.*

Jesus had associated the two commandments as making up a single supreme class of precepts (Mt. 22:36–40). St. Paul had summed up Christian morality in fraternal charity (Rom. 13:8–10). St. John teaches that it is impossible to love God without loving one's brother. To pretend to have charity for God without extending it to one's neighbor would be a lie (1 Jn. 4:20). Worse still, the divine *agape* cannot live in a heart that closes itself to compassion for a brother in need (1 Jn. 3:17). *A priori,* when the objects of the two loves are so diverse, it is difficult to see why they cannot be dissociated. But the apostle declares that this is the divine ordinance: "We have received this command from God: He who loves God must love his brother also" (1 Jn. 4:21).

The command does not actually appear in the Gospel, so

it must be understood that St. John, by his apostolic authority, was interpreting and clarifying the Lord's will in a sort of theological conclusion to which he gave the force of law. In any case, it is easy to retrace the evolution of his thought. *Agape is a very particular kind of love, which bespeaks absolute initiative and anteriority, not reciprocity.* God has revealed his charity under this mode (4:11, 19). How then can Christians possess and exercise *agape* without themselves taking the first steps? *Vis-à-vis* God, their *agape* is necessarily response; only toward neighbor can it manifest authentic spontaneity. Perhaps it is in this sense that 1 Jn. 4:19 and 1 Jn. 4:12 should be understood: "We must take the initiative in loving our brothers since he first loved us"; and "No one has ever seen God, yet if we love one another, God abides in us and our love for him reaches its perfection," its full *ratio* of *agape*.

Another, more profound consideration is added to this one. The love which the believer possesses is infused (4:7). It is the charity with which God loves himself and all Christians. It keeps the same objects in our hearts, therefore, as it has in God, as 1 Jn. 5:2 suggests: "We know by this sign that we love the children of God, when we love God." What does this mean if not that the possession of the divine reality which is *agape* is enough to unite us *ipso facto* with God and his children? Charity accomplishes this communion because it is its nature to do so, and that is why it is unthinkable that anyone could be attached to God and exclude his neighbor, or *vice versa*. This dichotomy, which could be valid in human affections or in certain mystiques, is contrary to the very notion of charity, which is a love that is proper only to God and to his own.

We arrive, then, at St. John's ultimate reflection, one already made by Peter and Paul. According to St. John, the proper fruit of faith is not justification or even obtaining eternal life, but, first of all, becoming the child and sharer of the divine life. "Everyone who believes that Jesus is the Christ is born of God" (1 Jn. 5:1; Jn. 1:12). God is love, the manifestation and gift of love (1 Jn. 4:8, 16). When he begets children, he gives them the *agape* which characterizes his nature. From the gift, it is easy to deduce the consequence: the child of God is "naturally" loving; charity is the rightful possession of every disciple who is reborn of God. "Everyone that loves is a child of God" (1 Jn. 4:7).

This is certainly the supreme motive of fraternal love. Christians are exhorted to love their neighbor because of the loving nature they received at baptism. "Beloved, let us love one another, *because* love is from God" (1 Jn. 4:7). St. John tells us that this love is a family love. God is the Father; he loves his children; and each of them must consider the others also children of their common Father and must love them as their brothers. "Everyone who loves the parent loves his child also" (1 Jn. 5:1). This notion makes everything clear, and we can understand why St. John united charity for God so intimately with charity for neighbor, or rather for other Christians. Fraternal *agape* is much less a love prescribed for the sake of resembling God and conforming to Christ's example than it is a sharing and application of God's love of predilection for all the disciples of Jesus.

That is why our fraternal charity is a proof that God lives in us (1 Jn. 4:12). To distinguish between the children of God and the children of the devil, it is only necessary to observe who loves his neighbor and who does not (1 Jn. 3:19). Only those who do are sure of "being born of the truth" (3:10) and of having passed from death to life. "We know that we have passed from death to life, because we love our brothers. He who does not love abides in death" (3:14). The charitable person is truly alive (v. 15); he possesses God's own life in him and he walks in the light (1 Jn. 2:10).

Although St. John multiplies statements about the duty of manifesting love of neighbor and about the reasons love is necessary, he is silent about the acts and modes of its being carried out. He emphasizes only that it must be effec-

tive, because effectiveness is the characteristic of charity
which God and Christ have revealed to him.[34] Since true
love consists in the Father's giving the Son and the Son's
giving his life (4:10; 3:16), the essential sign of fraternal
love is that it does not love "in word or tongue, but in deed
and truth" (3:18). It dedicates itself to the kind of humble
and fervent service of which our Lord gave a very concrete example when he washed his disciples' feet (Jn. 13:15;
cf. Lk. 22:26). A good spirit is not enough; we must really
give ourselves to others in a union of heartfelt love and
self-sacrifice—"happy are you if you do these things" (Jn.
13:17). Consequently, just as God sacrificed his only Son
out of mercy for us, so the disciple will feel himself full of
pity for those in need and will share everything he has with
them. He must even be ready to give his life, following the
Savior's example (1 Jn. 3:16) and the law of infused charity.

Furthermore, when Jesus was told that his friend Lazarus
was sick, he let him die—"Jesus loved . . . Lazarus" (Jn.
11:5)—and he even rejoiced because he had not helped him
sooner (Jn. 11:15, *chairō*), because Lazarus' sickness and
death were to manifest God's glory (v. 4). Attachment to
neighbor is subordinate to the demands of divine love. If it
is a matter of God's honor (cf. 9:3–4), we must agree to the
most painful trials for those we love—"your dear friend is
ill" (v. 3). Then, however, we will taste the joy of being
in full accord with the Father's will (*echarēte;* 14:28), in
direct contrast to the Jews who, not having charity within
themselves (5:42), "cared more for the approval of men
than for the approval of God" (12:43).

8. The progress and fruits of *agape*

Because *agape* is God's nature in us, nothing is more stable
than our love. Whether it is charity for God, Christ, or
neighbor, the person who possesses it is assured of being

[34] 1 Jn. 4:11; Jn. 15:9–10, 12–13.

forever established in God or in Christ, in life eternal and heavenly light. "He who abides in love abides in God and God in him." [35] The moral life is seen as a walking under the inspiration of charity (2 Jn. 6), and the Christian is sure that he will never stumble (1 Jn. 2:10). Where there is *agape*, there is also security.

But stability, permanence, or even fixedness are not synonymous with inertia. Johannine charity, like Pauline, is extremely active, proving itself above all in the practice of the commandments.[36] Diligent fidelity arouses the delight of the three divine Persons and wins new gifts, first of all the coming and indwelling of the Holy Spirit: "If you love me you will keep my commandments. And I will ask the Father, and he will give you another Advocate to be with you for all times to come" (Jn. 14:15–16). The believer's first reaction before the divine ambassador is to "receive" him (Jn. 1:11–12). Only those who love God "welcome Jesus." [37] The person who gives himself and attaches himself to Christ has the assurance that both the Father and Christ will return his love. Just as the faithful person's charity expresses itself in works, so Jesus' charity is shown in his gifts: "He who has my commandments and keeps them—he is the one that loves me. And he that loves me will, in turn, be loved by my Father; and I will love him, and will manifest myself to him" (14:21; cf. vv. 19–20). The disciple's loving obedience brings him deeper into the divine intimacy. As the charitable person proves the sincerity and force of his *agape*, the Father and the Son draw nearer and their indwelling in the soul becomes more profound. "Anyone who loves me will keep my word, and my Father will love him, and we shall come to him and make our home with him" (14:23).

In these three texts (14:15–16, 21, 23) the fervor of *agape* is proved by fidelity. Everything depends on "keeping the commandments" or "the word." John 14:21 accentuates

---

[35] 1 Jn. 4:16; cf. Jn. 15:9–10; 1 Jn. 4:12; 2:10; 3:14–15, 17.
[36] Jn. 15:10; 1 Jn. 3:23–24; 4:21; 5:2–3, 2 Jn. 5–6.
[37] Jn. 5:43; 13:20.

even more the notion of practical realization and perseverance: "he who has my commandments and keeps them."
The disciple receives, keeps, and accomplishes the will of
Jesus. As he does so, his charity not only proves itself but
also is strengthened by use; consequently, his divine participation becomes even fuller. Christ shows him still more
love (Jn. 14:21). With his Father, he establishes himself
permanently in the soul (1 Jn. 14:23), and, if we may dare
to say so, the stay of the Holy Spirit becomes even more
active (Jn. 14:16).

Since the coming and abiding of the Trinity are presented
as something new with respect to the first divine indwelling
within the convert (1 Jn. 4:16), the whole Christian life
may be considered an incessant, always-increasing manifestation and reciprocity of love between the disciple and God.
On God's side, this is self-evident, since he is charity and
charity is pure gift and communication. God never stops
loving, manifesting his love, and lavishing his gifts upon his
children. On the Christians' side, however, since their charity is received from God—"the love of the Father in him"
(1 Jn. 2:15; cf. 4:7)—the problem is to increase love by a
more generous sharing in the divine *agape*. St. John calls this
God's *agape* among us (4:17) or in us (v. 12) or in this
person (2:5). Charity itself cannot grow, since it is already
all fullness, but it can make progress in the soul that assimilates it. It occupies or inhabits the soul with greater sovereignty. Its mastery increases until it becomes "finished"
or consummated, until it is "perfect love," *he teleia agape*
(1 Jn. 4:18).

St. John writes several times that God's *agape* reaches
perfection in us (1 Jn. 4:12, 17; 2:5). This amounts to
saying that we grow and become perfect in *agape* (4:18).
We should understand that the disciple of Jesus Christ assimilates more and more profoundly the entity which is
"the *agape* that comes from God." He gives it full place
in his soul. He "realizes" it better and better in himself,
so that he exists integrally in *agape* and, like God himself,

arrives at identifying himself with love. Certainly that is his ideal and the direction of his progress.

Thus the participation in the divine nature that the child of God received at his engendering in baptism is intended to grow. The essence of its nature is love; its acts are manifestations of love: observance of the commandments and fraternal love. Its progress, linked to its concrete activity, is progress in charity. Its perfection is the perfection of love itself, and finally it is consummated in the unity, which will be complete only in heaven, of all those who participate in *agape*—of God, Christ, and the children of God (Jn. 17:23, 26). Heaven and earth could not be brought closer to each other. *Agape* is at once link and place of meeting. This is is true only because *agape* is God himself.

As *agape* grows and acts, the psychology of the Christian changes; he no longer fears God. If we really understood the content of this revelation, we would have to call it a miracle. After all, God is the holy one, the transcendent one, and before him every creature is seized with fear (Lk. 4:36). Furthermore, ever since the flight of the first guilty man before God (Gen. 3:8–10), every man feels himself a sinner (Lk. 5:8–9). His instinctive reaction is to see God as a judge whose punishments he fears. He is afraid. But the immense manifestation of God's love in the merciful coming of the Savior teaches man that God is a father and that he does not want to lose any of his creatures (Jn. 3:16–17) but on the contrary wants to associate them with his own life and make them share his intimacy (1 Jn. 1:3).

The realization of the immensity of God's love ought to dissolve all apprehension and "reassure our heart" (3:19). Even when he is conscious of his sins, the Christian still dares to approach God, because he knows that God is "greater than our heart" (v. 20), that he is magnificent in his pardon, and that he does not treat us according to our iniquities (1:8–2:2).

However, this conviction given by faith does not seem to be enough to eliminate the instinctive terror of the human heart before the divine majesty and holiness. There can be no question of establishing a *koinōnia* between the Father and his children until fear has first been dissipated. St. John attributes the psychological victory of confidence over fear to *agape*. He declares, "There is no fear in love" (1 Jn. 4:18). He understands clearly that the two feelings can coexist only in souls that are not sufficiently evolved. When *agape* succeeds in establishing its reign profoundly and the disciple understands what God's manifestations of love for us mean (4:16), then he attains to authentic, perfect charity, *hē teleia agapē*, which casts out fear. For St. John, the triumph of divine love in the human heart is the criterion of perfection. "In this has *agape* become perfect in us: that we have full assurance, *parrēsia*, against the day of judgment. . . . He who fears has not yet reached the perfection of love" (1 Jn. 4:17–18; cf. 3:21). *Parrēsia* is not only the daring confidence of the innocent who appear before the tribunal with their heads held high, but also the liberty, clarity and intimacy of the relationships which have been established in an atmosphere of joy between the Father and his children. When *agape* raises the children to the level of their Father, it allows them a true "society" and a perfect intimacy.

The contrast between the Church and the synagogue can be summarized in the substitution of loving assurance for fear and of filial piety for servility. It is not that life in the Church is easier or obedience to precepts any less constraining. On the contrary, in the Church it is necessary to sacrifice one's life totally and to be strictly faithful to the commandments. But Christ took Moses' place as mediator (Jn. 1:17), and *agape* replaces the Law; consequently, "his commandments are not burdensome" (1 Jn. 5:3).

According to St. John, not only is *agape* the first reality and the foundation on which everything else rests, as it is for St. Paul, but also it is the very essence of the Gospel, stated in Jn. 3:16 and repeated in 1 Jn. 4:9. The relationship between God and man, which is what religion is, has been revealed and established by the mediator Jesus Christ. "No one comes to the Father except through me" (Jn. 14:6–9). Christ's love for his disciples desires that God's love for him should extend to his own, and he accomplishes his desire by making his disciples dependent on the divine paternity (1:12), by making them begotten of the Father (17:26). The teaching and life of Jesus are summed up in his manifestation of God's true name—Father. His religion is a loving relationship between father and children, between God and the Word, between the Word and his adopted brothers, and between the Father and children.

St. John knows only one love, *agape*, unlike St. Paul and St. Peter, who also mention *philanthrōpia, chrēstotēs, philadelphia* and *philoxenia*. *Agape* is the love which God alone possesses and, consequently, with which he loves himself and in which he envelops his incarnate Son and all his children. He communicates his charity to them, so that Christ's disciples love God, Christ, and their brothers by a law of nature and not because they have been commanded to. Consequently, it is correct to say that *agape* is a reciprocal love. However, the reciprocity is first of all the relation of effect to cause, since it is God's charity in the Christian that returns to God and extends to neighbor. Besides, reciprocity or mutual exchange are not strong enough to express the intimacy of the *koinōnia* or, especially, the unity among the persons who love and are loved. Johannine *agape* is more than a link. *Agape* is God himself in whom the Christian is and lives. By love, the Christian participates in God and in his nature; consequently, it is he and his Son who love in the Christian. That is why to live in charity is the same thing as to live in Christ, as Christ lives in the Father and the Father in him.

The "theonomic" moral life, according to St. John, depends on this essential conviction. Since to live is to act, it reconciles in a marvelous harmony the double fundamental requirement of "living in God" and "acting in God." The

Christian's activity is in the line of the structure of his being. "We are born of God and his need is in us" (1 Jn. 3:9). By faith the disciple of Jesus Christ is removed from the kingdom of darkness and admitted to the light of life (Jn. 17:3). Clinging to the word made flesh, he has become a child of God (1:12) or a child of the light (12:36). The Christian life will be perseverance in this attitude of soul which is oriented toward Christ—or, rather, united with Christ, who is the way, *hodos* (14:6)—and faithful to the light, *en tōi phōti peripatōmen.*[38]

Practically speaking, walking in the Savior's footsteps according to his example [39] consists in fulfilling God's will and observing his commandment. It is called "walking in truth," *peripatein en agapēi* (2 Jn. 6) or *en alethēiai kai agapēi* (2 Jn. 3). Just as to hate is to be the son of the devil and walk in the darkness (1 Jn. 2:11; cf. 3:10–11), so to love is to behave as a son of God and walk in the light.

In short, St. John knows only two virtues which can animate the Christian life. More exactly, since faith is primarily the initial condition and fundamental decision, all the dynamism and fidelity of the Christian's actions are attributed to *agape*. Faith itself consists of "believing in love" (1 Jn. 4:16), and its conviction first arouses adherence to the divine will and then inspires conformity to it. Thus the precept or law is inherent in faith and not superimposed upon it. The unique normative principle is truly the love of God manifest in Jesus Christ. The Christian is confronted less with the task of determining his duties than with the necessity of understanding better and better the meaning and implications of *agape*. Johannine charity is life, overflowing richness, and fecundity (Jn. 15:4–11). All the disciple's "fruits" as well as his permanent "living in Christ" must be attributed to *agape*'s intensive nature. Unlike St. James, St. John tells very little about the details of Christian works. His panoply of virtues—*agathopoiein* (Jn. 5:29);

[38] 1 Jn. 1:6–7; cf. Jn. 8:12; 11:9–10; 12:35.
[39] 1 Jn. 2:3, 4, 6; 3:22, 24; 5:2.

poien tēn dikaiosynēn (1 Jn. 2:29; 3:7, 10)—is considerably poorer than that of the Synoptics, of Peter, and especially of Paul. Except for Apoc. 2:19, he has no "catalogue of virtues," no *Haustafeln,* and no traditional *topoi.*

This is not to say that for St. John the disciple is a pure contemplative or a mystic who is disinterested in morality. No one insisted more than St. John on the connection between the theological virtues and practical conduct. He is the specialist of observance. He knows no love except in "deed and truth" (1 Jn. 3:18), and he is the one who consecrated the meaning of *agape* as the manifestation and effective proof of love. However, St. John is more interested in the basic inspiration, the fundamental principles, and the main axes of the new morality than in the details of practical applications. No one had a greater sense of the hierarchy of values or of their synthesis. His great merit is to have organized the Christian ethic as a function of *agape* conceived as total gift of self. "We know what love is from the fact that Jesus Christ laid down his life for us. We, too, ought to lay down our lives for our brothers" (1 Jn. 3:16). Everything is in this statement. To love is to forget oneself, to give oneself without reserve, to sacrifice oneself.

This kind of heroism or sanctity, carried out in the variety of everyday circumstances, can come only from God. Therefore, just as St. Paul prayed without ceasing that divine charity might grow in the souls of the faithful, so St. John has only one desire, that we may share perfectly in God's *agape* and that his *agape* may act without impediment "in us and with us." All the rest follows of itself. There is no real danger on the way (*skandalon;* 1 Jn. 2:10–12). His commandments seem light (1 Jn. 5:3). Untouched by fear, our hearts are filled with the confidence and assurance (*parrēsia, tharsein*) of one who triumphs (1 Jn. 5:4). Our joy is complete (Jn. 15:11; 16:24); it is the very joy of the glorified Lord (14:28). The disciple in St. John has nothing taut or strained about him; he is calm and radiant and all on fire.

Such a psychology is understandable if "this love is a vital movement, a form of existence, an actualisation of God in this world." [40] It is understandable if God is charity and if he inspires the person who loves him and in whom he dwells. Truly, *agape* is everything. To know means to experience and to possess, and "everyone that loves is born of God and knows God" (1 Jn. 4:7).

[40] E. Stauffer, "*Agapaō, agapē,*" G. Kittel, *Theological Dictionary of the New Testament*, I, p. 53.

APPENDICES

The verb *philein* and its derivatives in the Synoptics

The verbs *eraō, stergō,* and their derivatives do not appear in the Synoptics; neither does the noun *philia.* However, the verb *phileō* is used eight times and the noun-adjective *philos* sixteen times. Fifteen of these uses are in St. Luke, who also has the only two examples of the noun *philēma.*[1] A brief account of these usages will be helpful in explaining the vocabulary of love in the Gospels.

The three synoptic writers conveyed faithfully the Savior's insistence on the hypocrisy of the Pharisees and the danger of their example. The sentence which Matthew inserts in the Sermon on the Mount, "And when you pray, do not be like the hypocrites, for they love (*philousin*) to pray standing in the synagogues or at street corners to attract the attention of their fellow-men" (Mt. 6:5), is developed under this form by the same Evangelist: "They love (*philousi*) the places of distinction at meals and front seats in the synagogues" (Mt. 23:6). Similarly, Luke 20:46 has, "Beware of Scribes, who fancy (*tōn thelontōn*) fine robes for outdoor wear, and crave (*philountōn*) ceremonious greetings in public places, and front seats in the synagogues, and places of honor at meals." It may be granted that in this case *philein* is a synonym of *agapan,* since *philoutōn* in this doublet of Luke replaces *agapate* in the exactly parallel passage of Lk. 11:43. However, we have shown that in this last text, the nuance of *agapaō* was somewhat special, corresponding to *thelō,* "To have a taste for, to take delight in," in Mk. 12:38, which was Luke's source. At any rate, the meaning is classical and has no theological significance.

Mk. 10:37 is more notable: "He who loves (*ho philōn*) father or mother more than me is not worthy of me." Since it is a question of choice or preference and of a love that

[1] Lk. 7:45; 22:48.

implies personal renunciation, *agapaō* would seem to have been a better choice than *phileō,* and a writer like St. Luke, who was careful about exact meanings, would undoubtedly have used it. However, the two verbs are not synonymous, because the choice and meaning of *phileō* are determined by its objects: father, mother, sons and daughters. It is a matter of family affection and of the attachment that arises from ties of blood which are so strong that they can even become an obstacle to entrance into the kingdom of heaven. Specifically, the Lord demands a religious love for his person, a devotion which surpasses all other bonds and is capable, if it should become necessary, of breaking them. Separation and sacrifice for the sake of adhering to the Lord arise from *agapan.* "The Lord urges that he be preferred to all human love. . . . God is to be loved before all else" (St. Thomas).

There are three texts in which *phileō* is used in the sense of "to kiss." When the Master was arrested in the Garden of Olives, Judas gave a signal: "The one I shall kiss, *hon an phileso,* that is the one. Arrest him." [2] The traitor carried out his plan to "approach Jesus to greet him with a kiss," *philēsai auton* (Lk. 22:47). Where Luke has *philēsai auton,* Mt. 26:49 and Mk. 14:45 have *katephilēsen auton.* Luke has avoided the verb which he always used in a tender, noble context.[3] That two witnesses of the scene should choose to use it seems to suggest the extent of Judas' gesture. Not content with giving Christ a kiss, he put his arms around him (cf. Acts 20:37) to point him out more clearly. Perhaps the traitor, sensing that Jesus understood him, wanted to disguise his treacherous intention by emphasizing a gesture of friendship. We might even suppose that as he embraced the Lord, Judas felt his soul hesitate as he experienced his first remorse. Frozen, he could not loosen his embrace for several moments.[4] Certainly, the Master made him realize

---

[2] Mt. 26:48; Mk. 14:44.   [3] Lk. 7:38, 45; 15:20.
[4] *Kataphilein* can have this triple meaning: to kiss tenderly, to clasp

the horror of his gesture. "Judas, with a kiss (*philēmati*) you betray the Son of Man." [5]

St. Luke liked to describe a man surrounded by friends who pay him the tribute of their affection, confidence, and, if need be, devotion. Friends will help out in necessity, because their gratitude can be trusted. They are invited to dinner with parents and neighbors, and they are honored by having a good place saved for them (Lk. 14:10, 12). Good meals are a pleasure only because friends are there (Lk. 15:29). The great joys of life are increased by being shared with *philoi* (15:6, 9).

These are the friends of the parables, as are the *hetairoi*. The centurion had sincere and devoted friends (7:6), and St. Luke notes that Pilate and Herod, who had not been on good terms, revived a more confident and cordial relationship after the trial of Jesus. "They became mutual friends again that very day" (Lk. 23:12). As for the Lord, his adversaries reproached him for his association with the disreputable publicans and sinners and for his sympathy with them—*philos telōnōn kai hamartōlōn* (7:34; cf. Mt. 11:19). According to the context and the other uses of *philos*, it must be understood that Jesus ate with them and did not hide his pleasure at being with them. His eating with them seems so habitual and accepted that it might be concluded that these people without morals constituted the social milieu preferred by the Savior. However, the Master lived day in and day out with a group of intimates who were even more dear to him. They were his apostles, and when he had to reveal to them the heavy trials they would have to undergo, his heart was moved and he could not help softening the cruelty of the future by revealing his tender attachment

---

in one's arms, to embrace over and over. According to Philo (*Quis rer. div.* 41), none of these demonstrations necessarily signifies a real affection.

[5] Lk. 22:48; cf. 7:45. The solemn designation "Son of man" emphasizes the sacrilegious character of the betrayal. Jesus is not only betrayed by a friend; the Messia is betrayed by one of the twelve!

for them: "I tell you, my friends (*philoi*), do not fear those
who kill the body and, that done, have no power to inflict
anything worse" (Lk. 12:4). *Philoi* here has its strict sense
of very close and dear friends. The depth of affection comes
from a life completely shared by those who love one
another. The twelve must share their Master's trials precisely because they are so closely united with him.

It is clear, then, that *philein* and *philos* are almost always
used in their profound sense by the Synoptics. They never
refer to God's love for men or men's love for God or to
the religious love of men for one another. The language of
the Synoptics, which was the expression of the Lord's revelation, had already fixed its vocabulary in function of the
epourania of the new Covenant. Various texts of the Sapien-
tial books may seem almost to equate *philein* and *agapan*,
but from the time of Jesus, the word *agapan* is strictly reserved to the love of charity.

"And who is my neighbor?"

The Evangelists never define "neighbor." When the Scribe asked the Lord, "And who is my neighbor?" *kai tis estin mou plēsion* (Lk. 10:29), the Master evaded the speculative question and showed through the parable of the good Samaritan that it is possible to draw near to anyone through love, even to a foreigner or a stranger. It is not forbidden, however, to try to make the notion of *plēsion*, "neighbor," more explicit, on condition that the attempt remain on the plane of language and usage and not seek a strict or a philosophical definition in the revealed text.

In speaking to the Scribe, Jesus referred to the precept of Leviticus 19:18: "Thou shalt love thy neighbor as thyself." In Hebrew the word "neighbor" is designated by *rê'a* and in the Septuagint by the adverb *plēsion* used as a noun. The Vulgate translates this incorrectly by the superlative *proximus*. However, the idea is certainly one of some spatial or temporal proximity: "in the neighborhood of" or "what is about to happen." In both cases "near" is opposed to "distant." In fact, in showering his kindnesses even on sinners, God shows himself good to those who are the most removed and the most dissimilar, those who differ the most from his sanctity. In the same way, the good Samaritan, in contrast with the priest and levite, drew near an unknown, wounded man who was nothing to him. This is the fundamental notion of biblical *plēsion*. Only the context can determine the degree of proximity of "the other" to the interested person.

In most cases, both Hebrew and the Septuagint use the word "neighbor" where we would say "another person" or simply "a being" in the most impersonal sense. Thus, for example, Ruth did not get up until it was light enough for one person to distinguish another (Ruth 3:14). *Ho plēsion* can be a synonym of *ho heteros*, then, and mean simply "someone else." This is the authenticated sense of most of the uses of the word in legislative texts forbidding injustices against "the neighbor" [1]—bearing false witness (Ex. 20:16), coveting a house,[2] taking the wife of "another." [3] It has this sense in establishing what should be done if one man's ox injures another's [4] or, especially, in anticipating the case of a man who hates his "neighbor" and kills him.[5] In all these instances, the "neighbor" has no bond or kinship or affection for the person concerned, who may be a stranger or even an enemy.

However, the precepts given in Exodus and Deuteronomy with regard to the *rêᶜa* are often formulated in an identical way in Leviticus with regard to the *ᶜâmît*, the *socius*, the "person-who-lives-with-one," the compatriot. The Septuagint translates this word, also, by *plēsion*.[6] When Leviticus 19:18 (cf. Sir. 28:7) prescribes love for neighbor, it designates neighbor by *rêᶜa*, but the commandment is parallel to another: "You will harbor no rancor against the children of your people," so that *plēsion* is explained as "the children of your people."

Proximity can refer to a smaller area than nationality; it may be based on neighborhood. In this case *ho plēsion* is synonymous with *ho geitōn* (Jer. 6:21). For the Passover, "If any household is too small for a sheep, it shall provide one along with its neighbor who is nearest to its own household," *ton geitona ton plēsion autou* (Ex. 12:4). "You must not move your neighbor's landmark, which the early inhabitants put in place." [7]

More often, "neighbor" is a passing companion or fellow-workers [8]—those who make bricks together (Gen. 11:3),

---

[1] 1 Kings 8:31; 2 Chr. 6:22.   [2] Ex. 20:17; Lev. 19:13; 20:10.
[3] Deut. 22:24; Ez. 18:6, 11, 15; 22:11; 33:26; cf. Lev. 18:20.
[4] Ex. 21:35; 22:8–14.
[5] Ex. 21:14, 18; Lev. 19:16; Deut. 19:4, 11; 22:26; Sir. 34:22.
[6] Lev. 18:20; 19:11, 13; 24:19; 25:14, 15, 17; cf. Ex. 2:13.
[7] Deut. 19:14; cf. 23:25, 27:17.
[8] Hab. 2:15; Sir. 6:17; 9:14; 10:6; 15:5.

woodcutters who fell trees together (Deut. 19:5), an employer and his employee (Jer. 22:13), the contracting parties to an agreement (Ruth 4:7), a creditor and his debtor,[9] two persons telling each other their dreams (Judges 7:13, 14). All these relationships are temporary and arise from the circumstances of social necessity.[10]

Plēsion has a genuinely affective value only when it refers to a friend; then it is a synonym of *philos*. After the episode of the golden calf when Moses said to the people, "Let each kill his brother, his friend, and his neighbor" (Ex. 32:27), he put "friend," *ton plēsion*, between "brother," *ton adelphon*, and "neighbor," *ton eggista*. The union of "neighbor" and "brother" is quite frequent [11] and was considered very close. Hatred and dissension are odious between those who ought to love one another: "They shall fight brother against brother and friend against friend" (Is. 19:2).

In making his own formulation of the precept of loving one's *rê'a*, Jesus wanted first of all to disengage the notion of "neighbor" from the notion of relationship of family, friendship, or nationality. He used the traditional term because it lent itself perfectly to this extension. It can actually mean anybody one meets or has some business with; "neighbor" is everybody else, even enemies. Like the good Samaritan, we must love the other person, whoever he is, as soon as we approach him. Liberated from its social and affective limitations, the biblical concept of *plēsion* becomes an absolute. In Christian language, "neighbor" is "everyman." "In all respects do to your fellow men exactly as you wish them to do to you. This, surely, is the gist of the Law and the Prophets" (Mt. 7:12).

The notion of *plēsion* is extended to the whole human race because it is henceforth intrinsically associated with *agapan*. In the Old Covenant, "neighbor" was considered from the point of view of justice, and the many precepts

[9] Deut. 24:10; Sir. 29:1, 2, 5, 14.   [10] Ps. 28:3; 45:15.
[11] Deut. 15:2; Ps. 15:3; 35:14; 38:11; 122:8.

determining duties toward neighbor were negative: do not harm another, do not wrong him or do evil to him. In promulgating the new morality as a function of the love of charity, the Lord necessarily affirmed the primacy of neighbor and formulated positive precepts about him, because *agape* is essentially generous. It is defined by both its object and its act—"the one who pitied him" (Lk. 10:37). It can be concluded, then, that according to the Gospel a "neighbor" is anyone to whom it is possible to do good. Furthermore, according to Mt. 5:43–48, the "other" is seen as already loved and blessed by the Father who is in heaven. We love him with *agape* in order to imitate and prolong the divine love he has received from the beginning. Finally, according to Mt. 25:31 ff., to the eyes of faith every person in need will forever represent the suffering humanity of Christ. The neuter *plēsion* of the Old Testament has become theological and Christological, we may say. That is why *plēsion* is exalted as the privileged object of the love of the sons of God and even more of their compassion. It is understandable, then, that in loving neighbor we love God, with whom we are united in the one will, one object, and one set of acts of *agape*, and we love Christ who is identified with our brothers (Mt. 10:40, 42). It is even explained that "proximity" with Jesus is established through charity.[12] According to the new revelation, *agape* draws men close to one another and unites them. Since it is always active, their union will never end.

[12] Mt. 12:50; Mk. 3:35; Lk. 8:21.

The origin of the triad: faith, hope, charity

The association, already made in the first epistle of the Pauline *Corpus*, of the virtues which Clement of Alexandria called "the sacred triad," *hē hagia trias* (*Strom.* 4:54), and which later came to be called "the theological virtues," [1] has led several historians to pose an aporia of literary criticism: what is the origin of the triad? Is the grouping a result of chance, a deliberate creation of St. Paul, or a borrowing from some unknown source? An adequate solution to such a problem would call—before any recourse was made to possible parallels—for reference to the mystique of numbers and to a definition of the psychological rules which govern the rhetorical development of a "formula." However, it is important to recall, first of all, that St. Paul has nothing in him of the stylist picking over his vocabulary and still less of the *comestor* plundering his contemporaries or copying from his predecessors. He is essentially a thinker, whose language must be interpreted more on the doctrinal plane than on the literary. When the Apostle chooses a particular word or expression, he always does so because of the notions he wants to express and not for the sake of the sound or the harmony of his phrase (2 Cor. 11:6).

In the present case, it would be impossible to overemphasize the fact that St. Paul's religious language depends primarily on the Septuagint, in which *agapan*, expressing both persevering love and religious fidelity, is associated several times with faith and hope. Moreover, in his own theology, the Apostle uses *pistis* to designate the fundamental attitude of soul attaching the Christian to the Savior and governing his entire moral life. Faith is completely impregnated with love. To adhere to Christ is not only to recognize his divinity but also to give oneself to him wholeheartedly

[1] 1 Thess. 1:3; 4:8.

and to consecrate one's life to him. Consequently, it is natural for St. Paul to have distinguished faith and charity as the two governing virtues which summarize the Christian life. Sometimes he reserves faith for relations with God and charity for love of neighbor;[2] other times he simply wants to emphasize the two major components of the new life.[3] The revelation of Christ had put *agape* in a unique position. There are thirteen passages in St. Paul's epistles where *pistis* is mentioned along with *agape*[4] without their mutual relationships being made clear.[5]

Moreover, the life of intimacy with the Lord is only sketched in here on earth; it presses on with hope toward the heavenly encounter. On the moral level, our present existence is nothing but waiting and faithful patience. Six different times St. Paul was led to associate faith with hope,[6] although in a less intrinsic way than he associated it with charity.

Two observations must be made about these groups of quotations. First, the virtues are not always listed in the same order. Faith is usually given before charity, but there are three cases where charity comes first.[7] Secondly, none of these statements is a stereotype. Even the shortest are not strictly identical with one another[8] and, consequently, do not correspond to any pre-established "formula," which might have been imposed by tradition, a borrowing from an authority, or a liturgical text. Furthermore, the groupings are not limited to just two virtues. To faith and charity are

---

[2] 2 Thess. 1:3; Eph. 6:23. In Philem. faith itself is associated with *agape* in fraternal service.

[3] 1 Thess. 3:6; Eph. 3:17; cf. 1 Tim. 2:15; 4:12.

[4] In chronological order they are: 1 Thess. 3:6; 2 Thess. 1:3; 1 Cor. 16:13–14; 2 Cor. 8:7; Gal. 5:6; Eph. 3:17, Eph. 6:23; Philem. 5; 1 Tim. 1:14; 1 Tim. 2:15; 1 Tim. 4:12; 2 Tim. 1:13; 2 Tim. 2:22; cf. 1 Pet. 1:8.

[5] With the exception of Gal. 5:6; Eph. 6:23; and still more vaguely 1 Cor. 16:13–14.

[6] 2 Thess. 1:4; Gal. 5:5; Rom. 4:8; Rom. 15:13; Col. 1:23; Tit. 1:1–2.

[7] Eph. 6:23, Philem. 5; 1 Tim. 4:12; cf. Rom. 15:13.

[8] 1 Thess 3:6; 2 Thess 1:3; Gal. 5:6; Philem. 5; 2 Tim. 1:13.

added peace,[9] justice,[10] zeal (2 Cor. 8:7), grace (1:14), purity (1 Tim. 4:12), and sanctification and prudence (1 Tim. 2:5). There are combinations of three (1 Tim. 1:14), four (1 Tim. 2:15; Tit. 1:1–2; 2 Tim. 2:22), five (2 Cor. 8:7; 1 Tim. 4:12), six (1 Tim. 6:11), and even nine (2 Tim. 3:10) virtues.

St. Paul liked to name faith and love or faith and hope together in the most varied contexts, combining them sometimes with still other qualities, and it was perfectly natural that he should be led to mention the three virtues together. In fact, he mentions the triad ten times [11] with an even greater freedom of expression than in the other formulae. Not only the order of the virtues but also their names vary.[12] Moreover, it was not only the pastoral epistles which added three or six other virtues to the "theological" virtues (1 Tim. 6:11; 2 Tim. 3:10), for Rom. 5:1–5 had already interpolated grace, peace, and patience. Finally, in 1 Thess. 1:3 and 4:18, the "triad" is mentioned only in terms of its works. Beginning with 1 Cor. 13:13 each virtue is exalted for itself. This is the major text and the equivalent of a catechism definition: "Now there remain these three, faith, hope and charity; and the greatest of these is charity."

According to these observations, then, this last formula is the outcome of a frequent and varied use of the terms "faith," "hope," and "charity." This kind of juxtaposition often happens in preaching. After having treated some theme of moral theology under the most diverse aspects, the preacher will arrive at a happy phrase which summarizes

[9] Eph. 6:23, 2 Tim. 2:22; cf. Rom. 15:13.

[10] 2 Tim. 2:22; cf. Gal. 5:5.

[11] Besides 1 Thess. 1:3; 4:8; cf. 1 Cor. 13:13; Rom. 5:1–5; Eph. 1:15–18; Eph. 4:2–5; Col. 1:4–5; 1 Tim. 6:11; Tit. 2:2; 2 Tim. 3:10; cf. Heb. 6:10–12; 10:22–24; 1 Pet. 1:21–22; and 1 Cor. 16:13–14 where *grēgoreite* is a precept of hope.

[12] *Elpis* in 1 Thess. 4:8; 1 Cor. 13:13; Rom. 5:1–5; Eph. 1:18; 4:2–5; Col. 1:4–5; *hypomonē* in 1 Thess. 1:3; 1 Tim. 6:11; Tit. 2:2; 2 Tim. 3:10.

and clarifies all he has previously said, making plain the hierarchy of values within a complex notion. From the beginning of his ministry St. Paul had presented the Christian life as the work of one or another of the "theological" virtues. Here he wanted to make it clear that these three virtues are the major ones among all the others and that charity is always supereminent. The definition is so clear and so unexpected that some commentators wonder whether it was original with St. Paul or was borrowed from some Christian or pagan source.

A. Resch holds firmly that the triad comes from the Lord himself.[13] As proof he quotes the beginning of a homily of the Egyptian monk St. Macarius (+ 392) *On Paradise*,[14] which says that this *logion agraphon* comes from Christ. Actually, this apophthegm is more than suspect. Macarius is a late and edifying author, who represents no personal, traditional authority. His vocabulary is as far removed as it is possible to be from the Gospel. Furthermore, his sentence appears to be a condensation of Christian doctrine; it is probably a reproduction of the common teaching of the primitive Church rather than a revelation of its source.

In 1913 Ed. Norden,[15] considering the manner of expression and the number of the words more than the thought, mentioned the relationship between the "triadic" Pauline formula and certain formulae of Hellenistic mysticism. The comparative method was at its height at that time, and R. Reitzenstein, taking up the suggestion a little while later,[16] discovered a parallel for 1 Cor. 13:13 in Porphyry, an author of the third century A.D.

[13] *Agrapha*, Leipzig, 1906, p. 155. It must be noted that A. Resch understands by *agrapha* not only the extraevangelical sentences of the Savior, but every fragment of a discourse or even of history given later as scriptural. Cf. L. Vaganay, art. *Agrapha* in DBS, I, col. 161–163.

[14] Hom. 37:PG. 34:749.

[15] *Agnostos theos*, Leipzig-Berlin, 1913, pp. 352–354.

[16] *Historia Monachorum und Historia Lausiaca. Eine Studie zur Geschichte der Mönchtums und der frühchristlichen Begriffe Gnostiker und Pneumatiker*, Göttingen, 1916, pp. 100–102.

There are four first principles that must be upheld concerning God—faith, truth, love, hope. We must have faith that our only salvation is in turning to God. And having faith, we must strive with all our might to know the truth about God. And when we know this, we must love him we do know. And when we love him we must nourish our souls on good hopes for our life, for it is by these good hopes that good men are superior to bad ones. Let then these four principles be firmly held.[17]

Does this series of four elements—faith, truth, love, hope—permit us to believe that an analogous formula of the *stoicheia* of "the interior man" was current in Corinth two centuries earlier? Reitzenstein thinks so. Saint Paul could have used this hypothetical formula with a polemical intention, substituting *agape* for *erōs* and suppressing *alētheia*, which had too many Gnostic overtones. Finally, "there remain Faith, Love, and Hope, these three (and only these three)."

Hypotheses so gratuitous and unlikely could not go unanswered. A. von Harnack immediately pointed out six things: [18] 1) The improbability of a Pauline borrowing from pagan mysteries; 2) The anachronism and paradox of the reference. If there were a borrowing, it could only have been Porphyry's borrowing from Paul and not Paul's from Porphyry. The preacher of the Gospel could not have borrowed from a successor, who had had to be first informed of Christian doctrine. 3) The inexactness of the parallel. With Porphyry the "four elements which refer to God" are developed successively, whereas "the three" of Paul are simultaneous. 4) The psychological impossibility in the presupposition that common persons, slaves, and women knew a "current expression" of neo-Platonic literature and philosophy. 5) The frequency of the triad in the other Pauline epistles, which Reitzenstein seems to overlook. 6) Although

[17] Porphyry, *To Marcella*, 24, trans. Alice Zimmern (London, George Redway, 1896), p. 71.
[18] "Über den Ursprung der Formel 'Glaube, Liebe, Hoffnung'" in *Preussiche Jahrb.* 1916, pp. 1–14, reprinted in *Aus der Friedens-und Kriegsarbeit*, Giessen, 1916, pp. 3–18.

v. 13 seems poorly connected with the context, it is simply a recalling of a doctrine which was well known to the converts and often repeated in Pauline preaching. On the positive side, Harnack believes with good reason that Paul arrived at "forging the triadic formula" through the combination of the pairs "faith and charity" and "faith and hope," in such a way that there can be no doubt about the truly Christian origin and creation of the three fundamental virtues. A thorough investigation of the "erotic," pre-Christian literature leads to the same conclusion. There is no affective or religious triad there, even when words are used which are more or less closely related to Paul's words. "Faith, hope and charity" are as proper to the new religion as "Father, Son, and Holy Spirit" and "Our Father."

Despite the rejection of his theory, Reitzenstein reaffirmed his judgment as pure philologist many times and at length, and his originality and subjectivism led him to many an astounding conclusion.[19] For example, he says that faith, charity, and hope—he prefers this sequence—cannot represent Christian ideas, since *agape* and *elpis*, hope, which he arbitrarily distinguishes from *hypomenē*, are not found in the Synoptics. Moreover, he says that the pairs "faith and charity" and "faith and hope" are not true formulae. After analyzing many religious dyads or triads in the New Testament or in primitive Christian texts, R. retains only a very few which he says are true "formulations," and this because they were influenced by non-Christian models which arose more from popular thought than from philosophical systems. The only authentic formulation in the Pauline corpus, he says, is 1 Cor. 13:13, which is related to a "Hellenistic system" of four "forces," reduced by the Apostle to three. Instead of being dependent on *gnōsis*, these forces are henceforth subject to *agape*. Certainly, each philologist is free to decide the categories of his analysis and to choose his own

---

[19] "Die Formel 'Glaube, Liebe, Hoffnung' bei Paulus" in *Nachrichten von der königlichen Gesellschaft der Wissenschaften zu Göttingen Philologische-historische Klasse*, 1916, pp. 367–416.

vocabulary. R. has the right, then, to distinguish *Freie Verbindungen* or *Quasi-Formeln* and *Echte Formeln*, and, strictly speaking, one can agree that 1 Cor. 13:13 belongs in this last category. But how can one not see that the constant interplay of the relationships faith-hope, faith-charity, faith-charity-hope, was bound to lead to the stabilizing of the grouping and hierarchy of the three virtues, a stabilizing which came very naturally at the end of the only development in which *agape* is exalted for itself? The contrary is what would have been surprising. There is no need to resort to profane parallels to explain the formulation. All that is necessary is to follow the vital evolution of a doctrine which seeks its own internal coherence and adequate expression. Its evolution will necessarily lead to precisions first in the notions involved and then in the terminology which expresses them. Finally, R. concentrates his entire interest on 1 Cor. 13 and neglects both the importance of the first triad (1 Thess. 1:3) and its later reappearances. 1 Cor. 16:13–14, for example, may not correspond to the canon of "formula-type," but it nevertheless expresses the fundamental Christian attitude under the dominion of charity perfectly.

Undaunted, Reitzenstein took up his thesis a last time in his great work on the mystery religions.[20] He pushed it to the extreme, for he noted the evolution of an originally Iranian formula of five elements into the Hellenistic type with four elements which was then reduced by Philo and St. Paul to a triad. St. Paul's intention of arguing against his adversaries in Corinth shows clearly, R. says, that the pagans themselves could understand as divine forces faith, love (*erōs, agapē*), truth, knowledge.

Approval for this erudition was not lacking. In particular, J. Geffcken[21] furnished new texts of the same Coptic-Gnostic and Manichean type. H. Lietzmann declared it impossible that the strongly circumscribed trinity—faith,

[20] *Die hellenistischen Mysterienreligionen*[3], Leipzig-Berlin, 1927, pp. 383–393.
[21] *Der Ausgang des griechisch-römischen Heidentums*, Heidelberg, 1920, pp. 271–272.

hope, charity—should have been created by St. Paul. In virtue of the parallels mentioned above, he conceived of the
agape of 1 Cor. 13:13 "as a spiritual fluid poured into us." [22]
R. Bultmann, although he rejects certain invalid parallels,
explained that St. Paul was combating a formula of Gnostic
origin in which *gnosis* was seen as a divine force which, in
union with other forces (faith, hope, charity), constituted
the spiritual man. *Gnosis* was the foundation of his immortal
nature. St. Paul rejected the description of these entities as
dynameis (or *stoicheia*) and he removed *gnōsis* from them.
Finally, W. Theiler, after having noted the "strong bond"
between the expressions of 1 Cor. 13:2—*pistis, gnōsis, agapē*
—and of Porphyry, *Ad Marc.* 23—*therapeia theou*—goes
on to gather and compare the sparse references to *pistis,
elpis, agapē* (*erōs*) from among the most dissimilar neo-
Platonicians: Philo, Posidonius, Proclus, Jamblicus, Dio
Chrysostom, etc.[23]

The accumulation of texts and verbal analogies is always
impressive and even intoxicating, at least if one is not too
particular about the chronology of the quotations or the
psychology of the authors or, in the present case, even about
the existence of Corinthian Gnosticism in the middle of the
first century. C. Clemen has shown that Reitzenstein's thesis
was nothing but a succession of hypotheses. He grants that
pistis and *elpis* are used in 1 Cor. 13:13 in a sense somewhat
different from their usual meanings, but, returning to the
essential, he denies that Reitzenstein has furnished any proof
that Paul borrowed from an earlier "formula." [24] He refers
to Wettstein, who had already cited literary parallels to *ta
tria tauta*, "these three," and shows that they could not be
understood as signifying "*only* these three" without violence being done to the texts. Even if this were the nuance,

[22] *An die Korinther*², I–II, Tübingen, 1922, pp. 68–69.
[23] *Die Vorbereitung des Neuplatonismus, Problemata* (Forschungen
zur klassichen Philologie, 1), Berlin, 1930, pp. 147–153.
[24] *Religionsgeschichtliche Erklärung des Neuen Testament*², Giessen, 1924, pp. 328–330.

it would not follow that Paul was engaging in polemic and trying to reduce a formula of four terms to a formula of three. Not only is it not established, but also it remains highly unlikely that the Apostle would have known a Manichean or Gnostic formula and still less likely that he would have used it. For his part, R. Schütz notices the arbitrariness of the suppression of *agape* in Lk. 11:42 and Mt. 24:12. His special merit is to have recalled that the appearance of the triad in 1 Cor. 13:13 poses no real problem if it is related to the language of the Septuagint and to the religious conceptions of Rabbinism.[25] E. von Dobschutz makes a positive contribution to the discussion in studying the psychological and linguistic process of the development of binary and ternary formulae in the New Testament.[26]

Consequently, an extra-biblical explanation of 1 Cor. 13: 13 is superfluous. To look for one would be barking up the wrong tree, as the proverb says. Therefore, E. B. Allo judges correctly that the triad, which goes back to the earliest times of the Church if not to Jesus himself, is the fruit of the essence of Christian life and experience.[27] Both the way the triad is introduced and its mention in 1 Thess. 1:3 and 5:8 show that this grouping of virtues was well known to the faithful and already consecrated at Corinth by time and custom. Consequently, it was not forged by St. Paul during the Corinthian controversy.

If one desires to understand the language and vocabulary of St. Paul in terms of contemporary literature, the theological "triad" and the lists of virtues in the New Testament should be considered a customary device of style in the Hellenistic diatribe. Often even the vocabulary of these lists appears dependent on the terminology of popular moral phi-

[25] "Der Streit zwischen A. v. Harnack und R. Reitzenstein über die Formel 'Glaube, Liebe, Hoffnung', I Kor. XIII, 13," *Theologische Literaturzeitung*, 1917, col. 454–457.

[26] "Zwei—und dreigliedrige Formeln. Ein Beitrag zur Vorgeschichte der Trinitätsformel," *Journal of Biblical Literature*, 1931, pp. 117–147.

[27] *Saint Paul. Première Épître aux Corinthiens*. Paris, 1934, pp. 351–353.

losophy, even when their meanings were profoundly altered. J. Dupont, after making a minute literary analysis of the Pauline lists, concluded that *agape* is the echo of a truly Christian theology,[28] unlike *gnōsis*, which was inserted among the virtues under the influence of Judaism. Its excellence and primacy are not mentioned in any of the known documentation. *Cuique suum*. Neither Hellenism nor Judaism inspired St. Paul in the "determination" of this fundamental point of doctrine. The teaching and the life of the Lord, especially in the Sermon on the Mount, and the fruit of the Holy Spirit in the soul of the converts (Gal. 5:22) are all abundant and fruitful sources well able to account for the formula "faith, hope, charity, these three things" and for its many applications in the Pauline epistles.

[28] *Gnosis. La Connaissance religieuse dans les Épîtres de Saint Paul.* Louvain, Paris, 1949, pp. 379–417.

APPENDIX IV

Benignity

It is very difficult for anyone who reads the New Testament today to grasp the depth and variation in meaning of terms which express some moral quality. For one thing, the context does not often allow their exact meaning to be determined; for another, these words which were assumed into the sacred language had a wide gamut of extremely varied meanings in their profane uses. What nuance is correct in a particular passage of the Gospels or of St. Paul? The problem arises for *chrēstos-chrēstotēs*, particularly, which St. Paul liked so much to use, and even more for *chrēsteuesthai*, which appears only once in the Bible in 1 Cor. 13:4. These terms have such an affinity with *agape* that the theologian of charity is obliged to define them as clearly as possible. How did the first Christians understand them?

For a Corinthian of the first century the terms *chrēstos-chrēstotēs* meant first of all the "good quality" of things, either in the sense of usefulness, something that could be used, or, if it described food, something that was healthful or agreeable to the taste. From these meanings *chrēstos* came to describe good news or a happy outcome, as well as a favorable judgment or a profitable counsel. Later the adjective and the noun were used in a moral sense with a triple meaning. First they were a designation pure and simple of virtue, whether they described a good master, a good citizen, or good behavior. Then they became an expression of integrity, with the nuances of bravery, loyalty, nobility and honor. In this sense, *chrēstos* is a designation of excellence and *chrēstotēs* is an honorific title of state etiquette. Finally, the accent came to be on that which renders service, and *chrēstos* meant "obliging, kind, attentive." This moral sense, which was very common, conveys the liberality of the good

215

<u>person</u>, from the devotion of a slave to the aid given by beneficent gods. Benignity is especially a manifestation of disinterested benevolence composed of gentleness or mercy. It is the birthright of magnanimous hearts; it is the virtue of the great Lord. When St. Paul uses *chrēstos* and *chrēstotēs* together with the *agape* of God or the Christians,[1] he must intend to convey th<u>is meaning of generous and spontane</u>ous <u>kindness, but</u> in 1 Cor. 13:4, the nuances of virtue strictly <u>speaking, magnanimity and honor, are not absent</u>, and the readers of the Epistle were surely aware of them. St. Paul, nourished by the Septuagint, undoubtedly recognized a more complex meaning in the word, however, a meaning for which we must now look.

<u>Hebrew vocabulary</u> is very poor, especially in words expressing abstract notions, and it had only one word to con<u>vey the idea of kindness</u>, *tôb*. By taking the context into consideration, the Alexandrine translators specified the nuance of *tôb* and translated it about thirty-eight times by *chrēstos, chrēstotēs*, which from then on assumed a moral and religious meaning. When the adjective refers to human kindness, it <u>qualifies kindness with exquisiteness</u> and brings out the many elements it contains when it is perfect—benevolence, affability, <u>gentleness, obligingness, service</u>, devotion. The <u>Vulgate understood it in this</u> way and often translated *chrēstos* by <u>dulcis</u> and <u>suavis</u>, and *chrēstotēs* by *dulcedo* and *benignitas*. This last translation is particularly happy if it is true that *benignus* is derived from *bonus* and *gignendus* and, according to etymology, means "good-natured."

Applied to things, benignity refers to their quality, utility, and especially their sweetness. Jer. 24:2, 3, 5 speaks of baskets of "good" figs—excellent, ripe, or sweet and sugary figs in contrast to very bad and inedible ones. When it is applied to human beings in a figurative sense, therefore,

[1] 2 Cor. 6:6; Gal. 5:22; Eph. 2:4–7; 4:32–35:2; Col. 3:12–14.

benignity must make the same kind of impression on the mind and heart of others that sugar and honey make on the taste. Benignity is not an entirely interior feeling; it tends to manifest itself and render service. Beneficence is an essential part of benignity, under the special mode of humaneness, gentleness, indulgence, or condescendence.

That is why the Old Testament assigns benignity to God as his special attribute. In himself and in his name, in his favors and in his commandments, Yahweh in his person and his works is *chrēstos*. He eminently possesses a benevolent and helpful kindness. From the Psalmist [2] and Nahum (1:7) to the Book of Wisdom (15:1) and the priests of the Maccabean period (2 Macc. 1:24), all proclaim that the kindness of the God of Israel is particularly sweet and helpful. They ask that Yahweh be praised, blessed, celebrated, and thanked because of his benignity; [3] that the divine sweetness be contemplated and tasted (Ps. 34:9); and that his people, assured of God's loving welcome and sweet kindness, [4] approach him and pray to him. Because Yahweh is all benignity, we must trust him (Ps. 52:11), rely on his Providence, [5] beg for his help, seek refuge with him in the day of distress (Nah. 1:7), listen to his prescriptions, and obey his decrees (Ps. 119:39, 68).

If God's transcendence, omnipotence and holiness are the object of "the fear of God" and of worship, the just man also remembers in his prayer the marks of the divine kindness which he has received. The memory of these favors aroused the admiration and enthusiasm of the Psalmist: "How great is thy benignity which thou hast in store for those who fear thee" (Ps. 31:20). "Thou didst prepare in thy benignity for the poor, O God" (Ps. 68:11). "Thou crownest the year with thy benignity and thy paths drip fatness" (Ps. 65:12). "They shall publish the memory of thy great benignity" (Ps. 145:7). The pious soul comes to

[2] Ps. 25:8; 119:68; 145:9.
[3] Ps. 100:5; 106:1; 107:1; 136:1; Jer. 33:11; Dan. 3:89.
[4] Ps. 69:17; 86:5; 109:21.   [5] Ps. 109:21; cf. 51:20; 25:7.

know the divine *chrēstotēs* through the generous manifestations of God's tender love.

God's generous kindness is sometimes associated with his uprightness (Ps. 25:8), his fidelity (Wisd. 15:1), his power (2 Macc. 1:24), and especially with his mercy. Because the relation of God to man is that of creator to creature, master to servant, and holy one to sinner, every manifestation of the divine love for man is a mercy. Pity is an essential part of biblical *chrēstotēs*. "Thou hast treated thy servant with benignity, O Lord" (Ps. 119:65). The good God is compassionate to all his creatures, but especially to those who call upon him.[6] The exhortation is chanted unceasingly: "Praise the Lord, for he is benignity, his mercy is everlasting."[7] The parallel construction shows that *chrēstotēs* and *eleos* are synonymous, and it can be said with equal correctness that God's benignity is merciful or that his mercy is all benignity.[8] Finally, the divine perfection is described by four attributes which express a single disposition of heart: God is "compassionate, merciful, slow to anger, and rich in kindness."[9] The prophet could exhort the Israelites to return to Yahweh their God, for he is propitious and reserves a favorable welcome for them. The fundamental notion of biblical benignity includes all these notions—delicate goodness and exquisite kindness which manifest themselves above all in loving, eager welcome. This is exactly the same attitude as is expressed by *agapān*, verb of gracious and generous hospitality.

This benevolent, helpful kindness is very suitable for men who are in a position to help their neighbors by lending them money without interest (Ps. 112:5), especially the rich, and even more for rulers, who have greater means and more frequent occasions for magnanimity. They are more able to imitate the generous benignity of God. It is striking that nearly all the characteristics of benignity proper to

---

[6] Ps. 86:5; 145:9; Wisd. 15:1.   [7] Ps. 100:5; 106:1; 107:1; 136:1.
[8] Ps. 69:17; 109:21.
[9] Ex. 34:6; Ps. 86:15; 103:8; 145:8; Joel 2:13.

princes which the Old Testament records express a benevolent, generous welcome. Thus the Babylonian king, Evil-Marodach, treated King Jehoiachin with benignity, speaking to him kindly and providing for his support. The chancellor of state, Heliodorus, was received cordially by the high priest of the city when he arrived at Jerusalem.[10] On his deathbed, Antiochus Epiphanius declared that he had always treated his subjects with benignity (1 Macc. 6:11), and he recognized that they had shown him unmistakable signs of good will (2 Macc. 9:21). Whether it refers to God, princes, or the most humble man, *chrēstotēs* always has the two characteristics of kindness and liberality, of warm welcome and generous beneficence. *Chrēstotēs* is a love of well-wishing that proves itself in works which display charm and tact, urbanity and delicacy, always right for the circumstances.

In the New Testament as well as in the Old, benignity is a divine attribute and an aspect of mercy.[11] Rom. 11:22 contrasts the severity of the God who punishes (*apotomia*) with his benignity toward those who have remained faithful. As in the Psalms, Rom. 2:4 associates *chrēstotēs* and *makrothymia:* "Do you despise the wealth of his benignity, patience, and long-suffering? Do you not know that God's benignity is meant to lead you to repentance?" The sinner is importuned by *chrēstotēs*, which is full of pity; it is inclined to pardon and leads him (*se agei*) to the welcome of reconciliation.

One of the innovations of Pauline theology was to conceive the entire plan of salvation in function of the benignity of God, who is not only benevolent and merciful but also helpful and effectively active. It was in order to show throughout the ages to come the overflowing riches of the grace springing from his benignity to us in Christ Jesus, that God, who is rich in mercy, was moved by the intense love with which he loved us and made us live with the life of Christ; he raised us up together with Christ Jesus and

[10] 2 Mach. 3:9. Cf. Acts 28:7. [11] Lk. 6:35; 1 Pet. 2:3.

enthroned us in the heavenly realm (Eph. 2:7). The same idea is repeated in Tit. 3:4: When the goodness and kindness of God our Savior toward all mankind was manifested (*epephanē*) by the birth of Jesus, we were saved in virtue of his mercy. According to the context, *chrēstotēs* has a special nuance of pity for the deplorable state of humanity described in v. 3. This compassion is more than a simple feeling in the heart; it is active and decrees the means of remedying the unfortunate situation. It decides to send a Savior. Christ is the living expression of the divine benignity; he is its incarnation. His life on earth was an "epiphany" of some thirty-five years of gentle, merciful, beneficent kindness—the tender welcome he gave to indiscreet crowds (Lk. 9:11) and repentant sinners (Lk. 7:37–50); the invitation he addressed to tired and heavily burdened hearts (Mt. 11:28); the pardon he granted the good thief (Mt. 27:38); the predilection he showed for the poor; the miracles he worked for the sick and the disabled; his pity for all distress.[12] *Chrēstotēs* is surely Christ's dominant trait and the best summary of his ministry.

Consequently, it is self-evident that the criterion which distinguishes the authentic apostle, the apostle who is the messenger of divine salvation and the witness to Jesus Christ, can only be benignity. We recommend ourselves as God's ministers, writes St. Paul, "in long-suffering, in benignity . . . in unaffected love" (2 Cor. 6:6). "In," *en*, means "by means of"; it is a Hebraism for the simple Greek dative used to express the feeling which inspires an action. The whole passage shows that the patient, benign behavior of the preacher of the gospel is simply a concrete manifestation of the divine charity. The Apostle's *chrēstotēs* gives, as it were, a human face to God's invisible *agape*.

Since Christians are sons of God, they must resemble their Father, and from the moment of the Sermon on the Mount the Master had demanded that his disciples love their neighbor in imitation of the benignity of God (Lk. 6:35).

[12] Mt. 14:14; 15:32; 20:34; Lk. 7:13; 10:33.

St. Peter mentions the trait of sonship (1 Pet. 2:3), but it is St. Paul, especially, who described the most expressive form of *agape* as *chrēstotēs*. In all the Churches—the Corinthian, the Galatian, the Ephesian, the Colossian—he asked the faithful to give proof of a perfect benignity. "As God's chosen ones, holy and well beloved, clothe yourselves with sentiments of compassion, kindness, humility, meekness, long-suffering. Bear with one another and forgive whatever grievances you have against each other . . . just as the Lord has forgiven you" (Col. 3:12). These terms are complementary and explain each other. Fraternal *chrēstotēs* presupposes a tender, pitying heart; merciful within, it willingly and smilingly pardons the wrongs or even the injuries it has suffered; patient, it knows nothing of revenge. All these responses, which would be impossible without humility to accentuate the note of sweetness and unalterable gentleness, are proper to Christians who are the objects and beneficiaries of the divine charity (*ēgapēmenoi*). Those who have received the grace and gifts of God's love ought to manifest them in turn to their brothers. The benignity of "the elect" is not just any kind of goodness; it is the very kindness of God participated in and reproduced by his "beloved."

Eph. 4:32 repeats: "Be kind to one another, and merciful, generously forgiving one another, as also God in Christ has generously forgiven you. Therefore, follow God's example, as his very dear children, and walk in love." To live in *agape* is to participate in God's love and consequently to show one's neighbor the tender, merciful benignity which characterizes truly divine charity. It presupposes a naturally gentle and sensitive temperament which is capable of feeling with real emotion (*eusplagchnoi*) the evils that happen to someone else; It also requires an appropriate ascesis, especially the perfect receptivity to grace which softens the heart and assimilates it to the heart of Christ, full of pity for sinners. In all the texts, *chrēstotēs* appears as the human expression of infused love. St. Paul had already opposed the fruit of the Holy Spirit to the works of the flesh: "It is charity, joy, peace (with one's neighbor), long-suffering, affability, goodness, fidelity, gentleness, self-control" (Gal. 5:22).

In order to understand what St. Paul meant by *chrēsteuetai hē agapē*, "love is kind" (1 Cor. 13:4), it is necessary to take all these texts into consideration. The verb *agapan* already signified a delicate welcome, affectionate care, and the signs of tenderness one shows a guest or very dear friend. To add that charity is kind is undoubtedly to emphasize the fact that it participates in the gentleness of the divine love, but, more, it is to strengthen singularly its nuance of sweetness and delicacy. According to St. Paul, a Christian should create an impression of charm and attractiveness. When the believer finds himself in some connection with his neighbor, he is predisposed in his favor from the beginning; he is ready to make allowances; he welcomes him graciously and is smiling and affable. He shows the joy he experiences at their meeting, listens patiently, and responds gently, so that the whole conversation is, as it were, impregnated with sweetness in the sense that this word is used of perfumes and colors which make a sweet and pleasant impression on the senses. *Christi bonus odor sumus!*

Both *agape* and *chrēstotēs* imply exterior manifestation and generosity. Benignity is more than a benevolent disposition; it includes willingness and liberality as essential parts. The charitable man shows himself eager to oblige his neighbor, to be "useful" to him, and to spend himself in his service. St. Jerome described these two characteristics. "Benignity or sweetness—the Greek *chrēstotēs* has both meanings —is a gentle virtue, caressing, tranquil, disposed to share all its goods. It invites entrance into its familiarity; it is sweet in its word and measured in its conduct. In short, the Stoics defined it as a virtue spontaneously disposed to beneficence. Goodness properly so-called (*agathosyne*) is not very far removed from benignity, for it too is disposed to beneficence. But it differs from it in that goodness can be a little somber and furrow its brow with an austere morality, doing good, no doubt, and giving what is asked of it, but without being sweet in its relationships or attracting the world by its sweetness.[13]

Thus, by *chrēstotēs* the invisible divine charity which lives in the soul of the Christian becomes plain to everyone, gives the Christian new features, and imparts a new style to his life. It is marvelous that this trait was so exactly reproduced by all the members of the primitive Church, who modeled themselves so successfully after the image of their Savior that the pagans exclaimed, "See how they love one another."[14] They pronounced the name "Christian" not *christianoi* but *chrēstianoi*.[15] It could be said of each one of them, "*Apparuit benignitas Salvatoris nostri Dei!*"

[13] *In Gal.* 5:22 (PL 26:420).   [14] Tertullian, *Apol.* 39.
[15] *De suavitate vel benignitate compositum* (ibid. 3:5; cf. *Ad Nat.* 1:3).

APPENDIX V

Philein and the other terms for love in the Acts and the Epistles of the New Testament

The verb *philein* appears eighteen times in the Gospels,[1] only twice in St. Paul, and not at all in the other epistles. It can be concluded, then, that this verb does not belong to the language of the primitive catechesis, or at least that it was supplanted by *agapan* in preaching to the communities whose language was Greek.

In signing his first letter to the Corinthians in his own handwriting, St. Paul set down an imprecation: "If anyone loves, *philei*, not the Lord, let him be accursed" (1 Cor. 16: 22). At first the reader is surprised and even a little disturbed that the epistle which is the theological place of fraternal charity should close with a curse. It is true that *agape* includes horror of evil as well as attachment to good (Rom. 12:9) and that this is not the first time the Apostle had thundered out an anathema,[2] but could a loving Father leave his small children[3] with such a heavy threat? Our astonishment grows when we notice the unusual use of *philein* in a religious formula, when all the parallel texts have the verb *agapan*.[4] Possibly the choice of *philei* was influenced by the word *philēmati* in the preceding verse. However, and especially if we take this possible influence into account, *philein* expresses primarily the interior sentiment of affection, the familiar union between two friends, not adoration, veneration, and the total belonging of the disciple to his Lord. We would expect its object in this verse to be "Jesus" rather than "the Lord." In this text, therefore, it is preferable to consider *philein* a synonym of *agapan*, and since the for-

[1] Ten uses are in the fourth Gospel; cf. in addition Apoc. 3:19; 22:15.
[2] Rom. 9:3; 1 Cor. 12:3 (cf. 5:1–5); Gal. 1:8.   [3] 1 Cor. 3:1; 4:14.
[4] 1 Cor. 2:9; 8:3; 1 Jn. 4:20; cf. Rom. 8:28 (vv. 35, 39); Eph. 6:24; 2 Tim. 4:8.

mulation of the verse is foreign to St. Paul's vocabulary, it is probably a quotation from some other source.

In 1926 E. Peterson demonstrated that the final anathema of 1 Cor. reproduces an ancient liturgical formula and resembles the *Didache*, 10:6; "May Grace come . . . If anyone is holy, let him advance; if anyone is not, let him be converted; Marana tha. Amen." (*elthetō charis . . . ei tis hagios estin, erchesthō; ei tis ouk esti, metanoeitō, maranatha, amēn.*[5]) G. Bornkamm, in his turn, observing that *philein ton Kyrion* is not a Pauline expression, pointed out the eucharistic terminology of Heb. 6:6; 13:10–15 and in particular the parallel of Apoc. 22:15–19 *hexo hoi kynes* ("outside are dogs") . . . *ho dipsōn erchesthō* ("let him who thirsts come") . . . *erchou kyrie Iēsou* ("come Lord Jesus").[6] Meanwhile, K. M. Hofmann recognized in the "holy kiss"[7] a rite of introduction to the Last Supper and concluded that the four elements of 1 Cor. 16:20–23: *philēma, anathema, marantha,* and the call to grace (v. 23) reflect the liturgy of the eucharist.[8] J. A. T. Robinson,[9] who curiously overlooks all his predecessors,[10] and K. G. Kuhn[11] understood the pericope in the same way.

Even if a particular argument of these authors or the eucharistic character of the whole pericope is rejected, it must be admitted, at least, that v. 22 is a quotation transcribed from the Aramaean and coming from the first Palestinian communities. The studies of A. Lemonnyer[12] and

---

[5] E. Peterson, *Eis Theos*, Göttingen, 1926, pp. 130 ff.

[6] G. Bornkamm, "Das Anathema in der urchristlichen Abendmahlsliturgie" in *Theologische Literaturzeitung*, 1950, col. 227–230, reprinted in *das Ende des Gesetzes*, Munich, 1952, pp. 123–132.

[7] 1 Cor. 16:20; cf. 1 Thess. 5:27; 2 Cor. 13:12; 1 Pet. 5:14.

[8] K. M. Hofmann, *Philema Hagion*, Gütersloh, 1938, pp. 23–26.

[9] J. A. T. Robinson, "Traces of a liturgical sequence in 1 Cor. 16: 20–24," *The Journal of Theological Studies*, 1953, pp. 38–39.

[10] E. Käsemann, "Sätze heiligen Rechtes im Neuen Testament," *New Testament Studies*, 1955, pp. 250 ff.; G. Bornhamm and Lietzmann, *Messe und Herrenmahl*, 1926, p. 229.

[11] Art. *maranatha* in G. Kittel, *Th. Wört*, IV, 470–475.

[12] A. Lemonnyer, *Theologie du Nouveau Testament*, Paris, 1928, pp. 151–161.

especially those of L. Cerfaux [13] have shown that the title
of Lord (*Maran, Kyrios*), which commonly described the
reigning sovereign in the protocol of the Syro-Hellenic
royalties, was applied from the beginning to Jesus, the Messia king, particularly by St. Peter at Jerusalem: "Therefore,
let all Israel know most assuredly that God has made him
both Lord (*Kyrion*) and Christ." [14] To affirm that "the
Lord" has come or that he is there is to make an essential
profession of faith in the person of Jesus, to submit to his
sovereign authority, and, consequently, to be inscribed in
the community of his disciples—like a soldier in the army
of his leader—or to be inserted into this religious society
which "invokes the name of the Lord." [15]

The liturgical meetings of the Church of Corinth included
charismatic manifestations, the celebration of the eucharist,
and occasionally the reading of an "epistle" of the Apostle. [16]
It sometimes happened there that certain converts were once
again seized by their former satanic or pathological inspiration and went so far as to cry *"Anathema Iēsous!"* (1 Cor.
12:3). St. Paul must have felt the horror of such a blas-
phemy, which, like all sacrilege, provoked the jealousy of
God (1 Cor. 10:22), and he curbed it by a juridical or
ritual formula which was already current: "Whoever curses
Jesus will be cursed by him" or, more exactly, "whoever
does not love the Lord." The negative form suggests more
than the simple absence of love; it is a litotes, analogous to
"I do not know you," which expresses rejection and repro-
bation. [17] Consequently, "whoever does not love the Lord"
suggests more than lack of warmth and gratitude; it expresses antipathy and positive opposition. The complement,
"The Lord," conveys the real horror of such a refusal of

[13] *Recueil Lucian Cerfaux*, Gembloux, 1954, pp. 3–188.

[14] Acts 2:36; cf. 1:3, 6, 22, etc.

[15] Acts 9:14–21; 22: 16; 1 Cor. 1:2; 2 Tim. 2:28.

[16] O. Cullmann, *Le Culte dans l'Eglise primitive*, Neuchâtel-Paris,
1944.

[17] Lk. 13:27; cf. Mt. 25:12; 1 Cor. 16:12; 2 Thess. 2:10.

love. It may be concluded, then, that the verb *philein* translates the Hebrew *'âhab* and signifies, exactly as *agapan* does,
adoration and religious consecration of the believer to his
God. It is almost a tautology to write: Whoever refuses
to belong to Christ—in Christian language, "whoever does
not love him" (Mt. 6:74)—is excluded from the Church,
from the eucharistic banquet, and from the heavenly kingdom, but legislative and liturgical texts often have the pe-
culiarity of affirming the obvious.

The only other Pauline use of *philein* also occurs among
the good wishes customary in letters, and it too appears to
be a synonym of *agapan.* "Greet those who love us in the
faith," *aspasai tous philountas hēmas en pistei* (Tit. 3:15).
Although this formula was original with St. Paul, it also
occurs very frequently in profane letters, at least in essence,
for example in the letter of Flavius Herculanus to Aplonar-
ion, "Greet all who love you," *aspasai tous philountas se
pantas,*[18] or of Ptolemaios to his brother Zosimus, "I greet
my sister especially and her children . . . and all who love
us," *aspazomai tēn adelphēn mou polla, kai ta tekna autēs
kai . . . tous philountas hēmas pantes.*[19] The participle
philountas, "Those who love," is the equivalent of the adjective *tous philous,* "our friends." [20] St. Paul is writing, as
most people do, "Greet our friends," but in doing so, he
Christianizes the conventional formula by adding *en pistei,* a
phrase which determines the quality and the mode of the
affection. To love "in the faith" or "in the Lord" is a peri-
phasis for "to love religiously" or "to love with charity"
—*agapē meta pisteōs* (Eph. 6:23). If the special vocabulary
of the Pastorals is considered, an element of truth and
authenticity will be noted in the phrase *philein en pistei,*
since *pistei* is associated with *gnēsios* (1 Tim. 1:2; Tit. 1:4),
alētheia (1 Tim. 2:7; Tit. 1:1; 13–14; 2 Tim. 2:18; 3:8) and

[18] *P. Oxy.* 14:1676:38–39 (3rd c.).
[19] *B.G.U.* 2:625:35 (2nd–3rd c.).   [20] *B.G.U.* 2:423:20.

with *anypokritos* (1 Tim. 1:5; 2 Tim. 1:5). Sincerity or authenticity is the major quality of *agape*.[21] Finally, the formula, *aspasai tous philountas hēmas en pistei*, can be translated, "Greet our true Christian friends." It identifies "those who love us," *philountes*, with "our people," *hēmeteroi*, in v. 14, contrasting them with the "disobedient men," *hairetikon anthrōpon* of v. 10. The exclusion of inveterate liars (1:12) from the final greeting corresponds to the anathema of 1 Cor. 16:22 and confirms charity's inseparability from true faith.

The adjective *philos*, used twenty-two times in the Gospels, appears only three times in the Acts and four times in the Epistles. Because of its affinity with Tit. 3:15, 3 Jn. 15 should be mentioned first of all: "*Aspazontai se hoi philoi. Aspazou tous philous kat' onoma*," "Your friends greet you. Greet my friends, each one in particular."

According to customary epistolary usage, the Christians of Ephesus—*hoi philoi*—join with John in greeting Gaius, and John instructs Gaius to greet those whom he knows, *tous philous*, in Gaius' circle. Certain commentators, observing that Christians in general are never designated by the term "friends," explain that here the word describes the brothers of the community who remained faithful to the Apostle and did not approve of the conduct of Diotrephes. Other commentators prefer a mystical interpretation. The author of the Epistle calls the Christians *hoi philoi* because he remembers that Jesus had called Lazarus his friend (Jn. 11:11) and said that he would confer the same title on all those who fulfill his will (Jn. 15:14–15). It is even suggested that the designation, "each one by his name," *kat' onoma*, refers to the name by which the good Shepherd knows his sheep (Jn. 10:3), so that the Shepherd of the Churches of Asia is imitating the good Shepherd.

And one might also be surprised that St. John, who used *agapētoi* so frequently, changed his vocabulary here and did

[21] Rom. 12:9; 2 Cor. 6:6.

not mention the love of charity in his conclusion. In reality, the examples of the papyri prove that the Apostle was using the conventional profane formula. He did not even take the trouble to Christianize it as St. Paul had done (Tit. 3:15), an omission which is normal enough in so personal a letter, which is not really an "epistle" at all, but a simple note. Moreover, he conformed to profane usage strictly in adding the stereotyped formula, *kat' onoma* to the wording of Tit. 3:15. There is no need to track down some nuance of tenderness or pastoral solicitude in this phrase; it is simply a cliché.

After quoting Genesis 15:6, "Abraham believed God, and it was reckoned to him as justice" (James 2:23), St. James adds, "and he was called God's friend," *kai philos theou eklēthē*. This explanation, although it is not found in Genesis, does reflect its spirit and express a traditional opinion in Judaism, that Wisdom makes holy souls "friends of God and prophets, for there is nought God loves, be it not one who dwells with Wisdom," *philous theou kai prophētas kataskeuazei; outhen gar agapai ho theos ei mē ton sophiai synoikounta* (Wis. 7:27). In this text *philoi theou* is clearly to be taken in its passive sense of "those loved by God" (cf. 7:14). Moses is exceptionally graced with this title of honor (Ex. 33:11), but it is Abraham who is the friend of God par excellence. Yahweh himself declared him so. "You, Israel, my servant (*pais mou*), Jacob, whom I have chosen, offspring of Abraham my friend, *hon ēgapēsa*" (Is. 41:8). Josephat, too, proclaimed, "Did not you our God give this land to the seed of Abraham your friend?, *tōi ēgapemenōi sou*" (2 Par. 20:7). Azarias repeated, "Do not take away your mercy from us, for the sake of Abraham, your friend, *dia Abraam ton ēgapemenon hypo sou*" (Dan. 3:35). The Septuagint always avoided writing *philos*, perhaps to put more stress on the religious and honorable characteristics included in being *ēgapēmenos*, the preferred of God. What is certain is that Abraham is the object of the divine charity, *agapai ho theos*, and that the justification of the *philos theou* is attributed to God's generous love. In any case the justified man, *dikai-ōtheis*, has a relationship of loving union with his Lord. It may be concluded semantically that *philos* is here a synonym of *agapētos* and doctrinally that what we call "the state of grace" is friendship with God.

In a severe apostrophe to Christians seduced by the pleasures of this world *en tais hēdonais hymōn* (4:3), St. James expresses a basic evangelical truth in his own terms: "Adulterers, do you not know that friendship with the world (*philia tou kosmou*) means enmity with God? Whoever, therefore, wishes to be a friend of the world (*philos tou kosmou*) makes himself an enemy of God" (4:4).

According to the traditional metaphor of the Old Testament, the relations of Yahweh and Israel within the Alliance are like the ties of marriage. God and his people are the married couple. Sin is an infidelity by which the "adulterous" spouse breaks his commitments and renounces his promises. Moreover, Jesus called his contemporaries "a headstrong and adulterous nation." [22] The word "adulterous," *moichalis*, which was unknown in secular language before this period and appeared in the papyri only in the sixth century, designates "a married woman who commits adultery" (Rom. 7:3). By his invective, "Adulterers!", St. James emphasized the violation of the contract, the breaking of the bond, and the refusal of an obligation. Christians are indeed already totally and definitively committed to God. Their whole life is subject to the precept to love God with all their hearts, all their souls, and all their strength. If they satisfy their passions (v. 3), they will be sacrificing to the *philia tou kosmou*, the friendship of this world.

It is impossible to determine the precise sense of *philia* in this phrase, its only appearance in the New Testament. It can signify simply "to be on good terms," but it can also have its proper sense of "reciprocal friendship." Here it seems preferable to give it its broad meaning of "attachment and delight." The term is undoubtedly chosen because it

[22] Mt. 12:39; 16:11; Mk. 8:38.

fits the conjugal metaphor in evoking the leaning and "inclination of the heart"; and, consequently, the sinning soul is represented as a woman who is enslaved by passion to her lord and master the world, source of all contamination. Philo declared that the soul which rejects all discipline becomes a lover of pleasure instead of a lover of virtue, *gegone philēdonos anti philaretou*.[23] Moreover, the Lord had said, "Where your treasure is, there, too, your heart will be" (Lk. 12:34). St. James is making the most radical contrast, therefore, between attachment to the world and its pleasures (cf. 1 Jn. 2:16) and the consecration of one's entire self to God which is an essential part of *agape*. More specifically, since the love of "friendship" is characterized by affinity of thoughts, tastes and sentiments, harmony of action and a living relationship, "friendship of this world" creates so profound a likeness to the sinful world that it implies radical opposition to God. *Theos* and *kosmos* are antithetically opposed, just as *echthra* and *philia* are. The stress of the phrase falls on the antagonism and incompatibility. That is why, using the synonymic parallelism by which Semite "proverbs" emphasize their main thought, St. James repeats, "Whoever wishes to be a friend to the world makes himself an enemy of God." There is no conciliation possible. Attachment to the one master excludes *ipso facto* a belonging to the other. Love of God and love of the world cannot exist in the same heart, as Jesus had already said very strongly (Mt. 6:24; Lk. 16:13). However, in his exhortation, St. James stresses the subjective choice which each Christian must make—"Whoever wishes . . . makes himself"—*boulēthēi . . . kathistatai*. Each person must understand that if he willingly takes his pleasure in the world, he places himself in a state of enmity with God.

The Acts of the Apostles have only three uses of *philos*, all in an ordinary sense and, for the first two at least, in a profane sense. While he was awaiting Peter's arrival at Caesarea, Cornelius had invited several of his relatives and

[23] *De lege alleg.* 2:90.

intimate friends, *synkalesamenos tous syggeneis autou kai tous anagkaious philous* (Acts 10:24). In classical Greek *hoi anagkaioi*, employed absolutely, refers to parents and relatives. These blood relationships—which do not allow one to refuse the responsibilities of an inheritance—are different from those one has with strangers. After the time of Euripides, the expression *philos anagkaios* was used for this idea,[24] and in the *Republic* (IX, 574, b, c) Plato contrasts the mother (*philē anagkaia*) with the courtesan who is desired in marriage (*philē ouk anagkaia*); the father, the nearest relative and the one whose relationship is the longest-standing (*philos anagkaios*) with the adolescent born yesterday (*philos ouk anagkaios*). Flavius Josephus mentions "intimate friends" ten times; but, oddly enough, these "intimate friends" are almost always the intimates of the king. At that time, *philos* was an aulic designation. Nebuchadnezzar's son, for example, releases Jechonias and holds him among his closest friends. The papyri finally testify to the common usage of *philos*. They extend from a letter of recommendation written in March, 257 B.C.—"Ptolemaios, who brings you this letter, is my friend and intimate, *estin mou philos kai anagkaios*" [25]—to letters of the second and third centuries A.D.—"I have an intimate friend in Alexandria," *echō en Alexandreiai anagkaion philon*.[26] These examples allow the vocabulary of St. Luke to be placed in relation to the contemporary language, and, consequently, the human nuance of friendship it conveys can be determined. It is the same type as that of 3 Jn. 15. It may be supposed that these "intimate friends" shared the dispositions of soul of Cornelius and that they, too, anxiously awaited the joyful message which Peter was coming to bring them. However, the expression which suggests a gathering of *suggeneis* and *philous*, "relatives and friends," around an important person is so common in chancellery usage and aulic protocol that it suggests Luke's desire to emphasize the solemnity of the recep-

[24] Euripides, *Andr.* 671.   [25] P. *Zenon* (Colomb.) 7:3.
[26] B.G.U. 2:625, 26.

tion at Caesarea, which was to make such a mark in the history of the primitive Church. For one thing, the audience was worthy of the head of the new Church; for another, and more important, the Roman officer appeared as an important person. Not only was his dignity symbolized and enhanced by the friends and relatives who surrounded him, but the whole assembly, described in such "official" terms, "prepared the foundation of the community at Caesarea." [27] Many souls would owe their faith to this centurion and to his *philoi anagkaioi* who were to become *adelphoi agapētoi* (cf. James 1:16).

The serious disturbance—*tarachos ouk oligos* (Acts 19: 23)—which Demetrius raised up against Paul at Ephesus is well known. Paul wanted to go into the middle of the maddened crowd to defend himself, but "some of the Asiarchs, who were his friends (*ontes autōi philoi*), sent a plea to him not to venture into the theatre" (Acts 19:31). The text is clear. The Asiarchs, who were responsible for order in the theatre, were sympathetic to Paul and respectful of his doctrine. They begged him not to expose himself to danger. The origin and quality of their relations with Paul are not known, but St. Luke emphasizes their intentions. It is out of friendship for him that they warned him of the seriousness of the danger and worried about his security. This is a good example of the *philia* and philanthropy of these great magistrates. Clearly, the historian of the Church wishes to contrast the kindness and respect shown by the highest persons of distinction in the Capitol with the popular hostility toward his hero. In other words, for Luke as for Flavius Josephus, *philoi* has a strong nuance of honor and prestige.

The same feelings of respect and courtesy inspired the centurion Julius. At the port of Sidon, Julius "treated Paul kindly, allowing him to go to his friends and to be cared for," *epetrepsen pros tous philous poreuthenti epimeleias tuchein* (Acts 27:3). All the commentators from Harnach to F. F. Bruce and E. Haenchen, with the exception of E.

[27] E. Haenchen, *Die Apostelgeschichte*, Göttingen, 1956, p. 302.

Jacquier, H. J. Cadbury, and J. Renié, have decided that *philous* with an article indicates a distinct category, the Christians. It is true that Phœnicia knew the gospel message from the beginning (Lk. 6:17) and that in the year 60 A.D. there was a Christian community at Sidon. Objectively, therefore, "the friends" that Paul was going to visit were his brothers in the faith. It is not certain, however, that this is the way the centurion understood the *philoi* of his prisoner. In this phrase, which is completely classical from the linguistic point of view, it seems preferable to understand "friends" as the "relations and acquaintances" that the Apostle could have had in the port; thus *philoi* has the same meaning it had in its previous uses in Acts.

It is unwarranted to suppose that "the brothers," having received news of the Apostle's arrival (cf. 28:15), would have come to the port to wait for him and meet him, for the ship's itinerary was not officially fixed and no one could tell exactly when it would put in at Sidon. Therefore it was on his own initiative that Julius had his prisoner disembark. Very likely he freed Paul on parole. This sort of kindness and confidence was so unusual that Saint Luke expressly mentions it—"Julius treated Paul kindly," *philanthrōpōs chrēsamenos*—and some have supposed that the centurion had known the Apostle for a long time.

The Roman officer's nobility and delicacy of heart are even more evident in his reason for granting this permission to Paul. It was not in the least so that Paul might find some way to relax but rather so that he could see his friends and be comforted by their love and services. This is the way we understand the biblical *hapax, epimeleias tuchein*. The noun *epimeleia*, which is not found anywhere else in the New Testament, is very frequent in classical and Hellenistic Greek, in particular in the sense of "to give all one's care to, to pay attention to, to accomplish one's duty." [28] It is applied to a *Curator (Epimelētēs)* who administers a property or supervises accounts; or to a manager who runs and super-

[28] *Letter of Aristeas,* 317.

vises a project; to the education of children, and, in particular, to the care given by a nurse. From this is derived the medical meaning, "to care for a sick person," which is the meaning retained here by several commentators. St. Paul, who had been sick on this difficult crossing, would have been cared for by the Christians of Sidon.

But, even in medical writings, *epimeleia* is frequently used in the sense of attention and devotion in the most varied domains, and the phrase *epimeleias tuchein,* recorded from the time of Isocrates,[29] means simply to receive attentive care. An example of this usage is the request of Servaeus Africanus that the *strategoi* watch over the state of the treasury, *hai tamiakai ousiai tēs prosekousēs epimeleias teuxontai.*[30] Finally, *epimeleia* in Acts 27:3 should be understood in terms of Julius' *philanthrōpia* and Paul's *philoi,* in other words in a context of urbanity, kindness, and affectionate respect. The Apostle is not "hospitalized" in the homes of the Christians of Sidon who would care for him to the best of their ability; rather, he receives the "hospitality" of his friends who surround him with kindnesses and do everything they possibly can for him. The expression evokes all the generosity and complexity of the oriental welcome of a venerated guest. The centurion's philanthropy is matched by the humble and active devotion of the brothers.

Finally, although the verb *phileō* is a synonym of *agapaō* in two uses (1 Cor. 16:22; Tit. 3:15), and *philos* takes on a religious meaning in James 2:23; 4:4, the adjective *philos* keeps the meaning it usually had in profane language in the epistolary salutation of 3 Jn. 15 and in Acts 10:24; 19:31; 27:3. It is not at all surprising that the Hellenist Luke should have used the language of the *kalos kagathos* or that, as a noble humanist, he appreciated the value of friendship. It gave him pleasure to present one or another of his personages surrounded by his friends and receiving their care. It remains true, however, that friendship, *philia,* plays only a secondary and episodic role in the epistolary *corpus.* That

[29] Isocrates, *Philip.* 154; *Areop.* 37.   [30] *P. Oxy.* 1:58, 22.

it is mentioned so few times proves that the disciples of Jesus did not think of themselves as contemporary *thiasoi*, groups; they were keenly aware of the change in values and in the ends of human life which their Savior had brought. Although they surely applied the great principle of *koina ta philōn*, "the goods of friends are held in common," more than ever in their community, and although fraternal union represented the summit of their *eudaimonia*, happiness, it was no longer "flesh and blood" or reason and heart which governed their relationship but rather the spirit and grace. Essentially, they formed a "family of God," where relationships were no longer those of one human being to another, but those which unite the children of a same Father. Christians are no longer associates or friends but brothers, and this *philadelphia* presupposes a new birth and a new life. Consequently, their love is no longer a more or less restricted friendship, but an *agape* that is essentially universal and permanent because it is divine. In other words, since believers can love one another only *en Kyriōi*, those whom they love are *agapētoi*.

To spend time on the numerous compounds with *phil-* in the New Testament would be without interest for clarifying the notion of *agape*. On the other hand, *epipothein* and *epipothētos* seem to have a rather close relationship with charity, at least according to 1 Thess. 3:6 and Philip. 4:1. Since neither R. C. Trench's *Synonymes* nor Kittel's *Dictionary* analyzes these terms, it will not be superfluous to determine their meaning.

The compound *epipotheō*, which is rare in classical Greek, did not become frequent in the literary *Koine* until the end of the first century A.D., and it was completely unknown in the papyri. If we observe that it occurs twelve times in the Septuagint and nine times in the epistolary corpus of the New Testament and that the derivatives *epipothēsis*, *epipothia*, *epipothētos* are used for the first time in the Greek language by St. Paul, we can rightly conclude that this family of words is strictly biblical.

The determination of its meaning is not on this account easy, for in the ten cases in which *epipothein* is used, it corresponds to eight different Hebrew verbs. When it is used with *pheidomai*, it means compassion,[31] hence the note of anxiety, as for instance that of the eagle which flutters over its young (Deut. 32:11). However, in the Wisdom literature, *epipothein* has the basic meaning of "to desire" either good or bad things, often with an element of intensity, which is usually rendered by "to long for," "to yearn for." Thus the holy soul longs for God as the hind longs for the running waters (Ps. 42:1). The Psalmist emphasizes the strength of the desire by using redundant expressions. Thus he yearns and pines for the courts of the Lord, *epipothei kai ekleipei* (Ps. 84:3); he is consumed with longing for his ordinances, *epepothēsen . . . ton epithumēsai* (119:20); and he gasps with open mouth in his yearning for the Lord's commands, *heilkysa pneuma hoti tas entolas sou epepothoun* (v. 131). So violent an aspiration presupposes that one is profoundly caught up; besides, this verse is parallel to verses 47–48, 127, 159, 166 which use the expression, *agapan tas entolas*. In Wisd. 15:19 or Sir. 25:21, where this desire is expressly aroused by beauty, *epipothein* can be translated "to love"; it is a synonym of *eran*. Similarly, but in a religious context, Ps. 84:3 places the notion of love and desire in a parallel construction: "How lovely are your tabernacles . . . my soul yearns and pines for the courts of the Lord," *hōs agapēta ta skenōmata sou . . . epipothei kai ekleipei hē psychē mou eis tas aulas tou kyriou*. It must be understood not only that the divine courts are desirable and that the soul longs to live there, but also that these courts are lovable, and, consequently, that the intense desire to reach them is the desire of charity, *epipotheō* being very close to *agapaō*. This twofold sense is best expressed in the *De Abr.* 87 where Philo says that those who seek God and aspire to find him

[31] Deut. 13:9; Jer. 13:14.

love the solitude which he loves, *hoi gar zētountes kai epi-pothountes theon aneurein tēn philēn autōi monōsin aga-pōsi.*

In the New Testament, St. Peter, comparing the neo-phytes to newborn babes, urges them to act like infants who long for their mother's milk and to aspire intensely to the pure and nourishing doctrine of the gospel, *to logikon adolon gala epipothēsate* (1 Pet. 2:2). The Vulgate accu-rately translates the aorist imperative *epipothēsate* by *con-cupiscite,* since *epipothēsate* has the same sense of desire and effort it had in Ps. 42:1–3. In both cases, there is a thirst and the quenching of the thirst by a divine drink; it is a matter of life or death.

The aspiration of St. Paul is equally intense. He groans, *stenazomen,* in his present condition, and ardently desires to clothe his body with a glory beyond that of his mortal flesh, but without having to be despoiled of this flesh by death, *ependysasthai epipothountes* (2 Cor. 5:2). The wait-ing includes anxiety, as in Deut. 32:11; it is a mixture of de-sire and fear.

In four Epistles *epipotheō* expresses a strong desire to be reunited with cherished persons from whom one is separated. When Timothy came back from Thessalonica, he brought good news of the community, and in particular of its faith and charity, *ten pistin kai tēn agapēn hymōn;* the brother kept a faithful memory of their apostle, *echete mneian hēmōn agathēn pantote,* and ardently wanted to see him again, *epipothountes hēmas idein* (1 Thess. 3:6). St. Paul wrote to the Romans that he desired very much to come to them, *epipothō gar idein hymas* (Rom. 1:11), and told Timothy that he was anxious to see him again and is unable to forget the tears of his dear child, *epipothōn se idein mem-nēmenos sou tōn dakryōn* (2 Tim. 1:4). He sent Epaphrodi-tus back to the Philippians "because he is yearning for all of you, and is distressed that you have learned of his illness," *epipothōn hēn pantas hymas kai adēmenōn* (Phil. 2:26). For one who knows the heart of Paul there is no doubt that in

these circumstances he chose the verb *epipothein* to express
the warmth of his good wishes and, it must be added, of his affection. In fact, in 1 Thess. 3:6 and 2 Tim. 1:4, his desire
arose because of the fidelity of their remembrance, in other
words, because of their love. In addition, remembrance and
desire are joined, in the first case, to the Thessalonians'
agape; in the second, to the Apostle's tenderness for his
child of predilection, *agapētōi teknōi* (2 Tim. 1:2). In these
texts, *epipotheō* expresses the desires of charity. Charity
alone can account for Paul's wish to see the Romans whom
he has never met; but, precisely, he hopes "to impart some
spiritual gift" to them (Rom. 1:11). Thus the trite expression so often used in letters, "I desire to see you" must be
understood in terms of the personality of the writer, who
knows only one love, the love which the Holy Spirit diffuses
in the heart of those who have been justified. The case is
the same in Phil. 2:26, where Paul says that he is sending
Epaphioditus back, *epipothōn hēn pantas hymas,* literally,
"because he had a desire for all of you" or "filled as he is
with desire for you." Taken alone, this has no great meaning,
so an addition is sometimes made, "he had such a desire to
see you again." However, according to usage in the Septuagint, the expression should be translated, "he was longing for
you," and, according to Pauline vocabulary, should be understood as "he loved you so much and tormented himself so
much because of you!" *Epipothein* expresses both the divine
quality of the love which united them and the painful desire
of the human heart longing for the presence of the person it
loves.

This interpretation is confirmed by 2 Cor. 9:14. The
Corinthians must generously help the saints of Jerusalem. In
return, as the "saints" pray for their benefactors, they experience a "lively inclination" toward the Corinthians, realizing what an extraordinary grace God has given to these
converts from paganism: *kai autōn deēsei hyper hymōn epi-
pothountōn hymas dia tēn hyperballousan charin tou theou
eph' hymin.* "They in turn in their prayers give vent to the

affection for you elicited by God's surpassing grace bestowed on you." As in Phil. 2:26, the human and the divine interpenetrate one another. In the hearts of Christ's disciples, spontaneous, natural gratitude was expressed in prayer; gratitude made the power of God's grace admired. The result was *epipothoutōn hymas*. How should this genitive absolute be translated? If the idea of desire is kept, one can gloss, "their heart reaches out, springs forth to you." [32] However, their strong inclination toward their benefactors is an affection, a *penchant*, and the most elementary psychology knows that nothing wins the heart more quickly than a kind deed. The Jerusalemites felt themselves bound and attached to the Corinthians, both according to the natural order of gratitude and according to grace (cf. Philem. 16), *i.e.*, to the divine love which had been lavished upon the neophytes of the Pauline Churches. They adjusted their warm feelings and response to the divine *agape*. We must therefore not hesitate to read, "They are filled with affection for you too" (E. B. Allo) or, "You have become the objects of their love." [33] That this is a case of authentic charity is taught by the very notion of charity in the Septuagint and in the New Testament, where the love of charity is usually based on gratitude. Thus *epipotheō* is here a synonym of *agapaō*, as in Ps. 84:3.

Finally, the most beautiful declaration of love that the Apostle ever made is decisive. He addressed it to the Philippians, his favorite disciples, while he was in prison, a situation in which sensibility is acute and the prisoner feels a great need to speak his heart without holding anything back. "I have you in my heart . . . God is my witness how I love you with the tender affection of Christ Jesus," *hos epipothō pantas hymas en splagchnois Christou*. "The object of my prayer is that your love may become richer and richer" (Phil. 1:8). The literal translation of the Greek words is, "How I love you in the entrails of Christ," for the

---

[32] M. Goguel, *Le Nouveau Testament*, Paris, 1929, p. 289.
[33] A. Lemonnyer, *Épîtres de Saint Paul*, Paris, 1905, I, p. 218.

entrails are the seat of the passions, especially of love. Today
we would say, "I love you in the heart of Christ." This
reference could have no meaning apart from the Apostle's
incorporation into the Lord, which is so profound and vital
that it is Christ who lives and loves in Paul (Gal. 2:20). He
who would ask the Philippians to have the same sentiments
as Jesus (Phil. 2:5) practiced what he asked of them. He
loved *in Christo Jesu,* with the love that is in Christ, with
agape. Consequently, *epipothō* joined to *en splagchnois
Christou,* has lost all sense of desire and even of vague cordial inclination. It is an intense love, with an element of
feeling and of the emotion proper to the entrails. It is a very
tender—one would almost dare to say passionate—love (cf.
Sir. 25:21), at the very least a love comparable to the extreme and gentle fervor of a mother's love for her little children. One thinks of that fire of *agape* which Jesus came to
spread in the hearts of believers. . . .

There remains a very obscure text in which James, having
just contrasted friendship with the world to love of God,
quotes the authority of Scripture, *pros phthonon epipothei
to pneuma ho katōikisen en hēmin* (Jas. 4:5). A few modern
commentators understand this to mean that the natural tendency of man with his corrupted nature is to envy his
brothers and struggle against them (Phil. 1:15), and they
refer to Ecc. 4:4. But this is to give *pneuma* a meaning it
does not usually have (cf. Gen. 6:5) and to make unintelligible the qualification, "the spirit which God made to dwell
in us." It would be better to translate, "It desires jealously,
this spirit which God made to dwell in us." If this *pneuma*
is not the Holy Spirit in person (Rom. 8:26–27), it is at
least a participation in him. This interpretation would allow
us to give *epipothein* a meaning similar to that in Ps. 42:2,
especially if we adopt Wittstein's correction of *pros ton
theon* in place of *phthonon.* However, one hardly sees the
meaning of this affirmation in the context; besides, no text
of the Old Testament records any such aspiration of the
Pneuma toward God (this is a strictly New Testament

revelation). Therefore, we prefer the reading of almost all the commentators: "Or do you suppose that the Scripture utters empty words when it says that it is with jealousy that he [God] desires the spirit he has made to dwell in us?" There is agreement that *epipothei* should be closely joined to *pros phthonon* which should be considered equivalent to *phthonerōs*, jealousy, exclusivity, in the characteristic of the divine charity for Israel (Ex. 20:5; 34:14). Its object here is the *pneuma*, which is understood in the same sense as in Ecc. 12:7 and Gen. 2:7 (*pnoēn zōēs*), not as a spiritual faculty but as the vital breath, life itself. The Creator, who made his creatures out of nothing and gave them life, has the right of absolute ownership over them, and he requires that his creatures direct their souls and all their activity toward him (Is. 42:5). The mention of loan or gift, *ho katōikisen*, suggests both the divine sovereignty and man's obligation to be grateful. God cannot tolerate a rival in the heart of his creature. St. James is referring to the first commandment (Deut. 6:5), perhaps, insisting on the totality of love which Yahweh demands; but it is more likely that he is referring to the whole of Scripture which reiterates the divine demand over and over again. To shirk it is to divide one's heart, to be an adulterer (Jas. 4:4).

Therefore, the reference to the inspired text is perfectly in order. *Epipothei* must have as its subject God, who has just been named at the end of verse 4, and it must be understood in terms of *moichalides*, "adulterers," and *philia-philos tou kosmou*, "friendship-friend of the world," in the same verse, *i.e.*, in an affective and religious context. Yahweh is both a Father and a lover, anxious about the choice of his children or his spouse, about their total fidelity. He repeats his jealousy to them, emphasizing that he has all the rights to exclusivity. In other words, *epipotheō pros phthonon* signifies "to love intensely and exclusively"; but since it is a question of God's loving for himself and demanding what belongs to him, the author could not use the verb *agapan* which suggests a love that is essentially disinterested and beneficent. Nevertheless, St. James explains that when we desire in this way, it is indeed a matter of true love. "God gives a great grace" (v. 6). He would be our enemy if he consented to the deviation of his creature. The *epipothēsis* of God is a *charis*, a love.

All these biblical uses indicate that *epipothein* expresses an intense desire which is in direct relationship with whatever kind of love aroused it. The Septuagint only rarely gives it the sense of covetous desire. The New Testament employs it only in a good sense, of the aspiration of the soul or heart, extending from a simple inclination to the most fervent fraternal tenderness. If one "desires" his neighbor, it is in order to be united to him and live in his presence; when one "desires" God or the gospel, it is in order to be nourished from the food that is of vital necessity to him. Given the strong emotional quality and the anxiety which is almost always present in *epipothēsis*, *epipothein* cannot be a synonym of *agapan*, which of its nature means contentment and happiness. But charity is certainly at its origin, communicating to it its *élan*, its expressiveness, its vehemence, and especially its specific characteristic of totality. As the hind yearns and languishes until it finds running water, as the converts cannot live without the food of the Gospel, as Epaphroditus cannot keep from seeing the Philippians again, so God himself is, as it were, impatient to possess without reserve or sharing the *pneuma* of his creatures. He loves them, he wants them, he desires them. All these sentiments are included in his *agape* for his *epipothētous*.

The best illustration of charity's manifestations of tenderness is furnished by 1 Thess. 2:7–8, "But in your midst we become as gentle as a nursing mother fondling her children. Such was our tender love for you that not only would we gladly have shared the gospel with you but even ourselves, because you had become so dear to us." The very human and tender words, "gentle," *ēpioi*, "as a nursing mother," *hōs trophos*, "tender love," *homeiromenoi*, are simply the expansion and manifestation of *agape* which bestows its riches, *dioti agapētoi hēmin egenēthēte!*

St. Paul did not wish to assert himself at Thessalonica through his authority as an apostle, *en barei* (v. 7). On the contrary, he was gentle and irenic. This is how we understand *ēpios*, which does not occur in the Old Testament, and is found again in the New Testament only in 2 Tim. 2:24. "The Lord's servant must not quarrel, but be gentle toward all, qualified to teach," *ēpion einai pros pantas, didaktikon.* Contrary to what one might think, *ēpiotēs* is not a virtue of intimacy or family life—much less of the nursery, as some have thought. The Apostle requires it of a head of the Church and usage makes a great many men its object. In the *Invocations to Isis,* written in the second century, it is an attribute of the divinity,[34] similar to *philostorgia,* the virtue of sovereigns. Assuerus had claimed it by the same token as *epiekeia* (Esth. 3:13), and in the fifth century A.D. Leontios, the prefect of Illyria, considered it a title of glory to have been gentle and kind to honest judges and terrible to the abettors of injustice, *krintērsi gar eimi ēpios eithydikois, tois d'adikousi deos.*[35]

In fact, in his treatise on royalty, the Pythagorean Sthenidas of Locri wrote: "It is natural that the first god was considered to be the father of gods and men especially for this reason, that he is good-natured toward all the beings he has created—*hoti ēpios pros panta ta hyp' autōi genomena enti*—and for all indiscriminately he is the foster father, the master—*tropheus, didaskalos*—who teaches all that is good."[36] The same idea is expressed in a treatise on the good king in which Philodemos of Gadara, in the first century, attributes gentleness to the prince, *dia krisin phoinētai praos, dia men tēn ēpiotēta philētai.*[37] Finally, J. Pollux, consecrating a chapter in his *Onomasticon* to royal titles,

[34] *P. Oxy.* 11:1380:11.
[35] *Epigramme de Gortyne,* line 4, published by L. Robert, *Hellenica,* Paris, 1948, pp. 14–16.
[36] Stobaeus, 7:63: t. IV, p. 271.   [37] 7:13–14; cf. 6:24.

Peri Basilikōn onomatōn, begins it by the following praises: *Peri basileōs epainōn lege, patēr, ēpios, praios, hēmeros, pronoētikos, epieikēs, philanthrōpōs, megalophrōn.*[38]

Indulgent and gentle, St. Paul was almost maternal toward the Thessalonians. He warmed them with his own fervent tenderness (*thalpō*) and surrounded them with his kindness. That was his method of teaching his new converts. He was *trophos*, an educator, just as Zeus, according to Sthenidas, was *tropheus, didaskalos*. He cherished his children. The rare *homeiresthai* should certainly be considered a synonym of *epipothein*, since it means "to desire impatiently," "to languish," but also "to love paternally or maternally," "to cherish." This interpretation is borne out by an inscription of the fourth century, in which the priest and priestess of a local Lycaonian cult wrote on the tomb of their son Zotikos: *"hou charin estēsan gonees homeiromenoi peri paidos."* [39] The *houtōs homeiromenoi hymōn* of 1 Thess. 2:8 should therefore be translated, "Cherishing you in this way"; with *houtōs* referring to *ēpioi* and to *hōs ean trophos thalpēi.*

One could not discover a way to be more gently affectionate. The Apostle explains why he feels such warm tenderness: *dioti agapētai hēmin egenēthēte.* We must not understand, as is ordinarily done, "so dear have you become to me," as if *agapētos* were a term for just any kind of love, on the same level as the preceding terms. To understand *agapētos* in this way would weaken the liveliness of Paul's affection, since *agapan* and *agape* do not express the warmth of passion. Actually, the Thessalonians' fidelity and holiness of life (vv. 9 ff.) aroused an increase of charity in Paul's soul, and they became the "object of his *agape*," of his religious respect and love. The Apostle's esteem for so courageous a Christian faith brings him to devote himself to them in the most generous way possible. Authentic charity is characterized by its depth and by its gift of the greatest of goods: the gospel and, especially, the sacrifice of self (cf. Jn. 15:13). The proper verb to express this kind

[38] 1:2, 40. [39] *C.I.G.* 3:4000:7.

of giving is *metadidonai* or *didonai* (1 Tim. 2:6; Tit. 2:14), *paradidonai* (Gal. 2:20; Eph. 5:2). *Agape* is by nature heroic. The marvel—and this is St. Paul's contribution to the semantic of austere *agape*—is that *agape* can arouse an exquisite tenderness and warm emotion in the heart of believers. The good Samaritan was "moved in his entrails" at the sight of the wounded man (Lk. 10:33). The Lord had objectively compared charity to a fire (Mt. 24:12), but this is the first time since the spouse of the Canticle that the resonance of *agape* within the inferior faculties is expressed as it appears in everyday life. Born on Calvary, *agape* consists first of all in dedicating oneself and giving one's own life; but, in doing this, the Christian is led to cherish the object of his love with an unlimited fervor. This is the marvelous union of grace and nature in the religion of the incarnate Word!

APPENDIX VI

Bibliography of
agape in the New Testament

Allen, E. L., "A Christology of Love," *The London Quarterly and Holborn Review*, 1950, pp. 295–301.

Appasamy, A. J., *Christianity as Bhakti Marga. A Study of the Johannine Doctrine of Love*, Madras, 1926.

Aubert, A., "De Ecclesia in quantum est communitas caritatis," *Collectanea Mechliniensia*, 1950, pp. 59–63.

Balducelli, R., *Il concetto teologico di carità attraverso le maggiori interpretazioni patristiche e medievali di I ad Cor. XIII*, Rome, 1951.

Ballantine, W. G., " 'Lovest Thou Me?' ", *Bibliotheca Sacra*, 1889, pp. 524–542.

Barr, A., "Love in the Church. A Study of First Corinthians, chapter XIII," *Scottish Journal of Theology*, 3, 1950, pp. 416–425.

Bassett, S. E., "I Cor. XIII, 12," *Journal of Biblical Literature*, 1928, pp. 232–236.

Bauer, W., "Das Gebot der Feindesliebe und die alten Christen," *Zeitschrift für Theologie und Kirche*, 1917, pp. 37–54.

—— "Ἀγάπη," *Wörterbuch zum Neuen Testament*[4], Berlin, 1952, col. 8–10.

Baumann, E., "Die Bruderliebe im Neuen Testament," *Junge Kirche*, 1936, pp. 1119–1128.

Beeking, J., *Die Nächstenliebe nach der Lehre der Heiligen Schrift*, Düsseldorf, 1930.

Belcher, F. W., "A Comment on Mark, XIV, 45," *The Expository Times*, LXIV, 8; 1953, p. 240.

Bernard, J. D., *The Central Teaching of Jesus Christ. A Study and Exposition of the Five Chapters, XIII to XVII inclusive*, New York, 1892.

Bethge, Fr., *Das Hohelied der Liebe (I Kor. XIII)*[3], Kassel, s.d.

Biard, J., *Les vertus théologales d'apres les Epîtres de saint Paul*[2], Paris, 1924.

Bischoff, E., *Jesus und die Rabbinen. Jesus Bergpredigt und*

247

248 *Appendix VI*

"*Himmelreich*" *in ihrer Unabhängigkeit vom Rabbinismus,* Leipzig, 1905.

Bolelli, Tr., "Caritas, Storia di una parola," *Rivista di Filologia e di Istruzione classica,* 1950, pp. 117–141.

Bonnard, P., "Amour," J. J. von Allmen, *Vocabulaire biblique,* Neuchâtel-Paris, 1954, pp. 14–17.

Bornkamm, G., "Der köstlichere Weg (I Cor., 13)," *Jahrbuch der theologischen Schule Bethel,* 1937, pp. 132–150; reedited, *Das Ende des Gesetzes. Paulusstudien,* Munich, 1952, pp. 93–112.

——— "Das Doppelgebot der Liebe," *Neutestamentliche Studien für R. Bultmann,* Berlin, 1954, pp. 85–93.

Bowen, R., "Love in the Fourth Gospel," *The Journal of Religion,* 1933, pp. 39–49.

Brandt, W., *Dienst und Dienen im Neuen Testament* (Neutestamentliche *Forschungen,* 5), Gütersloh, 1931.

——— "Die geringsten Brüder," *Jahrbuch der theologischen Schule Bethel,* 1937, pp. 1–28.

Brisebois, L., "L'Eucharistie sacrement de la charité," *XXXV Congreso Eucaristico Internacional,* Barcelona, 1953, I, pp. 453–457.

Brunner, E., *Eros und Liebe,* Berlin, 1937.

Bultmann, R., "Aimer son prochain, commandement de Dieu," *Revue d'Histoire et de Philosophie religieuse,* 1930, pp. 222–241; reedited in German in *Glauben und Verstehen,* Tübingen, 1953, I, pp. 229–244.

Bunch, T. G., *Love. A Comprehensive Exposition of I Cor. XIII,* Washington, 1952.

Buonaiuti, E., "I vocaboli d'amore nel Nuovo Testamento," *Rivista Storico-critica delle Scienze Theologiche,* V, 1909, pp. 257–264.

Burr, J., *The Lordship of Love. Studies in First Corinthians, Chapter XIII,* London, 1932.

Burton, H., "The Breakfast on the Shore," *The Expositor,* V, 1, 1895, pp. 450–472.

Caspari, W., "Die altruistische Gegenseitigkeitsregel und die Bergpredigt," *Zeitwende,* 1928, 2, pp. 161–169.

Ceresa-Gastaldo, A., "ΑΓΑΠΗ nei documenti anteriori al Nuovo Testamento," *Aegyptus,* 1951, pp. 269–306.

——— "ΑΓΑΠΗ nei documenti estranei all'influsso biblico,"

Rivista di Filologia e di Istruzione classica, 1953, pp. 1–10.
—— "Ancora sull'uso profano di ΑΓΑΠΗ," *ibid.*, 1954, pp. 1–2.

Cerfaux, L., "La charité fraternelle et le retour du Christ (Jo. XIII, 33–38)," *Ephemerides theologicae Lovanienses*, 1948, pp. 321–332.

Cope, M., "Στοργή, ἔρως, φιλεῖν, ἀγαπᾶν," *The Journal of Philology*, 1868, pp. 88–93; repeated in *The Rhetoric of Aristotle with a Commentary*, Cambridge, 1877, I, pp. 292–296.

Cranfield, C. E. B., "Love," in A. Richardson, *A Theological Book of the Bible*, London, 1950, pp. 131–136.

Cremer, H., Kögel, J., "Αγαπάω-ἀγάπη," *Biblisch-theologisches Wörterbuch der neutestamentlichen Gräzitat*[10], Gotha, 1915, pp. 9–18.

Cross, J. A., "On St. John XXI, 15–17," *The Expositor*, IV, 7, 1893, pp. 312–320.

Dartigue, A., "Amour," *Dictionnaire encylopédique de la Bible*, Paris, 1932; I, pp. 43–47.

Debrunner, A., "Lesarten der Chester Beatty Papyri," *Conjectanea Neotestamentica*, 11; 1947, pp. 37–42.

Decourtray, A., "Renoncement et Amour de soi selon saint Paul," *Nouvelle Revue Théologique*, 1952, pp. 21–29.

Descamps, A., "Justice et Charité dans les Evangiles synoptiques," *Revue diocesaine de Tournai*, 1952, pp. 239–245.
—— "La Charité résumé de la Loi," *ibid.*, 1953, pp. 123–129.

Dibelius, M., "Joh. XV, 13. Eine Studie zum Traditionsproblem des Johannes-Evangeliums," *Festgabe für A. Deissmann*, Tübingen, 1927, pp. 168–186; repeated in *Botschaft und Geschichte*, Tübingen, 1953, I, pp. 204–220.

Dirlmeier, Fr., "ΘΕΟΦΙΛΙΑ-ΦΙΛΟΘΕΙΑ," *Philologus*, 1935, pp. 57–77; 176–193.

Dobschütz, E. von, "Zwei-und dreigliedrige Formeln," *Journal of Biblical Literature*, 1931, pp. 117–147.

Dodd, C. H., *Gospel and Law. The Relation of Faith and Ethics in Early Christianity*, New York, 1951.

Dölger, F. J., "Der Feuertod ohne die Liebe . . . Ein Beitrag zu I Kor. XIII, 3," *Antike und Christentum*, Münster, 1929, pp. 254–270.

Dublin, J., "Continue ye in my Love," *The Expository Times*, XLII, 1935, pp. 91–92.

250 Appendix VI

Duguet, J. J., *Explication des caractères de la charité selon saint Paul dans l'Épître aux Corinthiens*[2], Geneve, 1824.

Eichholz, G., "Glaube und Liebe im I Joh.," *Evangelische Theologie*, 1937, pp. 411–437.

―― *Jesus Christus und der Nächste*, Neukirchen, 1952.

Festugière, A. J., *L'enfant d'Agrigente*, Paris, 1941, pp. 121–129.

Fiebig, P., "Jesu Worte über die Feindesliebe im Zusammenhang mit den wichtigsten rabbinischen Parallelen erläutert," *Theologische Studien und Kritiken*, 1918, pp. 30–64.

Finding, R., *Agape. Die Göttliche Liebe im Johannes-Evangelium*, Stuttgart, 1936.

Findlay, J. A., "The Agape and the Eucharist in the New Testament," *The London Quarterly and Holborn Review*, 1950, pp. 113–120.

Fridrichsen, A., Charité et perfection. Observation sur Col. III, 14," *Symbolae Osloenses*, 19; 1939, pp. 41–45.

―― "Alska, hata, förneka (försaka)," *Svensk Exegetisk Arsbok* (Upsal), v, 1940, pp. 152–162.

Friedlaender, G., *The Jewish Sources of the Sermon on the Mount*, London, 1911.

Frieling, R., *Agape. Die Göttliche Liebe im Johannes-Evangelium*, Stuttgart, 1936.

Fuchs, E., "Was heisst: Du sollst deinen Nächsten lieben wie dich selbst?" *Theologische Blätter*, 1932, col. 129–140.

Fuerth, M., *Caritas und Humanitas. Zur Form und Wandlung des christlichen Liebesgedankens.* Stuttgart, 1933, pp. 42–65.

Graeff, H. C., "Ερως et 'Αγάπη," *La Vie Spirituelle.* Supplement 4, 1949–50, pp. 99–105.

Grail, A., "Eucharistie, sacrement de la charité dans le Nouveau Testament," *La Vie Spirituelle*, LXXXV, 1951, pp. 369–387.

―― "L'amour du prochain. Essai de Théologie biblique," *Cahiers de la vie spirituelle*, Paris, 1954, pp. 11–31.

Gray, J. R., "Whom Jesus Loved," *The Expository Times*, LXII, 10, 1951, pp. 291–294.

Grünhut, L., *Eros und Agape*, Leipzig, 1931.

Gspann, J. C., "Die Nächstenliebe im Neuen Testament," *Der Katholik*, XXXV, 1907, pp. 376–391.

Guardini, R., "Die christliche Liebe. I Kor. XIII," *Drei Schrift-Auslegungen*, Würzburg, 1949, pp. 53–76.

Güdemann, M., *Nachstenliebe. Ein Beitrag zur Erklärung des Matthäus-Evangeliums*, Vienna, 1890.

Haas, H., *Idee und Ideal der Feindesliebe in der ausserchristlichen Welt*, Leipzig, 1927.

Harbsmeier, G., "Das Hohelied der Liebe," *Biblische Studien*, 3; Neukirchen, Kreis Moers, 1952.

Harnack, A., "Das hohe Lied des Apostels Paulus von der Liebe (I Kor. XIII) und seine religionsgeschichtliche Bedeutung," *Sitzungsberichten der kgl. Preuszischen Akademie der Wissenschaften*, 1911, 1; pp. 132–163.

——— "Über den Ursprung der Formel 'Glaube, Liebe, Hoffnung,'" *Preussische Jahrbucher*, 1916, pp. 1–14. Reprinted in *Aus der Friedens- und Kriegsarbeit*, Giessen, 1916, pp. 1–18.

Harrelson, W., "The Idea of Agape in the New Testament," *The Journal of Religion*, 1951, pp. 169–182.

Hauck, Fr., "Die Freundschaft bei den Griechen und im Neuen Testament," *Festgabe Th. Zahn*, Leipzig, 1928, pp. 211–228.

Hauret, Ch., *Les Adieux du Seigneur. Saint Jean, XIII–XVII*, Paris, 1951.

Highfield, H., " 'Αγαπάω and φιλέω: A Rejoinder," *The Expository Times*, XXXVIII, 1927, p. 525.

Hitchcock, F. R. M., "The Structure of St. Paul's Hymn of Love," *The Expository Times*, XXXIV, 1923, pp. 488–492.

Hoffmann, E., "Pauli Hymnus auf die Liebe," *Deutsche Vierteljahrsschrift für Literaturwissenschaft und Geistesgeschichte*, 1926, pp. 58–73.

——— "Zu I Cor. XIII und Col. III, 13," *Conjectanea Neotestamentica*, 1938, pp. 28–31.

Hofmann, K. M., *Philema hagion*, Gütersloh, 1938.

Hogg, C. F., "Note on ἀγαπάω and φιλέω," *The Expository Times*, XXXVIII, 1927, pp. 379–380.

Höhne, E., "Zum neutestamentlichen Sprachgebrauch: I. 'Αγαπᾶν, φιλεῖν, σπλαγχνίξεσθαι," *Zeitschrift für kirchliche Wissenschaft und kirchliches Leben*, III, 1882, pp. 6–19.

Hum, J. M., "La Manifestation de l'Amour selon Saint Jean," *La Vie Spirituelle*, 382, 1953, pp. 227–253.

Hunt, H. A., "The Great Commandment," *The Expository Times*, 1944, pp. 82–83.

Jedzink, P., "Das Gebot der Nächstenliebe im Evangelium. Ein

252 *Appendix VI*

Beitrag zur neutestamentlichen Ethik," *Verzeichnis der Vorlesungen an der kgl. Akademie zu Braunsberg im W.S.* Braunsberg, 1916.

Jessop, T. E., *Law and Love. A Study of the Christian Ethic,* London, 1948.

Joannidis, V. Chr., " Ἡ καινὴ Ἐντολὴ τῆς Ἀγάπης καὶ ὁ Ὕμνος αὐτῆς ὑπὸ Ἀπ. Παύλον ἐν I Κορ. 13," Ἐπιστημονικὴ Ἐπετηρίς, ἐκδιδομένη ὑπὸ τῆς θεολογικῆς Σχολῆς τοῦ Πανεπιστημίου θεσσαλονίκης" (*Revue scientifique de la Faculté et Universite de Thessalonique*), 1, 1953, pp. 197–265.

Joüon, P., "Matthieu, V, 43," *Recherches de Science religieuse,* 1930, pp. 545–546.

Kalt, E., "Liebe," *Biblisches Reallexikon,* Paderborn, 1939, II, col. 56–71.

Kattenbusch, F., "Über Feindesliebe im Sinne des Christentums," *Theologische Studien und Kritiken,* 1916, pp. 1–70.

Keating, J. F., *The Agape and the Eucharist in the Early Church. Studies in the History of the Christian Love-Feasts,* London, 1901.

King, G. Br., "The 'Negative' Golden Rule," *The Journal of Religion,* 1928, pp. 268–279.

Kleinert, P., "Vorausschattungen der neutestamentlichen Lehre von der Liebe," *Theologische Studien und Kritiken,* 1913, pp. 1–30.

Kroner, R., "A Meditation on I Cor. XIII," *Anglican Theological Review,* 1948, pp. 216–218.

Kuss, O., *Die Liebe im Neuen Testament,* Breslau, s.d.

Laroche, J., "Charité," *Dictionnaire encyclopédique de la Bible,* Paris, 1932, I, p. 183.

Lee, E. K., "Love and Righteousness. A Study of the Influence of Christianity on Language," *The Expository Times,* LXII; 1; 1950, pp. 28–31.

Leenhardt, Fr. J., *Morale naturelle et Morale chrétienne,* Geneva, 1946.

Lehmann, E., Fridrichsen, A., "I Kor. 13. Eine christliche-stoische Diatribe," *Theologische Studien und Kritiken,* 1922, pp. 55–95.

Leeuwen, C. van, *Le développement du sens social en Israël avant l'ère chrétienne,* Assen, 1955.

Levertoff, P., *Love and the Messianic Age,* London, 1923.

Loisy, A., "Le grand Commandement," *Morceaux d'Exégèse,* Paris, 1906, pp. 163–181.

Lund, N. W., "The Literary Structure of Paul's Hymn to Love," *Journal of Biblical Literature,* 1931, pp. 266–276.

Lutgert, W., *Die Liebe im Neuen Testament. Ein Beitrag zur Geschichte des Urchristentums,* Leipzig, 1905.

——, "Liebe im N. T.," R.G.G.², III, col. 1638–1641.

——, "Nächstenliebe und Hamanitätsideal," *Ethik,* 1937, pp. 82–88.

——, *Ethik der Liebe,* Gütersloh, 1938.

Marett, R. R., *Faith, Hope, and Charity in Primitive Religion.* Oxford, 1932.

Martin, I. J., "I Corinthians XIII Interpreted by Its Context," *Journal of Bible and Religion,* 1950, pp. 101–105.

Michaelis, W., " Ἡ ἀγάπη οὐδέποτε πίπτει," *Paulus-Hellas-Oikumene,* Athens, 1951, pp. 135–140.

Michel, O., "Das Gebot der Nächstenliebe in der Verkündigung Jesu," *Zur sozialen Entscheidung* (hersg. von N. Koch), Tübingen, 1947, pp. 53–101.

Moffatt, J., "Exegetica. I Cor. XIII, 3," *The Expositor,* VIII, 8, 1914, pp. 190–191.

——, *Love in the New Testament,* London, 1929.

Moraldi, L., *Dio è Amore. Saggio sul concetto di amore in S. Giovanni con introduzione al IV Vangelo,* Rome, 1954.

Moulton, J. M., art. " Ἀγάπη," *The Expository Times,* 1914, XXVI, p. 139.

Nar, J., *Caritas in der hl. Schrift,* Augsburg, 1934.

Normann, Fr., *Die von der Wurzel ΦΙΛ-gebildeten Wörter und die Vorstellung der Liebe im griechischen,* Münster, 1952.

Nygren, A., *Eros und Agape. Gestaltwandlungen der christlichen Liebe,* Gütersloh, I, II, 1930–1937.

Ohm, Th., *Die Liebe zu Gott in den nichtchristlichen Religionen,* Krailling vor München, 1950.

Olivier, B., "La charité," *Initiation Théologique,* Paris, 1953, pp. 596–621.

Orr, J., "Love," *A Dictionary of the Bible* (J. Hastings), III, pp. 153–167.

Paeslack, M., "Zur Bedeutungsgeschichte der Wörter ΦΙΛΕΙΝ 'Lieben,' ΦΙΛΙΑ 'Liebe, Freundschaft,' ΦΙΛΟΣ 'Freund' in der Septuaginta und im Neuen Testament (unter Berücksichtigung ihrer Beziehungen zu ΑΓΑΠΑΝ, ΑΓΑΠΗ, ΑΓ-ΑΠΗΤΟΣ," *Theologia Viatorum, v. Festschrift D. M. Albertz,* Berlin, 1954, pp. 51–142.

Peterson, E., " 'Αγάπη," *Biblische Zeitschrift,* 1932, pp. 378–382.

――――, "Der Gottesfreund," *Zeitschrift für Kirchengeschichte,* Neue Folge, v, 1923, pp. 161–202.

Philippides, L. J., *Das Liebesprinzip im Buddhismus und im Christentum,* Athens, 1938.

Plé, A., "Un Mystère de Dieu: Le Prochain," *La Vie Spirituelle,* 300, 1945, pp. 225–241.

――――, "Église et Charité," *ibid.,* 1952, pp. 339–347.

Prat, F., "La charité dans la Bible," *Dictionnaire de Spiritualité,* fasc. 9, col. 508–523.

Preisker, H., "Die Liebe im Urchristentum und in der alten Kirche," *Theologische Studien und Kritiken,* XCV, 1924, pp. 272–294.

――――, *Die urchristliche Botschaft von der Liebe Gottes im Lichte der vergleichenden Religionsgeschichte,* Giessen, 1930.

――――, *Das Ethos des Urchristentums,* Gütersloh, 1949.

Rad, G. von, "Die Vorgeschichte der Gattung von I Kor. XIII, 4–7," *Geschichte und Altes Testament* (Festschrift A. Alt), Tübingen, 1953, pp. 153–168.

Rade, M., "Der Nächste," *Festgabe für A. Jülicher,* Tübingen, 1927, pp. 70–79.

Ramlot, L., "L'amour du prochain gage de notre amour du Christ," *Cahiers de la Vie Spirituelle,* Paris, 1954, pp. 33–62.

Ramsay, P., *Basic Christian Ethics,* New York, 1954.

Ramsay, W. M., "The Word ΑΓΑΠΗ," *The Expository Times,* IX, 1898, pp. 567–568.

Ratschow, C.H., "Nächstenliebe und Bruderliebe," *Zeitschrift für systematische Theologie,* 1950, pp. 160–182.

Reicke, B., *Diakonie, Festfreude und Zelos in Verbindung mit der altchristlichen Agapenfeier,* Uppsala, 1951.

Reitzenstein, R., "Die Entstehung der Formel 'Glaube, Liebe, Hoffnung,' " *Historische Zeitschrift,* 1916, pp. 189–208.

――――, "Die Formel 'Glaube, Liebe, Hoffnung' bei Paulus," *Göttingen Gesellschaft der Wissenschaften phil. hist. Klasse.* Nachrichten, 1916, pp. 367–416.

———, "Die Formel 'Glaube, Liebe, Hoffnung' bei Paulus. Ein Nachwort," *ibid.*, 1917, pp. 130–151.

Riesenfeld, H., "Etude bibliographique sur la notion biblique d'ΑΓΑΠΗ surtout dans I Cor. XIII," *Conjectanea Neotestamentica*, 5; 1941, pp. 1–32.

——— "La voie de la charité," *Studia Theologica*, Lund, 1948, II, pp. 146–157.

——— "Note bibliographique sur I Cor. XIII," *Nuntius*, 6; 1952, pp. 47–48.

Risch, E., Mette, H. J., Αγαπάζω, ἀγαπάω, B. Snell, *Lexikon des frühgriechischen Eros*, Göttingen, 1955, I, col. 45–46.

Rittelmeyer, F., "Die Liebe bei Plato und Paulus, Symposion und Korintherbriefhymnus," *Archiv für Religions Psychologie*, 1914, pp. 10–44.

Roach, S. N., "Love in Its Relation to Service. A Study of φιλεῖν and 'Αγαπᾶν in the New Testament," *Review and Expositor*, 1913, pp. 531–553.

Rotureau, G., "Charité," *Catholicisme*, II, 959–976.

Salafranca, S. G., " 'Agape' en San Juan XVII, 26," *Cultura Biblica*, 1955, pp. 272–281.

Salet, G., "Amour de Dieu," *Nouvelle Revue Théologique*, 1955, pp. 3–26.

Sanday, W., Headlam, A., "The History of the Word ἀγάπη. The Christian Teaching on Love," *The Epistle to the Romans*[4], Edinbourg, 1900, pp. 374–377.

Sander, R., *Furcht und Liebe im palästinischen Judentum*, Stuttgart, 1935.

Sauer, J., "Agape," *Lexikon für Theologie und Kirche*, I, 122–124.

Shepherd, W. G., "The Problem of Love," *Anglican Theological Review*, 1949, pp. 171–175.

Schlatter, W., *Die Liebe Gottes in der Mannigfaltigkeit ihres biblischen Selbstzeugnisses*, Berlin, 1935.

Schlier, H., "Ueber die Liebe. Eine Exegese," *Hochland*, 1949, pp. 235–243.

Schmidt, J. H. H., *Synonymik der griechischen Sprache*, Leipzig, 1879, III, pp. 474–491.

———, *Handbuch der lateinischen und griechischen Synonymik*, Leipzig, 1889, pp. 756–766.

Schnackenburg, R., *Die sittliche Botschaft des Neuen Testamentes*, Munich, 1954.

Scholz, H., *Eros und Caritas. Die Platonische Liebe und die Liebe im Sinne des Christentums*, Halle, 1929.

Schubart, W., *Religion und Eros*, Munich, 1941.

Schumann, F. K., "Natürliche Liebe und christliche Liebe," *Um Kirche und Lehre. Gesammelte Aufsätze und Vortrage*, Stuttgart, 1936, pp. 175–201.

Schutz, R., "Der Streit zwischen A. v. Harnack und R. Reitzenstein über die Formel 'Glaube, Liebe, Hoffnung' I Kor. XIII". *Theologische Literaturzeitung*, 1917, col. 454–457.

———, *Die Vorgeschichte der johanneischen Formel: ὁ θεὸς ἀγάπη ἐστίν*, Göttingen, 1917.

Scott, J. A., "The Words for 'Love' in John XXI, 15 ff.," *The Classical Weekly*, 1945, pp. 71–72; 1946, pp. 60–61.

Smith, M., "Mt. v, 43, Hate thine Enemy," *The Harvard Theological Review*, 1952, pp. 71–73.

Söhngen, G., *Die Offenbarung der Liebe Gottes in Jesus-Christus*, Cologne, 1946.

Souter, A., ΑΓΑΠΗΤΟΣ, *The Journal of Theological Studies*, 1927, pp. 59–60.

Spicq, C., *Agapè. Prolégomènes à une étude de Théologie néotestamentaire*, Louvain, 1955.

———, "La Morale de l'Agape," *Lumière et Vie*, XXI, 1955, pp. 103–122.

Stauffer, E., "'Αγαπάω, ἀγάπη," G. Kittel, *Theologisches Wörterbuch zum Neuen Testament*, I, 34–55.

Steinmueller, J. E., "ΕΡΑΝ, ΦΙΛΕΙΝ, ΑΓΑΠΑΝ in extra-biblical and biblical Sources," *Studia Anselmia*, 27-28. *Miscellanea biblica et Orientalia R. P. A. Miller oblata*, Rome, 1951, pp. 404–423.

Steinmueller, J. E., Sullivan, K., "Love," *Catholic Biblical Encyclopedia*, New York, 1956; *Old Testament*, p. 645; *New Testament*, pp. 398–405.

Sustar, A., "De Caritate apud sanctum Ioannem," *Verbum Domini*, 1950, pp. 110–119; 129–140; 193–213; 257–270; 321–340.

Tarelli, C. C., "'Αγάπη," *The Journal of Theological Studies*, 1950, pp. 64–67.

Thimme, W., "Eros im Neuen Testament," *Verbum Dei manet*

in aeternum. Festschrift für O. Schmitz, Witten, 1953, pp. 103–116.

Tillich, P., *Love, Power, and Justice,* London, 1954, pp. 107–125.

Tittmann, J. A. H., "Remarks on the Synonyms of the New Testament," *The Biblical Cabinet,* III, 1833, pp. 90–97.

Trench, R. Ch., *Synonyms of the New Testament*[12], London, 1894, pp. 41–45.

Tromp De Ruiter, S., *Gebruik en beteekenis von* ΑΓΑΠΑΝ *in de griekesche Literatur,* Gronigen, 1930 (Vidi, non intellexi). [*A.'s comment.*–Transl.]

Turner, C. H., Ο ΥΙΟΣ ΜΟΥ Ο ΑΓΑΠΗΤΟΣ, *The Journal of Theological Studies,* 1926, pp. 113–129.

Ubieta Lopez, J. A., "Caridad fraterna en las parenesis de Ef. IV, 25–V, 2 y Col. III, 8–17," *Cuadernos Pont. Colegio Español,* II, Rome, 1955, pp. 63–95.

van Imschoot, P., "Liebe," *Bibel-Lexikon* (edit H. Haag). Zurich, 1953, col. 1027–1034.

van Oyen, H., *Evangelische Ethik, I. Grundlagen. Die Anwaltschaft des Geistes,* Basel, 1952, pp. 115–215.

Viard, A., "La charité accomplit la loi. Commentaire de Rom. XII, 9 à XIII, 10," *La Vie Spirituelle,* 303, 1946, pp. 27–34.

———, "Le Fruit de L'Esprit," *Ibid.,* 384, 1953, pp. 451–470.

Vitti, A., "Excellentior Via: Caritas," *Verbum Domini,* 1929, pp. 43 ff.

Vogtland, Fr., "Die paulinische Lehre von den theologischen Tugenden," *Der Katholik,* 1917, pp. 315–331; 1918, pp. 1–15.

Vos, G., "The Scriptural Doctrine of the Love of God," *The Presbyterian and Reformed Review,* 1902, pp. 1–37.

Walter, E., *Glaube, Hoffnung und Liebe im Neuen Testament*[2], Fribourg in B., 1942.

Walterscheid, J., *Das grösste Gebot des Evangeliums,* Cologne, 1941.

Warfield, B. B., "The Terminology of Love in the New Testament," *The Princeton Theological Review,* 1918, pp. 1–45, 153–203; reprinted in *Biblical Doctrines,* Oxford, 1929, pp. 511–597.

Warnach, V., *Agape. Die Liebe als Grundmotiv der neutestamentlichen Theologie,* Dusseldorf, 1951.

Weber, H., *Das Wesen der Caritas,* Freiburg-im-B., 1938.

Wehrung, G., *Welt und Reich. Grundlegung und Aufbau der Ethik*, Stuttgart, 1952, pp. 277–283.

Weinel, H., "Die Nächstenliebe," *Archiv für die gesamte Psychologie*, 1932, pp. 247–260.

Weinrich, Fr., *Die Liebe im Buddhismus und im Christentum*, Berlin, 1935.

Whitaker, G. H., "Love Springs No Leak," *Expositor*, ser. 8, t. 21; 1921, pp. 126–128.

Wikenhauser, A., "Die Liebeswerke in dem Gerichtsgemälde Mt. XXV, 31–46," *Biblische Zeitschrift*, 1932, pp. 366–377.

Winterswyl, L. A., *Mandatum Novum. Über Wesen und Gestalt christlicher Liebe*, Colmar, 1941.

Winzen, D., "Agape bei Paulus," *Der Kathol. Gedanke*, 1938, pp. 14–18.

Volkl, R., *Die Selbstliebe in der Heiligen Schrift und bei Thomas von Aquin*, Munich, 1956.

Wood, H. G., "The Use of ἀγαπάω in Luke VII, 42, 47," *The Expository Times*, LXVI, 10; 1955, pp. 319–320.

Woolsey, T. D., "The Disciple Whom Jesus Loved," *The Andover Review*, 1885, pp. 163–185.

X., ΑΓΑΠΗΤΟΣ, *The Journal of Theological Studies*, 1919, pp. 339–344.

Zenker, E. V., "Platonisches Liebesideal und das Christentum," *Freie Welt*, 1934, pp. 11–18; 144–151.

List of Texts Analyzed

List of Greek Words

Index